GOD'S FEBRUARY

Archie and May: The Moderator of the General Assembly of the Church of Scotland and his wife — an official portrait 1961.

GOD'S FEBRUARY

A life of Archie Craig

1888–1985

Elizabeth Templeton

BCC/CCBI
Inter-Church House
35-41 Lower Marsh
London SE1 7RL

ISBN 0-85169-210-9

© 1991 Elizabeth Templeton

Published by BCC/CCBI
Inter-Church House
35-41 Lower Marsh
London SE1 7RL

Cover design by Tony Cantale Graphics

Typeset and printed by
Dramrite Printers Limited
129 Long Lane
Southwark
London SE1 4PL

Ref 50 GS

iv

This book is dedicated
in gratitude to my parents
who gave me room to grow.

"There is a time of the year in Scotland — it is about the middle of February — when you will see a dream in the eye of the garden-lover; a dream which is not the bastard of wishful thinking, but the lawful offspring of the garden-lover's knowledge of sun and soil and seed."

A.C. Craig. Sermon

Contents

Preface *by Lesslie Newbigin*   ix
Introduction   xi

                    PART ONE
Chapter 1   Boyhood   1
Chapter 2   Student days   10
Chapter 3   Wartime   22
Chapter 4   Parish ministry   29
Chapter 5   University chaplaincy   43
Chapter 6   The London years   55
Chapter 7   Return to Scotland   72
Chapter 8   The clatter of arms   86
Chapter 9   Moderator   100
Chapter 10   Retirement and old age   108

                    PART TWO
Chapter 11   Of lightning and of music   119
Chapter 12   The risks of establishment   132
Chapter 13   Towards symphony   141
Chapter 14   Caesar, Christ and conscience   148
Chapter 15   Life in a straight line   157

Appendix 1   Acknowledgements   170
Appendix 2   Bibliography   171

Index   173

Illustrations   Archie and May: the Moderator of the   Frontispiece
                    Church of Scotland and his wife – an
                    official portrait 1961

                    University Chaplain at Glasgow,   Between pages
                    sketched by Betty Bartholomew 1930   82 and 83

                    Walking and talking with Glasgow
                    University students in the thirties

                    At Doune with John Campbell his gardener

                    Preaching at Kelso 1966

PREFACE

The friends of Archie Craig, and they are a large and varied company, have wondered — ever since his death — whether anyone would be found capable of writing an account of him which would be worthy of the subject. I think that Elizabeth Templeton has done it, and I — for one — am grateful. The story which is told here illustrates not only the character of a great and loveable Christian man. It also illustrates important chapters in the early history of developing ecumenical relations in Britain. As the first General Secretary of the British Council of Churches and as its leader through the years of war, Archie played a vital role in the religious life of the country. As an ecumenical leader in his own native Scotland he had to suffer the rejection of the plan for closer union between the national churches of Scotland and England and the extraordinary bitterness of the conflict which these plans evoked. The story of his later years is also an important part of the story of religious life in Scotland during those years. But above all the book will be prized as a portrait of a very remarkable man, a man whose importance in the lives of people was far greater than his tenure of public offices might suggest. Archie combined in a unique way the depth, the strength, the firmness that came from his Calvinistic heritage, with the breadth and the gaiety of a fully human person. He combined the best of the Calvinist tradition with the best of the liberal mind. To be asked to pray with him as he knelt devoutly in his sitting room (for 'kneeling is the only proper position for praying') was to be drawn into the awesome presence of God who is infinitely great and glorious. But before you left there was always one more story to be told and more uproarious laughter. There was always the holding together of the goodness of human life and the depths that lie within it. Archie's relish for the absurdities of life was rooted in his awareness of the amazing grace of a holy God who is ready to deal with people like us. Those who knew him will not need an invitation to read this book. Those who did not will find here both a fresh perspective on important chapters of ecumenical history and also an introduction to a rich human character.

Selly Oak   Lesslie Newbigin
July 1990

INTRODUCTION

To be invited to write about Archie Craig is to be rather like a pond-minnow engaged to describe the life-cycle of an Atlantic salmon. Even though I had been privileged to know him for the last twenty years of his long, full life, I had not known him, so to speak, with a biographer's eye. On reflection, he seemed to have talked very little of himself in any conversation I could remember, so great was his interest in whoever he was meeting, and what was going on with them. Besides, I felt much less comfortable inside my Calvinist and Presbyterian skin than he had done, and wondered if I could do justice to the "insideness" of those aspects of his existence. And to complete my misgivings, I was innocent of biographical method and practice, except as an occasional reader.

As I began to read the fascinating and voluminous papers which Archie left, the shape of my unease changed. There was no lack of stuff, for in spite of octogenarian pruning, there were boxes and boxes of papers, letters and postcards going back to 1907, all the correspondence from father, mother and sisters which had been kept and brought back from the trenches, and bundle on bundle, not only of Archie's sermons, broadcasts, addresses, poetry and incoming correspondence, but of his father's sermons, and of committee documents relating to many stages of his career. To fillet and present even a selection of these would surely be enough to give something of the flavour of this rich life.

But there was the rub. Questions I had not had before in the forefront of my consciousness crowded in, the more I read. How should I select from thousands of pages of data in a way which did not distort, especially as I started off with the possible handicap of committed sympathy towards Archie's pacifist and ecumenical convictions? How could I encompass in print someone who in flesh transcended most of our assumed polarisations? Evangelical and liberal? Traditionalist and adventurer? Devoted churchman and fiercely anti-clerical? Intellectual and warm human being? Charmingly genial and robustly Puritan? Lover of Jeremiah and raconteur of jokes? For those who had known him, the coherence was earthed by memory and love, but how was it to be made convincing to those who had never met the man, without giving them the feeling that they were reading some unreal hagiography? How was an existence credible, if diligent enquiry could unearth no enemies, no personal animosity, even among those who fiercely disputed his policies on this or that? How would his life strike those who not only didn't know *him*, but were not part of the faith-world he inhabited?

Then there was the question of discretion. Archie's papers contained almost nothing of his long relationship to May before they were married, yet it was probably the most important human relationship of his life. Should it be dug out beyond the surface information? And if so, how? On the other hand, the papers did contain many references to people which were of a "pastorally sensitive" nature, and which would have been abused by public quotation, even though they shed significant light on aspects of Archie's life or work. Both the biographer's itch for omniscience and the dangerous professional ambition to reveal the truth, the whole truth and nothing but the truth had to be resisted. (Bonhoeffer's essay on "Telling the truth" was a great help here!)

Even when I tried to corroborate the paper-insights by talking with some of the scores of people who had known and loved Archie, there were so many aspects of the man which one saw as dominant and another as negligible, that I had the sense of a man who comfortably contained ten men. One said, "Don't, whatever you do, make him into an intellectual. He was great fun to be with." Another said he was an intellectual giant, possibly the outstanding one of his generation. One old friend said confidently that he would have had no time at all for the present Bishop of Durham; yet the head of BBC Scotland's Religious Broadcasting found him, in his nineties, the willing patron saint of a series called "*The Quest*", to which David Jenkins and his kind of questions were vital. People who couldn't stand each other's company both felt at one with him. Almost the only common factor was that almost everyone responded to his name with a story, a joke or an epigram which they had heard from him or remembered of him!

Those were perceptions enough to juggle with, and sometimes dilemmas enough to have to resolve. In the end, this can only claim to be a public biography of the public life of a man, culled largely from his public self-disclosure and from the generous imparting of privileged knowledge which many of his friends have been willing to share with me over the last two years. Doing the research has been a great pleasure. The paper work was made even more enjoyable by the unfailing hospitality of the New College Library Staff, and the interviewing introduced me to armies of people whose desire to celebrate Archie encompassed me with generous friendliness. The book properly belongs to all of them. Some of them are listed in Appendix 1.

Undoubtedly, more still might have been consulted, for the lives that were touched by this man in one or other of his various roles were legion. The failure to track them all down is not mere culpable incompetence, but cosmic limitation. And, sadly, some like Kathleen Bliss, who must have been a significant witness to Archie's Second World War years in London, were too ill to be interviewed. It was cosmic limitation too, in terms of the publishers' need for a manuscript in finite time, which prevented me from reading through all the papers twice, after as well as before the interviewing of friends. I am clear, from having re-read some of them, that the second run defines the focus of many details in crisper relation to the whole than was possible first time round. I hope the ensuing distortion is not mortal biographical sin.

Archie was wont to recall an episode in Glasgow Art Gallery, where he once observed a "misshriven little runt of a man" looking up at a statue of Apollo. It became for him a recurrent illustration of the distance we are from Christlikeness. No-one, I think, could have attempted this biography without a growing consciousness of unCraiglikeness. Archie deplored public spiritual striptease, so the details of the present writer's comparative defects remain for higher shriving than readers can perform. But I am unobsequiously clear that huge areas of Archie's life, his detailed botanical love, his musical insight, the disciplined precision of his private spirituality, to name but three, are handled here as by a clumsy and rather tone-deaf observer. The only point of mentioning something so manifest is by way of apology to those who are "further ben" in those areas of deep re-creation where I can do Archie too little justice.

Most people who knew him were glad that this book was being undertaken. By about the end of chapter three, my children were not. I owe Kirsten, Alan and Calum apologies and gratitude for their umpteen constrained disappearances, and hope that one day they may understand and retrospectively forgive. Douglas, who has mothered and fathered them through countless motherless excursions, and has been magnanimous about the growing symbiosis between me and the word-processor should really be acknowledged as the co-efficient cause of this production. He is owed much wifely time, private space and a lot of darned kilt-socks.

Though I was hesitant about undertaking this venture, I am now immensely grateful to the British Council of Churches for entrusting me with it. I owe to those I have met in that orbit so much of my own ecumenical nourishment, that this portrait of one of their founding fathers is a very small return. I hope − with Archie's ghost, I trust, very near my shoulder, − that the new ecumenical instruments, devoted to the vision of "a whole church for its whole task" will fruit sweetly and generously.

PART ONE
1 Boyhood

"The pathways of the air were still the monopoly of the birds and a few rather comical balloonists. There was no penicillin, no tranquillisers, no atom split."

When Archibald Campbell Craig was born, on Tuesday, 3rd December, 1888, Kelso was preparing for Christmas.

John Scott, the fruitmonger, was advertising oranges from Florida, and German eggs were available at one shilling a dozen. The Depot for Ceylon and India teas was boasting the superiority of its product, where "all the operations are conducted under the immediate superintendence of Europeans" to the teas of China and Japan, where the tea was cultivated in small patches by the peasantry "who gather the leaves and prepare the tea in their huts in a most slovenly manner." Walter Young respectfully invited inspection of his New Purchases in FANCY GOODS for Xmas and New Year Presents at 6d and 1s, advising customers of special values in Mantles, Paletots, Ulsters, Dolmans, Waterproof Mantles, Stays, Underclothing, Furs, Laces, Frillings, Ribbons, Gloves etc.

The primary domestic political issue was how to deal with Irish unrest, a question firmly bound up with the retention of authority in the colonial empire; but the townsfolk of Kelso, bustling market-centre of Roxburghshire, spent rather more of that week's newsprint on the list of wedding-presents given to the young Master of Polwarth, and to the trial and sentencing to death by hanging of one William Wardle, for a nasty and titillating murder.

In this small, thriving country town, the influence of the churches was palpable, set within the firm parameters of social stratification. In the week of Archie's birth, for instance, the First United Presbyterian Church Mutual Improvement Association was announcing a forthcoming season of lectures, which included poetry readings and such midweek talks as "Time and the methods of measuring it" and "The martyr sage of Athens." The same body, in conjunction with the Free Church Literary Society was holding a debate on the subject: "Is Mr. A L. Brown's Fishing (Scotland) Bill worthy of support?" The organist of St. Andrew's Church was offering music lessons, and the Free Church of Scotland was inviting competition for a £9 per annum School Bursary. On Sundays the range was more restricted, but still affording choice. Apart from worship itself, the Sunday evening of that winter week offered a public missionary meeting on the evils of the slave trade, or a Christadelphian lecture on "The Son of Man and the Son of God."

In this securely religious world, Archie was born, the last of eleven children of Alick and Margaret Craig, *nee* Forrest. His oldest sister, Bessie was already eighteen, and the rest had followed at regular intervals, five brothers and six sisters in all. Four years before Archie was born, an older brother, Alexander, died at the age of two, and in 1892, when Archie was four, his fourth sister, Hester, died at the age of fifteen. But the impression given by family letters and recollections is of a sturdy and happy family, in which the new baby grew up in an environment of steady and robust affection.

His father was the Free Church minister of Kelso East, carrying on a family tradition of ministry which went back to Archie's granduncle, George Craig, who had "come out" at the Disruption from Sprouston Parish Church with the words

> "I have a solemn persuasion that to conform to the Established Church as now subjected to the supremacy of the Civil Courts would be practically to disown the supremacy of the Lord Jesus Christ as King and Head of His Church: and to do this would to my mind be no less a sin than to deny his divinity."

Archie loved and cherished the integrity and reverence of this to the end of his days, and, for all his commitment to a re-united church, confessed that if anyone spoke a word against the Free Church, there was a frisson in his spine.

What it meant in day to day terms was a fairly Spartan life, plenty of plain food, fresh air and soap, morning and evening family prayers, and a strong sense of discipline in relation to money, pleasure and the use of time. His father tithed, a practice which Archie later came to think carried the risk of being too legalistic, and the family's running budget was obviously fairly tight. One memory which catches the feel of it for Archie was being taken into town by his father, seeing an enviable slate in a stationer's window, and creating a huge tantrum when his request for it was refused. When they got home his father produced his purse and showed him the twopence-halfpenny in it. "That is all the money I have until next Thursday, when the Sustentation Fund cheque is due; otherwise I should have loved to give you that slate." Somewhat wryly, Archie later recalls the episode as having taught him the virtue behind apparent parental cruelty, and the saving grace of something called the Sustentation Fund!

It seemly likely that this was not in fact the family's last twopence, for a neighbour of the manse in Forestfield testifies that the family had social access to the big house, and the style of dress which is manifest in the sepia family portraits of the 1890s, even if they are all wearing carefully looked-after best clothes, suggest good quality cloth and fine tailoring. In addition, travel seems to have been no problem for the family. In the 1870s there are letters home from Alick Craig apparently on holiday in Menton, and others from Rome just before Archie was born; and the boys as they grew were able to travel to visit scattered members of the family, or for educational purposes, to Germany, to Moscow, and even to the Far East. That this came from savings out of the Sustentation Fund is improbable, however relatively cheap travel was in those days. So it may have been that the routine living costs were strictly monitored against a background of adequate capital sufficiency which could be tapped for purposes deemed legitimate – but slates were not among them!

At any rate Archie remembered the whiff of his Free Church manse as "slightly astringent". As he writes of it in retrospect:

"The school of Presbyterian churchmanship to which I owe the unrepay-able debt of Christian nurture may have been, doubtless was, defective in some respects – too rigid, too much palisaded against the impact of the secular world and its problems, insensitive to the place of beauty in worship and of gaiety in character – yet its central aim was as clear as a diamond and as precious: it was at all costs, and by a well-ordered regimen of life in home and congregation, to reveal and exalt and uphold that way of life which Jesus Christ, worshipped as the Son of God, is the expositor, the central substance and the living dynamic. And this, in no small measure, it did."

In the case of the Craig family, the discipline was clearly balanced by geniality and tenderness. One catches the flavour of it in a letter written to Madge in 1878 from her father in the South of France:

"My dear Madgie,
   I begin with you as you are our little invalid. [She had polio which left her lame.] Mama must read this letter for you as you cannot read it for yourself. Papa is now far away but he often thinks of you. He has your photograph before him now as he writes this little letter".

He then continues with a lively description of the tidelessness of the Mediterranean, and of the diversity of trees and fruits, referring especially to those like gourds and locust trees named in the Bible, and moves on to talk about the voice in the bluebells singing, heard by the ear within:

"I hope that you and Bessie and Willie and Hetty too will have the love of God in your hearts, so you will hear God speaking to you when others perceive no sound at all. I don't know if you will understand this, but Mama will try and explain it to you."

He then gives an account of his nine mosquito bites and encloses two dead mosquitoes, with the reassurance that they cannot hurt her, and goes on to describe an amazing picnic outing by donkey. The letter ends:

> "I did wish my bairnies had been there. But Madgie must be well first. She must not run or walk till her leg be better, and then how nice it will be. Meanwhile Papa sends much love and many kisses, as many as the envelope will carry to you."

Mrs Craig was clearly a gifted, resourceful and devoted mother, who, like so many of her contemporaries, seemed to take the rearing of eleven children in her stride, though the youngest daughter, Alice, seems to have been a cause of many heartaches as she reached her twenties. Archie recalled finding one day a portfolio of his mother's drawings and paintings, done before her child-rearing, and commented on the unobtrusive sacrifice involved in her dedication to her family, which left little time for recreational pursuits. But it was a family which accepted that most worthwhile things required some sort of sacrifice, and took this as a formative principle for the children to appreciate. Yet Mrs Craig must have remained an animated and intellectually versatile reader at least, since she seems to have coped, in her seventies, with reading and enjoying the theological books with which Archie presented her for the odd birthday or Christmas, "new theology" like that of Joe Oldham or David Cairns.

The explicit reminiscences of childhood and boyhood in Archie's addresses and papers are relatively few, but remarkably even in tone, with a slightly rueful appreciation of the role of parental sanity. He recalls, for instance, an escapade when he was in his early teens:

> "When I was about thirteen or so, a gang of us who were reading Henty and Ballantyne formed a wonderful association called the Robbers. We dug an underground cave, and armed ourselves with weird weapons, and planned all sorts of thrilling deeds. It seemed the height of wellbeing, not to say bliss, to clamber up and down the tunnel or to crowd over the cave fire. And then our very sensible parents very firmly put an end to it. It seemed to us refined cruelty. It really was providential care, in circumstances where health was being risked and clothes ruined and schoolwork neglected."

Even more significant in his later reconstruction of his past was a moment in his early childhood, in which he read the anticipation of a life-long excitement about truth:

> "I once thought I had made a startling scientific discovery. It was when

I was a small boy of about five years of age. I happened to be standing on the front doorstep of my home on a brilliant winter's evening and I was gazing with pleasure at the spectacle of a young moon riding in the sky when I observed a phenomenon which caused me unbounded astonishment. In much the same fashion as the claws of a brooch's mounting may hold a pearl, or as the cup of an acorn embraces the fruit, so the glittering crescent clasped an orb of alabaster. I was dumbfounded by this immediate perception that the moon did not really wax and wane as certain hymns of the Church plainly asserted it did, but in fact persisted in its full rondure all the time. I rushed indoors to communicate my discovery, and was not a little dashed when it was coldly received. It appeared that it had been made before, and could be read about, along with much else of greater importance, in Chambers Encyclopaedia, and that, moreover, I had better go to bed and not be a nuisance. So off to bed I had to go, crestfallen and yet hugging to my bosom two consolations — the remembered vision of a sphere marvellously compounded of glittering crystal and ethereal alabaster, and the knowledge that with my own eyes I had discovered something which learned professors had written about in very large books. I began to entertain a favourable opinion of learned professors which subsequent experience of them has not entirely undermined. Whatever an unsympathetic family circle might say, I felt it to be a profoundly satisfactory thing that my personal observation squared with that of the professors and theirs with mine. And so it was indeed; for through that childish experience I had had the first glimpse of the possibility of a fruitful interplay between the realm of private awareness and a traditional corpus of knowledge which is in fact a condition of vitality in both Science and Religion."

How much of the import of this was only retrospectively felt cannot be established, but it seems clear that, even as a small boy, Archie was someone who needed space and time for long, long thoughts. He was not, however, lopsidely cerebral, being at the same time happily nourished in the good physical life of the countryside beyond his bedroom window, where the fields and woods of Roxburghshire beckoned. Seventy years later these boyhood delights were still vivid: swimming in the Cobby Hole at seven o'clock on summer mornings; the initiation rite of his first swim across the Tweed — "a new era in life" — [an action now banned by order of Kelso Council]; and the glory of harvest afternoons on nearby farms.

It was also at a fairly tender age that he took to the gardening which was to be a consuming interest throughout his life, not just as a pleasurable hobby, but as a source of wisdom and patience and discipline and hope.

"I had a penny to spend, which, believe me, to the last of a long brood in a Scottish manse, was wealth and adventure and romance all rolled into one. Across the window of a shop in Kelso on an April morning there was stretched a string, and on it a row of seed packets. I was stirred to the marrow, I looked and was lost; eventually I surrendered my soul and my penny — they were one and the same thing at the moment — to a little darling called *Nemophila Insignis* whom to this day I ardently love."

When he came home with his seeds, his father, himself a keen gardener, gave him a small rough patch of ground in the manse garden, where he could do no great harm, and from then on the passion grew. By the time he was a young man in the First World War, after his father's death, his mother was writing to consult him about details of what and when things should be done in the garden in their retirement home in Troon, and it was certainly one of the major activities and pleasures of his old age. Something about the time-scale, the privacy, the process, as well as the sheer beauty of the result seems to have fired his imagination and invoked his energy. He couldn't be doing with vegetables, but confessed that he could be wildly extravagant when inflamed by a flower-catalogue.

While his childhood gave him the kind of space to explore his private universe, a pole which he always treasured in himself and others, he was simultaneously part of the gregarious world of family and school. Not many indications of his infant schooling exist; that may have been done at home. But from 1896, when he was eight, till 1906 when he matriculated in the Arts Faculty of Edinburgh University, he attended Kelso High School under the headmastership of John Kemp, who appears to have been a brilliant and inspiring dominie "of almost pontifical dignity". Though Archie ruefully summarised his educational philosophy as being "that man must learn Latin in the skin of his palm, and that if you sow wild oats you will reap rich leather", he seems to have respected him as a liberal educator, who cultivated all the gifts of mind and body which his pupils possessed. Classics, of course, was strong, and Archie was good enough at Greek and Latin to produce 70s and 80s in his first year university classes. But more unusually, the school was extremely strong in German, with a native German-speaker to teach it, and it was here that Archie first gained the competence that was to take him into intelligence work in the war.

The *corpus sanum* was also well catered for: cadet-corps, runs up the Pipewell Brae, football (in Kelso presumably Rugby), hockey and cricket, the last played in Shedden Park with such ferocious inter-border rivalry that Archie recalled being more partisan than he had ever been in either political or ecclesiastical affairs. As he recalled it, "The teams that came from Coldstream or St. Boswell's were just wicked enemies deserving to be annihilated." All of this Archie relished, and he went on playing cricket, hockey, rugby and tennis actively into his forties, and, when he at last capitulated to having television at home after his retirement, watched with enthusiasm soccer, rugby and, somewhat surprisingly, boxing. He appreciated male strength and beauty, and could speak of a "glorious young Scottish football team." It was then no milksop or one-sided intellectual who emerged from these early years, but a boy who lived with both mental and physical zest, and had a strong sense of European humanism in his bones.

The Kelso school log for October 13th and 20th reads:

> "The attendance and work have been good. Mr Cunningham who succeeded Mr Purdie on the staff has resigned, having obtained a post under the Edinburgh Board. A.C. Craig has done well in the scholarship competition at Edinburgh University: He stands twelfth in the general list: takes 10th place in another list & 7th in another.
>
> The afternoon of Monday was given as a half holiday in honour of A.C. Craig's success."

Christianity, of course, was taken for granted, and the fragmented character of the Christian institutions was also part of the fabric of life, registering in Archie's early consciousness only as the sound of umpteen different church bells filling the Kelso air on a Sunday morning. In 1885 there were in fact, for a population of 4,000, two Church of Scotland parishes, two United Presbyterian congregations, two Free Churches, one Episcopalian, one Baptist, one Roman Catholic, several Plymouth Brethren and a robust cohort of Salvation Army.

On a person to person basis, people in different denominations were not conspicuously *unfriendly*, but church adherence tended to determine the scope and pattern of people's friendships, and subliminal assumptions were made about the others. Thus,

> "We in the Free Church were taught to regard ourselves as the true evangelicals, the parish folk as culpably moderate, the Episcopalians as people who ought to have known better and the R.C's as downright dangerous idolators."

The dividedness of the church did not at the time strike the young Archie Craig as any matter for regret. Indeed the very intensity of ecclesiastical rivalry was a signal of how serious this God business was, how much it mattered to get it right, and not to treat casually the awful holiness of God. What he says never struck him till his late teens was the possibility that religion might be to do with *joy*. The idea of using gay colour, for instance, in the context of the church's central solemnities would have been deemed by many to be "not merely sacrilegious but positively episcopalian, the thin end of the scarlet woman".

It was this problem of how to relate the rich secular world of experience to the sacred which increasingly seems to have engaged the schoolboy's conscious thought. The permission given to read the *British Weekly* on Sunday afternoons as an alternative to the lives of missionaries, the existence of such bodies as the Y.M.C.A., and of such beings as beadles, suggested some sort of buffer state between the clearly sacred and the clearly secular. But how were the boundaries defined?

> "Most perplexing of all was the treatment accorded to the great composers: for it appeared that whereas Johann Sebastian Bach might, broadly speaking, be reckoned to belong to the realm of the semi-sacred, the titanic Beethoven, who could purge the spirit with pity and passion was irretrievably secular — again, however, only broadly speaking, since excerpts from his works might pass muster on ecclesiastical occasions, provided they were played at a sufficiently slow tempo and made to sound as much like psalm-tunes as possible."

By the time he was ready to leave school, the sense of troubledness was acute. Though he did not finally decide to be ordained until after the war, Archie was already thinking of studying for the ministry before he left Kelso High. One day during his last year, he was asked about his future plans by the cadet-corps instructor, a Herculean Irish regular who had fought in the South African war, and was a great hero in the boys' eyes. He recalls:

> "I told him with a boy's shyness that I was thinking of studying for the ministry, and this avowal brought over his handsome, confident features a look which I have never forgotten, and which has become for my mind a little private symbol for a broad range of fact. It was a look in which a strong man's natural virility and kindliness of expression were suddenly infused with concern, amusement and unmistakeably also contempt. Clearly for the genial and gallant sergeant-major, religion and life were antithetic conceptions — life a glowing, thrilling, passionate adventure: religion a sombre negation of life which threatened to bleach its brave colours, and take the sweet sting out of its excitements."

The same question was focussed at the same time by one of his classmates, referred to only as A.T., whom Archie admired for his sound morals, high character and intellectual ability. This boy was feeling, as he came to the end of his schooling, a revulsion of the deepest kind, affecting his whole being, from his Christian upbringing, which seemed to threaten to disinherit him from width and wealth of human experience, from intellectual freedom, from exuberance, from the poetry of life beneath the sun. As Archie recalled it becoming his own question too, he framed it with an acute sense of the potential tension between humanism and Christian faith:

> "Where exactly in the landscape of Paul's assertion that all things are yours lay things like the Tempest sonata and the Pastoral symphony and Keats and Greek sculpture? Did they veritably belong to the Christian? Were they only permissible relaxations, but to be enjoyed cautiously and without abandonment of spirit, lest they should dull the palate for things unseen and eternal?"

In a way, it was the passion of that "venomous problem" for the boy which nerved much of subsequent thought and action of the man.

2 Student days

"I remember how once, when I was an undergraduate of Edinburgh University, a professor caused my spine to thrill deliciously by describing Ecclesiastes as "that whining Alexandrian pessimist". I had never dreamed that anyone dared take such liberties with a Biblical author as to call him a whining pessimist, let alone an Alexandrian one – which sounded to my rural innocence as though it much aggravated the offence."

The young Archie matriculated two months before his eighteenth birthday, at the same time as the friend who was to share digs with him, and to remain probably the deepest of his lifetime friends. This was Hugh Walker, another son of a United Free Church manse from Langton, by Duns. Hugh was to graduate in English, and Archie in Mental Philosophy, but their range of shared delight in literature, in theology, in sport, in debate and political argument and in one another's company lasted till Hugh's death in 1958.

It was Andrew Seth Pringle-Pattison, the gentle philosopher, who seems to have caught Archie's intellectual imagination above all others, as well as thrilling his spine; but his range of undergraduate classes was, in the best Scottish university tradition, a wide one.

In his first year he stuck with the Latin and Greek which John Kemp had so thoroughly instilled, and in which he retained both competence and pleasure. (In fact, he amused himself in his old age by translating nursery rhymes into Latin, and was able in his eighties to translate medical Latin for a massive *History of the Royal College of Physicians* written by his nephew, Stuart.) In session 1907-8 he took Maths, Logic and Metaphysics and German; the following year Moral Philosophy and English, and, along with his reading for finals, Political Economics. Rather surprisingly, his class exam marks in philosophy were low 50s and 60s, whereas almost all the others were high 70s and 80s, but his ability must have impressed the Department beyond his marks, for Kemp-Smith later appointed him as a part-time assistant lecturer in Philosophy after the First World War.

There is too little evidence to reconstruct much of his life at this stage. In academic terms, he had a bad third year, and was himself disappointed by his II:1 in Honours, though he must have been even more distressed for Hugh, who inexplicably finished with a third, and confessed himself shocked. It seems that Archie had significant health problems at this stage, which culminated in an appendicitis operation in September 1913, and there is some evidence too of something more like stress. Hugh writes in the May of his final year, "It is bad to hear that you are bothering about the result, you especially who have every excuse for doing 'badly' ''; and references to his health are so uniform among his correspondence at this time that it must have been a conspicuous problem.

Among the voluminous letters Archie kept was a small batch from one, Esther G. Bell, who had been ahead of him at university, and was the most distinguished woman philosophy student of her day. She had been a good friend of Archie's in S.C.M. and later wrote to him from Canada, where she had gone after marriage and graduation. The fragments regarding his health are tantalisingly slight, but suggest significant problems:

14th October, 1909.

"My dear Auxiliary,
    . . . Let me know how you fare if Philosophy does not claim every moment,
    From your sincerely attached though now far distant Guardianess"

27th December, 1909.

"I was very sorry to hear from Mr Dorward and Mr Ross that you have had something in the nature of a breakdown and had to go home for the end of the session to recruit. . . . . . . As the exam is not till June you need not feel unduly hurried, and I do solemnly beseech you, don't overdo things. If you think on ahead 10 years, you will realise that it will matter very little to you then whether you took a 2nd or a first class."

11th March, 1910.

"' . . . I hope your headaches are quite things of the past now. I was much gratified to hear you had treated yourself so sensibly. . . . . . . "

28th September, 1910.

"' . . . I regret your second class, but it was obviously due to your state of health all winter: otherwise it would have been surprising."

There is also a letter from Pringle-Patterson, dated 25th October, 1911, in which he writes, clearly in response to a request from Archie, that he is willing to certify him as fulfilling the conditions for a certain Bruce and Frangehill Scholarship. It continues,

"The best part of your letter is that which says that you are at last getting into good physical form. I should think on that ground the additional year you propose to give yourself is likely to be beneficial."

What exactly happened next is somewhat obscure. Indeed the period from 1906 until the war is rather incoherent from the biographer's limited vantage-point.

According to the records of Saint Mary's School, the Melrose prep school founded by John Hamilton, Archie was on the staff as a teacher of Classics and English from 1907 until 1912. How he combined this responsibility with the attending of classes, and why he sought to is unclear. Even how he managed to commute between Edinburgh and Melrose is problematic, for he was clearly involved not just in the bare minimum of classes, but active in various extra-mural pursuits. At university, he was certainly in S.C.M., as Esther Bell's letters make clear, debated vigorously in the Dialectic Society, wiping the floor with less able opponents, and was active in the thriving German Society which flourished under the sustaining tutelage of Professor Otto Schlapp. In his third year, he edited the yearbook of the latter society, a prodigious task, which involved a good deal of collating, some writing, including a funny illustrated article on "*Die Deutsche Wurst*", and a massive amount of physical labour, since all the writing, illustration and binding was hand done.

At Saint Mary's too, his involvement was more than minimal tuition. The obituary by Gordon Hector in *Great St. Mary's*, the former pupils' magazine, draws on school archives which bear witness to him "doing the work of three men" for the school in a six-a-side hockey tournament in Kelso, and to hockey and cricket teams which he assembled to play against the school, called, with characteristic self-depreciation "Edinburgh Motleys" and "Campbell Craig's Crocks". In addition, the only letter which is extant from a pupil, a child called Kenneth who had to leave Saint Mary's on health grounds, is full of animated confidence that *Dear Sir* will be interested in all his news about stamp-collecting, the birds in his garden and the family's new motor-car, the kind of trust not inspired by teachers who don't spend time with their pupils beyond the bounds of academic duty. Another former pupil, still alive and vividly remembering his St. Mary's days, one Ritchie Gardiner, remembers him as a friendly teacher who gave the boys a lot of scope, letting them, for instance, choose essay topics for themselves. Even more tellingly, going to visit Archie in Doune decades later, for the first time since his schooldays, Mr Gardiner's impression was that he "hadn't changed a bit."

At this stage it seems that he was seriously contemplating teaching as a career, and debating with himself as to whether to defer his entry into Divinity Hall at New College. What seems to have happened is that he began his theology in session 1911-12, attending a minimum of classes in order to fulfil the Scholarship requirements, and then decided to take a year out, on what

12

seem to have been partly health and partly vocational uncertainty grounds. His friends offer him conflicting advice. Esther Bell writes, in the autumn of 1910:

> "I applaud your resolution to take a year off, as I share to the full your distrust of the over-young and over-wise parson. I think the more a man has seen of the world before entering the Church the better. The Church has a fatal tendency to dehumanise men, I think."

Hugh Walker, on the other hand, a couple of years later, when Archie is still manifestly undecided about the ministry or teaching dilemma, is strongly in favour of him getting through New College first, if only to know what he doesn't want to do.

> "While I appreciate fully your reasons for looking for a light two-term teaching post, I don't know that I want to encourage you. I feel that I want you to get through your New College course. . . . . . If you ultimately decide against joining with the ecclesiastics, you must have your first youth to take up the other great profession competitively and unamateurishly".

Three months later it seems, he had decided; for his father writes, on 2nd December, 1913, "You have devoted your life to a noble calling — the noblest of all — and I doubt not that tomorrow will be a renewed consecration." It was the eve of Archie's twenty-fifth birthday.

As far as one can gather, the family had not leaned on him. Three brothers before him had gone into other professions, yet there is no sense that his parents are breathing down his neck. His father's allusions to the decision are light, as when he writes in response to Archie's birthday greetings in 1911:

> "It is the fewest number who are spared to see the youngest of a large family attain the age of four and twenty, and I still hope we may be spared to see the said young man 'wag his head in a pulpit'."

Whether he did take a full year out in 1912 is unclear. What can be established is that in the summer of 1912, he set off on a sea voyage to visit his sister Bessie, now living in Ceylon with her husband, who was in the Colonial Service. Dick Wright, another Saint Mary's friend and colleague, writes, just before that, in June, of Archie's having fallen into the hands of doctors and such people who were dealing badly by him, of his being forbidden violent exercise and taking up photography as an alternative recreation. And Hugh Walker sends a letter that same September, to catch him at Port Said on the return journey, and to brief him on what he should and shouldn't do in Paris when he gets there a week later. (The shoulds include visiting the Opera and *of course* a Cinema House, and the shouldn'ts warn against going to the Scotch Church in Paris, "where we heard an absolute bastard of a man, shallow, fluent so long as his praying counters lasted, & withal thoroughly complaisant.")

The following May, he is again abroad in Germany, with his mother worrying about how his digestion is standing the German food, and reproaching him for not saying how his stomach is using him; and his father urging him to visit the Dresden Art Gallaries and the Luther country, which he himself had wanted but not managed to visit when he spent a year of his own theological training in Tubingen in 1867. This advice Archie followed, visiting a friend in Jena, and being struck in the Dresden galleries by two things: one, a head of Christ which, instead of being conventionally pallid and insipid, showed a ruddy and virile face, full of life and energy and laughter; and the other a German tourist, going round tied to her *Baedeker*, and precisely matching the nerve of her admiring comments to the number of asterisks ascribed to each painting by the compiler. It was a kind of bad faith with which Archie could have no patience, to fail to look with one's own eyes. (He seems to have had a natural scorn for the kind of cowardice often involved in not being truthful. Of all his fellow students, the only one on whom he ever comments adversely was a man who pretended to subtle perplexities on fine points of conduct, but if he wanted to back out of an engagement, would invent domestic deaths and tragedies among an apparently inexhaustible supply of grandmothers!)

The stomach trouble persisted, and in September, 1913, his appendix was removed, quite a major operation in those days; and friends congratulated him on having dealt with his offending member in the scriptural way. He seems to have enjoyed his convalescence, and recalls to David Cairns years later the pleasurable indulgence of reading what he liked, "not *ad hoc, hoc* being a degree examination, but whatever took one's fancy". (One of his first requests to Hugh was for a *Golden Treasury*.) But the hopes of friends and family that this would end the stomach trouble, and that he could subsequently eat what he liked were not to be realised. Hugh again, having enlisted early in Kitchener's army, writes to him in October, 1915, ". . . and you, old son, are still troubled by your damned constitution."

So little did Archie ever disclose health problems as a matter of general conversation, and so robustly did he work and play, that almost all who knew him as friends or colleagues all plead total ignorance of the fact that he was ever ill at all. Yet there were several major periods of sick-leave in his life. One came soon after he himself enlisted, while he was still doing officer training in England, which prompted his mother to write wondering if he were in fact strong enough for the trenches; and another in 1944, while he was with the British Council of Churches, and had letters to and from the office referring to quite serious, though unspecified, illness. His elder brother, Billie, thought nerves had a lot to do with the 1915 trouble, and various friends at different periods speak of his need to let off steam, and of his reluctance to do so causing him problems; so it may be that there was a psychosomatic component to some of the medical symptoms.

Though all this must have provided some kind of undertow to his student wellbeing, he was, as letters to and from friends in the vacations suggest, more preoccupied about other things than with his own health. And the early years of his New College course, together with his involvement in the Student Christian Movement, the most thriving and stretching student group of the day, were beginning to get in focus some of the concerns that were to remain central to him for seventy years longer.

One of these was the relation of Christianity to secular and political life. Hugh was a committed Socialist, a Fabian and a member of the Church Socialist League, and Archie was, with him, beginning to be interested in an analysis which did not explain the world's evils only in terms of individual fecklessness. That seems to have made him somewhat critical of some of his teachers, of whom he made negative comment both to his father and to Dick Wright, now teaching in Liverpool. Their reponses suggest the brunt of Archie's comments. From his father comes the gentler remark:

"I am sorry to hear that the Principal (Alexander Martin) is inclined to be downhearted" (about the chances of social improvement). "I have no doubt it is in measure owing to his long residence in an eastern climate which is almost sure to have an effect on the liver, and the condition of that affects the spirits more or less."

Dick, more ebulliently responds:

"Sorry, beassly sorry you are unhappy with your old theologian. To my mind a man of education and culture who thinks all well with the world except for the intemperance and idleness of the lower classes is a wonder and a sorrow."

All Archie's subsequent comments on his teachers, however, including Principal Martin, are in a tone of unqualified appreciation, amounting almost to grateful veneration. The outstanding ones were, for him, Harry Kennedy in New Testament, introducing them to the delights of T. R. Glover's *The Jesus of History*; Adam Welch in Old Testament; and in Systematic Theology, "that figure of incandescent granite, H. R. Mackintosh." He recalls, somewhat ruefully, "the mists into which they led as a precondition of climbing to higher levels in the understanding of Scripture and of God's ways with the world", but in all his own subsequent teaching and preaching he stayed faithful to their sense that truth was not to be had on the intellectual or moral cheap. Much later, at the age of eighty-one, he was to summarise his sense of what should be going on in a Divinity school:

> "The greatest problem of all theological colleges is to keep theological learning and living religion in effective relation with each other. For living religion in divorce from sound theological learning can go haywire, louping or rolling on the floor in an empty ecstasy, or fixing a precise date for the end of the world and so being better informed than was Jesus. On the other hand, learned theology apart from living religion is the shell of a dead walnut, encapsulating only shrivelled sterility."

On the whole, New College seems to have passed the test, in that he refers back to his teachers at various points in his later ministry, finding things they had said important, or confirmed by his experience.

At the same time, there were other sources of learning. It is almost impossible to over-estimate the impact of the Student Christian Movement on the university and church worlds of the day, and Joe Oldham, who was at this time so deeply involved with it, was already a kenspeckle [well-known] figure in United Free Church circles, having narrowly missed appointment as secretary to that Church's Foreign Mission Committee. (This was not because he was not thought the best man for the job, but because the Assembly reacted with hostility to the feeling that some of Oldham's supporters were acting as a caucus, and thought they had the appointment sewn up!) Archie was already keenly involved in S.C.M. as an Arts student, though he once reminisced caustically, "In my youth, I was nearly pawed out of the Student Christian Movement by a branch official who was doing his well-intentioned best to paw me in."

By his time at New College he was "far ben" enough to be involved with Oldham and W. P. Paterson in setting up S.C.M. in theological colleges. The context seems to have been a gentlemanly afternoon tea, for he remembered long afterwards "W.P. discoursing with his eyes shut, and emphasising his points with a jelly-spoon to which there clung fragments of a pink jelly until he stirred his tea with it." He was struck too on this occasion by Oldham's combination of efficiency and devotion as he prepared to pray by asking for a systematic list of topics for prayer. It was Joe Oldham's influence which Archie in later life credited as the direct force *ab extra* which had brought him into the Ecumenical Movement.

Church re-union was, of course, in the air. The historic 1910 World Missionary Conference had been held in the Free Church's Assembly Hall in Edinburgh just as Archie finished his Arts degree, setting the overcoming of ecclesiastical divisions in the context of effective mission. Oldham was based in Edinburgh through Archie's university years, and was sounding the clarion cry that faith and secular life had to fuse if there was to be any hope of making sense to the world outside the churches, or to the young churches of the missionary outreach from Europe.

It was also in 1919 that the conversations began between the United Free Church and the Church of Scotland, with a view to their possible reunion. The theological student was at the time apparently less than enthusiastic about the motives, though by the time the Union took place in 1929, he was fully behind it. In 1912, however, Hugh writes to him:

> "As you infer, the movement towards Church Union is less a fruit of the spirit than a business more forced upon failing institutions by the antagonism of apathy around. . . . It has small likelihood of bringing with it that honesty of thought and speech which would necessitate that creed revision of which you speak, and until these things come together the decent instincts of the commonalty will be against the church."

It sounds as if these sons of manses had some sympathy with the "atrabilious journalist" castigated in the reminiscences of the Free Church Assembly for 1909, who had alleged that "Our meetings were barren of interest, barren of thought and barren of enthusiasm, . . . and that the same barrenness . . . also afflicted the Church at large during the other eleven months of the year, because the Church was hopelessly out of touch with the masses, and with the vast body of intellectuals who were deeply concerned about questions of social well-being."

What particularly dissatisfied him in the institution seems to have been appeals to blind fideism. Dick Wright responds to a paper he has written with the comment:

> "Broadly speaking, the intelligent religion of your paper is non-existent here with us. The "religion" which I despise and denounce is exactly what you vitriolise in your paper, — ignorance which calls itself faith or priestcraft mysticism-ritual."

By the age of twenty-five then, Archie was deeply involved in the pursuit of an intellectually cogent and politically relevant faith, but uncertain still as to whether he should pursue it in the context of ordained ministry, or as a teacher. He had done two summer locums on Islay, and had, of course, all the experience of the Kelso manse behind him. On the other hand, he had the energetic schooling of Kelso High, and the happy cameraderie of his time on the staff of a devoted and friendly prep school. Nothing extant gives us precise access to the internal wrestling this dilemma involved, and he must have carried it lightly in most people's presence, if the bantering chatter of holiday letters from fellow divinity students swapping vacation locum notes is anything to go by. But with intimates like Hugh it is clear that he unburdened himself of quite deep distress. One cordial and tender letter back from Duns, tantalisingly undated, is written "to cheer thee up my dear, dear friend," and expresses the hope of taking his mind for a little away from the thoughts of his "infernal task". The letter goes on

> "this thing you are doing and worriting your spirit in has no compensations. Don't think it would be a good thing if you were never irritated with the old man & always felt nice and happy and at home in the place ... Believe me, that to have adapted yourself to a place like that would have gone far to plucking the manhood and individuality out of you."

It urges him to resist the horrid blasphemy of exhortations to be content in that place and position to which Providence has called him, and insists that his cross does not lie in patiently bearing petty troubles that thwart his spirit.

Who the old man in question is, father? teacher? placement supervisor? is unclear, and the place unspecifiable. But the letter is telling enough as an index of the kind of inner wrestling about duty and direction which recurred at several key points in Archie's career. His massive and growing sense of Providence as the root doctrine of Christian faith in no way acted as a short-circuit to the painful human struggle towards hard decisions. There was no clarity or guidance on the cheap.

At home, circumstances had changed. His father had retired in 1909, after three final years in the newly united St John's Free Church, where he had enjoyed a happy collegiate ministry with a relatively young man called John Laidlaw, "which neither disparity of age nor even ardent rivalry over the chessboard did anything to impair." Mr Laidlaw had two children, a son named Leslie and a daughter May, and it was on the day of their arrival in Kelso on 15th October, 1906, that Archie first set eyes on the girl he was to marry forty-four years later, and live with for the subsequent thirty-five. His job on that autumn day early in his first university term was to meet Mrs Laidlaw and May at Kelso railway station and escort them to the manse, while the menfolk arrived by bicycle.

If Presbytery retiral tributes are to be believed, Alick Craig had set high standards for any son contemplating ministry. He was reported to read his Greek and Hebrew Bible oftener than any minister in Tweedale, and to have worn out more shoe-leather in visiting than anyone else in the Presbytery (though he too had latterly taken to cycling!) He had, in forty-two years, missed only seven sabbaths preaching, and apart from encroaching deafness felt himself seventy years young. The fact that he maintained his reputation for judgment, tact and brotherliness through years of acting as Presbytery Clerk testifies to a generous and genial humanness, and a younger minister recalls him taking the whole presbytery back home after meetings to enjoy Mrs Craig's convivial hospitality.

Much as Alick Craig loved Kelso, the family decided to move in retirement to Troon, in the neighbourhood of his first charge in Dundonald, so that "when the old wood was out of the way, the plant had a better chance of vigorous growth." They named their retirement house *St. John's* and seem to have had a complicated family menage, which included an elderly and difficult aunt living nearby, who taxed the psychic strength of Mrs Craig and of Minnie, the eldest unmarried daughter still at home. Letters to Archie from 1912 till Aunt Kate died in 1919 are punctuated by references to nurses having, or being on the edge of having, nervous breakdowns, and to the problems of finding replacements. There were, however, regular and warm contacts with the Borders, frequent visits and keen interest in the friends left behind there.

By now all the children had left home, with the exception of Minnie and Madge. Mrs Craig complains about feeling useless and unemployed, though if she was as involved in the doings of the others as she was in those of her "Benjamin", she must have had hardly a moment to spare! Letters to Edinburgh all through Archie's student years are full of little signs of her maternal involvement, news of when she has despatched his clean laundry, her inability to find last summer's cricket flannels, injunctions to buy a new tennis suit or to remember to bring home his ginger-jar on his next visit for refilling with marmalade. The house at Troon seems to have been permanently full of visitors; grandchildren, nephews, nieces, cousins, friends, and such hospitality was additional to maintaining impeccable standards of decent housewifery, with jam-making, spring-cleaning and garden chores high on the agenda, as well as umpteen activities related to the church in Troon, where the Craigs enjoyed the ministry of a young Mr Brander.

Another domestic problem which seems to have occupied a great deal of the family's psychic energy at this time was what should be done about Alice, Archie's immediately older sibling, born two years before him. One neighbour of Kelso days remembers her even then being nicknamed "Lady Disdain", and she apparently drove her mother, Minnie and her elder brothers to distraction. Large tracts of family correspondence through the 1910-1920 period take up the Alice problem. She refuses to work, won't speak of Minnie, snubs the Lays (her eldest sister's family by marriage) and is generally seen to be making life hot for all around her. Forrest, Archie's elder by nine years, writes to John, the third surviving boy in 1911:

"Alice can't housekeep, she has no idea of the value of money, our maids could not put up with her, in short there would be unpleasantness in a fortnight.

Besides, you as dominie, Archie as pastor, — (Does he assume it at this point, where Archie himself was still far from clear?) — I as doctor could not introduce into our seminary, parish, practice such a quarrelsome piece of furniture without discomfiture of some sort.

So you see the only thing left is to give her an income of some sort and tell her to go where she likes. Now while I am delighted to dole out ducats for Madge, I beg to draw the line at Alice. The coolness of her attitude fills me with wrath unspeakable. She has had a good education, better than any of her sisters, and ought to be doing something for herself.

Her proud stomach will not look at a small thing. The house is a hell upon earth for mother when the excitement of the holidays is over; what with Alice's tantrums and the old lady's groans and grumbles.''

Apart from various letters in this vein from both Forrest and John to Archie, he is also recipient of his mother's more gently distressed worry that she has somehow spoiled Alice, and she appears to think that if anyone in the family can appeal to her better nature, it will be Archie alone. At some stage Alice comes to stay with him in Edinburgh, and they go together to a dance; and when he gets his first D.D. from Edinburgh in 1938, she writes instantly that she is bubbling with excitement, so it looks as though he did a fair job in keeping open at least one unsoured relationship for her, perhaps because there was no possibility of his playing the big brother, as Forrest and John seem to have done.

Before he had finished his theology course, the large events of Europe had lurched into the forefront of everyone's life, overshadowing domestic or personal vocational issues. As a divinity student it was open to him not to enlist, but as he later put it, "To me as a being of sort of normal loyalty and patriotism at the time, it was not open not to enlist." So he "just enlisted", though taking care to safeguard his entry into the ministry by passing a Hebrew exam first. Though, characteristically, he makes light of the decision, it too was, at the time, something of a dilemma. On 9th September, 1914, his New Testament professor, H.A.A. Kennedy writes to him in a vein of cautious guidance:

"I can well realise that you feel a conflict of duties. As regards health, does not past experience urge you to go very cautiously in making your decision. Remember what the strain of active service is bound to be. . . . If the best men resolve to go on military service, what is likely to happen in the affairs of the Kingdom of God? . . . I can't help feeling that men with special endowments of mind and heart will be sorely needed at home."

While meant not to pressurise, such a letter must have given Archie pause, but in the end, on 5th October, 1914 he enlisted into the Royal Scots Regular Army, aged 25, height 6 ft, weight 162 lbs. By Christmas he was off, as Private 17055, for an officer training course as was his elder brother John. The decision for the two older brothers, Willie and Forrest, seems to have taken slightly longer. The family appear to have accepted both his right to decide and his decision without demur, though his mother, of course, was concerned about his health, and his father retrospectively disclosed his mixed feelings about Archie's enlisting. They clearly had enough respect for him and his decision-making not to impose their ambivalence on him in any way.

Only much later, on New Year's Day, 1916, his father writes,

"Needless to say I have thought it in many ways a pity that your Hall Course has been interrupted and your entrance on Higher work delayed — but I have no doubt that the experience you are gaining in your present sphere will give its own contribution to your fitness for the other duties when you are called to them".

Hugh Walker had already enlisted in the Cameronians, and was writing with bleak dismay of what he feared the war would cost Europe, in contrast to some of the optimistic predictions of other fellow-students that the skirmish would be over in a matter of months. What Archie anticipated is not clear, but for the next four and a half years he was to learn what he later esteemed, even in his pacifist days, as a key virtue — that of "soldierly obedience in the dark."

3 Wartime

"War is like a medicine which eases local troubles, but at the same time poisons the cardiac muscles."

Perhaps the most distinctive thing about Archie Craig's recollections of the war was his reticence about it. Whatever crucible of experience was his in the trenches, it was not something he wanted to dwell on, and so the reconstruction of the years 1914-1918 has to be made with the minimal information he subsequently divulges, together with what can be inferred from family letters, all of which he saved and kept.

On the whole, even contemporary material from the actual time hardly ever alludes to direct information he had given them, and the scores of letters from his mother, his father and Madge shed much more light on *their* lives in wartime Ayrshire than on Archie's own.

It seems that he had made the crucial decision to enlist by the late autumn, and that the dilemma was rather about fighting or finishing his course than about any pacifist alternative. Indeed his first memory of the word is "when, along with other boys of patriotic instinct, I used it as a satisfying term of abuse for Mr Ramsay MacDonald". Certainly he seems to have been the first of the family to enlist. By Christmas, 1914, his mother is writing:

"I don't know whether I should wish you a happy Xmas or not when everything is so dark and uncertain. There is a place for John in Tavistock College . . . . . but I fear he will want to enlist. I hear you say, "How unpatriotic you are, mother". Well, I fear I am, and a coward to boot. Please remember that the cold weather has a great effect on my spirits."

By 1st January, 1915, Private Craig had won his commission, after training in Edinburgh, and was then moved to Basingstoke for further training before setting off for France. Very little of what he made of this experience can be read off the letters from his family, which are the primary source of information for this period.

One thing which he records as if it surprised him at the time is the sense that men who can swear like troopers, and are not above misappropriating petty cash are simultaneously capable of immense loyalty and courage when it comes to actual soldiering. It was his first extended contact with men of a quite different social, educational and religious − or non-religious − background.

Both his parents, and his sister Madge write to him weekly, the latter addressing him more often than not as *Dearest Archibaldus*. His father ends his letter of 3rd March, 1915 by saying, "I hope I have not wearied you. If I remember rightly, you said you wished to have as many of the details of home life as we wished to give." And details abound — who has been preaching at the local church since Mr Brander, their parish minister signed up, Mrs Craig's new bonnet, Queen Mary shape, with violets and a white osprey, the ups and downs of the invalid Aunt, and, perennially, the doings of Alice in relation to the rest of the family.

By 9th July, 1915, Archie's battalion is ready to leave for France, and Mrs Craig's letter that week expresses concern that "We could not make out where your battalion was being sent, although I expected it would be to the front". She continues, as if to muffle a little the awful open uncertainty of the future:

"I hope you left orders as to what was to be done with the pile of socks sent off addressed to you by passenger train on Monday night. There were 104 pairs of socks, 7 shirts and a few pocket handkerchiefs, and one of the workparty said, "I wish we had just managed 120 pairs to have given each of the men two pairs." You must write Mrs Currie a letter of thanks to be read at the work-party."

Two items, not particularly stressed at the time, are more portentous to aftersight. On 22nd October, just as he is leaving with a battalion of Royal Scots for the trenches, his mother writes that his father is doing gardening against Doctor's orders. Then, three weeks later:

"I wish he — [Forrest, who had enlisted with the Medical Corps in May, 1915] — were at home to give father an overhaul, for I don't like to see him so breathless after any exertion, and of course he doesn't like any notice taken of it."

A few weeks later, she writes, though without any emphasis suggesting it was a matter of importance to Archie:

"May has broken off her engagement, whether wittingly or at the instigation of her parents I am not sure . . . Evidently the whole business has caused them much pain and axiety."

In view of the universally held belief that Archie and Mary had been emotionally, if not formally, betrothed since their first meeting, this comes as a surprise, but it is corroborated by an erstwhile neighbour of the Laidlaws in Forestfield, Kelso, who remembers that the reason for breaking off the engagement was that the young man in question turned up at the manse a little under the weather, alcoholically speaking! (Archie too seems to have had an earlier student friendship intense enough to provoke an enquiry from Dick Wright as to his "fair one in Mayfield Terrace", and some teasing about matrimonial prospects.)

All that is clear about this time is that news of the Laidlaws, including May, was part of the regular budget of family news. But matters like the broken engagement, or May's fairly serious illness a little later, when she had pneumonia and suspected tuberculosis, were presented in a low-key tone, with no implication that they would be causing Archie significant emotional upheaval. [Almost none of the correspondence from May to him was left among Archie's papers, except for what one suspects to be odd oversights. With his intense sense of privacy of deep feeling, it is likely that he took pains to protect any intimate correspondence from public scrutiny. The state of affairs between them at this stage can, therefore, only be speculative.]

Of his actual military exploits, very little can be documented. In November, 1915, another of his mother's letters reads:

> "How thankful I was for your marvellous escape when the bullet passed through between your legs. It seems almost impossible that it could make holes in your underwear and not injure you in the least."

That seems to be the most spectacular near miss which was disclosed to the family. Apart from that, the only references to injuries are to a badly cut forehead, and a damaged finger, which may interfere with his music. It is clear also that Mrs Craig lives in permanent dread of his having a motor-bike accident, and her letters recurrently express the wish that he didn't have to ride one.

Sometime around September, 1917, he was moved to the Intelligence Corps, and with his knowledge of German, played a significant enough role in gathering information to earn an M.C. The specific grounds for this he skilfully refused to disclose to questioners, but since the award was made in the First World War only for conspicous physical bravery, and the citation says "For gallantry in France" there must have been more to it than his self-deprecatory "just for intelligence" conveys. The journalist Colin Maclean thinks he was once told by Ronnie Falconer, [former Head of Scottish Religious Broadcasting] that Archie had crossed into enemy lines behind No Man's land to reconnoitre alone.

At any rate, even if he escaped relatively unscathed, the family as a whole suffered sore loss. One winter Sunday, resisting the family's plea that he should stay at home, Archie's father set out for church with Mrs Craig. Madge writes, a few days later:

"Mother saw him take hold of the railings of the Tennis Club and managed to gently lay him down on the ground. One long sigh and it was all over."

Though he had, according to Madge been failing perceptibly, he had made so little of his chest pains, (which Minnie, a trained nurse, thought were angina) that they were unprepared for his death, especially since he had been out in the garden the day before trying to light a bonfire.

At almost the same time, on 28th November, Forrest was shot through the chest while walking a wounded horse up a ridge which was under Turkish fire. He was working with the field ambulance of the Mounted Corps of the Palestine Expeditionary Force. Ironically, he had written, only weeks before, that he was glad to be doing hospital work again, firstly because Anna, his fiancee of a few weeks, need have no anxiety about his safety, and secondly for the sake of taking up medical work again. Gravely wounded, he was carried a mile by his batman and a Q.M. sergeant who refused to leave him, and then transported to military hospital in Alexandria, weakened by the loss of pints of blood, but *compos mentis* enough to register the disgraceful state of transport and medical facilities. A fortnight later, when he was regaining strength, he wrote home that he was ashamed of his corps, and by the lack of co-ordination which meant that wounded men had to put up with days without food, and eventually be given such unsuitable fare as biscuits and tinned rabbit. "If the same lack of provision and arrangement prevails to any extent in the conduct of the army operations in the field," is his tart observation, "there's little wonder that we don't make more way."

For a month, all the news from Alexandria is good, and by late January he is deemed well enough to be transported home on a hospital ship, the S.S. Glengorm Castle. Then, on February 2nd, a letter comes from the matron of the ship to say that Forrest has had a relapse, and, after two days of feverish chill, pain and vomiting, has died.

Their brother's death makes the war even more sombre for the remaining ones. John and Archie exchange letters which they wish to go to their mother in the event of either's death, and work out financial provision for their sisters. In the event, though the family lives with great anxiety through the big German offensive in the spring of '18, there are no further casualties, and the only disappointment is that Archie, now a lieutenant in the Intelligence Corps, has to stay on in Cologne to complete work for the Intelligence Corps. He does not in fact relinquish his commission till 12th August, 1919.

His own voiced reminiscences of the years in the army are not to do with the actual fighting, or the horror of the trenches, but with small vivid personal encounters. He recalls, for instance, a route march with a fellow-officer who, after the war, became a landscape painter. This man would test Archie's colour vision. "What colour is that?" he would ask, as they approached the dark mouth of a railway tunnel. "It's black, of course." "Can't you see," he almost shouted, "that it's a glorious purple!" It remained with Archie as a vignette of what it meant to look with cleansed vision.

Most of all, these years taught him to appreciate the kind of decisiveness which was needed to act competently, a new perception for one who had spent most of his energy as an adult in the world of thought and letters. Years later, he refers more than once to one particular episode:

> "I happened to be at the H.Q. of an infantry division in April, 1918, at the most critical stage of the battle before Amiens, when a wounded sergeant-major rushed in in a panic with the news that German forces had outflanked the divisional front, and were within striking distance of Headquarters itself. I saw the veins swell out like a net of string on the General's temples, and then he quietly called the G.S.O.I., and within five minutes had dictated so many essential orders, and within seven was off on his horse."

Though his total experience of the war convinced him that it was impossible to be anything other than pacifist, he never lost his sense of esteem for the essential virtues of the good soldier, and wished that the church would sometimes take more seriously its appellation of church *militant* rather than church *ruminant*. Years later, he could write:

> "Military images are almost indispensable to bring home certain aspects of the Christian truth: for among all human affairs, the realm of war affords the most numerous, and perhaps the most vivid examples of self-sacrifice at the call of duty, and under the impulse of very noble virtues."

What these virtues were he articulates at many points in his preaching: comradeliness, cheerfulness, loyalty, bravery, discipline and above all the capacity for quick yet responsible decision-making. Nothing in his subsequent pacifism made him cynical about the goodness of the ordinary volunteer soldier doing his job.

What he did deplore was the terrible jingoism of certain army types, and of the politicians who endorsed their easy nationalism. Much later, he sends some verses to a friend which include lines of scathing intensity. They take the form of a dialogue between a colonel and an army padre.

> "I liked the speed with which you nipped your
> Way through that curious bit of Scripture
> About a blessing on the meek

And turning of the other cheek.
. . . .
YES, YES, . . . the source may be reliable,
BUT IN THE FORCES IT'S NOT VIABLE.
We never won a battle yet
With Bibles: it's the bayonet
Thrust through the belly to the back
That keeps afloat the Union Jack.
Where should we be if high morality
Paled the red blood of nationality?
Or if that Jewish God I AM
Dethroned John Bull or Uncle Sam?"
. . . . . . So spoke
The brick-faced, ribbon-gaudy colonel,
Since warfare's dawn a type eternal.
"I grudge no man his luxury
However odd his taste may be,
Provided — mark my words — provided
It doesn't make him undecided
Or squeamish when it comes to killing:
For that's the soldier's special function,
Lawful and blessed by pulpit unction.
Our total system of instilling
Into the raw recruits the gen
That turns them into fighting men
Is framed to anaesthetise compunction
And weld the matter-mind conjunction
Whereby unthought reflexes act
On a split second's sharp impact,
Hurl the grenade, plunge home the knife
To end the something someone's life."

If, as seems likely, this was a type which Archie encountered as a soldier, it clarifies the complexity of his feelings about the war; that he could see it as an environment capable of bringing out good in some people, but the worst in others. He records that he did not himself really shed tears for the *scale* of the losses in the First World War until he visited Anzio during his moderatorial year, and saw the rows on rows of crosses, but he was well aware of the wreckage of his own generation, of former classmates and fellow-students who didn't return to their classes. Kelso High School lost thirty-one former pupils.

After the armistice, he found the nine months of his stay in Cologne almost more awful than the war. The sense of "carnival and carnality" shocked and shamed him, and the frivolity of the reactions to wartime austerity seemed to him less tolerable than the austerity had been. Puritanism always struck him as a more tolerable fault than sensuous self-indulgence, which seemed to him a betrayal of the proper hierarchy of mind over body.

In this period, his outstanding memory was of one man who shared his mess, a pianist called John Petrie Dunn. This man, whom Archie regarded as a musician of genius, promised his messmates that by a certain date he would have mastered a certain Mozart sonata. For weeks he studied and practised, and, on the very day he had promised, gave a brilliant performance. The dedication and concentration of his energy on this one thing, and the precision of his self-discipline in naming and meeting his target date impressed Archie immensely. It was for him the polar antithesis of the sexual abandon of post-war permissiveness, and he later referred to it as a paradigm of what Christian fidelity should be. He himself was able to have access to a good grand piano at the time, and the letters from home reflect his pleasure at this.

Principal Martin had at this point written to all the New College students who had enlisted, to say that they might finish their course in five terms, so back Archie went, part, as he put it, "of the straggling remnant who returned to their savage interrupted studies, certainly sadder and perhaps wiser."

What impact the war years had on the faith or theology of the young man can't be isolated, but it seems to have sown the seed that was to grow into a resolute disavowal of any nationalistic god. What he regarded as *normal patriotism* before the war became impossible for him. He was also faced, in another context than that of foreign mission, with the impact of a divided church. Many years later he records the impact of a letter from a fellow-soldier who had written just after the war:

> "I've no more use for the Church. It was the one thing in the Army that split up our unit into little sections marched off on Sundays to their separate Church parades."

Out of his generation, many of the best men had died. The fact that a year of students which contained John and Donald Baillie just ahead of him, and his own year, could think of themselves as a rump indicates perhaps what a flowering of theological intelligence might have been if the war had not so decimated them. Archie himself was by now thirty, and still had his studies to finish. But whatever was to become of him, the context of security of the pre-war world was irreparably altered.

4 Parish ministry

"The one, central, commanding, controlling, decisive ministerial priority is that the minister should be a *'lover'* ".

Address given at Leighton House

By the summer of 1919, Archie was back in harness as a student in Edinburgh, and beginning to look around for his next position after college. This seems to have involved wrestling with several options, for his mother writes:

"It is a pity you have so much difficulty in deciding what you are going on for in the future, but no doubt your way will be opened up."

This seems to refer not to the actual decision about ministry, but to the more specific issue of what *kind* of ministry. Yet there seem to have been more basic questions for him a few months earlier before he was demobbed, for in February, 1919, she had written, "I am glad you are going back to New College for another year, and I do hope you will see your way to go on to the ministry." There may still have been some uncertainty in Archie's mind as to whether he should teach rather than preach.

In the event, he completed his B.D. and went ahead with his licensing by the Presbytery of Jedburgh and Kelso, but for the following year held three part-time jobs in conjunction, as if to keep his options open. The family reaction is a cross between pride and concern that he is overworking, and will damage his health again. He was deeply involved in the Free Church's work in the ineptly-named Pleasance, which was then one of the worst slum districts adjacent to the Royal Mile. Here he assisted the redoubtable Harry Miller in the Pleasance church, and was also sub-warden of the New College Settlement, the centre of what would now be called "inner-city mission" by the students for the Free Church ministry. His mother writes in March, 1920,

"We are a little surprised to hear of you throwing in your lot with Dr Harry Miller. It is rather flattering that you should have no less than three strings to your bow. Don't try to do too much and wear yourself out before your time."

The third string was a position as assistant lecturer to Professor Kemp-Smith in philosophy, of which his mother writes:

"We were interested to hear about your appointment to the University. I am sure it will be good practice if you don't find it takes too much out of you over and above your other work."

The Pleasance introduced Archie to a range of experience which had no precedent either in his bonnie Roxburghshire or in the toughness of army life, that of urban poverty and squalor. Harry Miller, whose ministry had transformed the place, apparently gave students highly practical tips. Norman Porteous, who came to New College in 1924, a few years after Archie's time, remembers him advising on the right way to help a drunk woman down the street — ("Don't take her arm, let her take yours, she feels less taken over!") One of Archie's switherings in the next few years seems to have been about whether to go into that kind of parish as his first charge, and Harry Miller actually suggested a few years later that he apply for Arthur Street, an adjacent church to his in the same area.

From the Pleasance days two pastoral episodes become paradigms which are subsequently quoted in many other contexts.

At one point Archie is addressing a street meeting, consisting of half a dozen men on a corner in the Pleasance. Among them he notices one man in particular, burly and of churlish manner, who, throughout his talking smokes and spits, spits and smokes. When he finishes, there is a disconcerting silence. To break it, Archie appeals for comment: "Well now, will you tell us what you think of that, and what we have said?" To which the burly man replies, "Crack awa' wi' yer whup, young man. Ye're on the richt side o'the dyke. We a' ken there's yin abune." The matter-of-factness of this reply out of the reticent faith of ordinary people who were normally silent about what they believed was, from then on, something that tempered the evangelical zeal of the young preacher with caution against presuming paganism in those not vocally devout.

Another incident stayed with him to be repeated many times as an illustration and a parable. One of the homes he visited in the Pleasance belonged to a Mrs Smith, and overlooked one of the foulest corners of one of the worst streets in the district. On entering, Archie made some comment on how depressing it must be to be so cramped in such a setting. Whereupon the lady took him through to the back of the house and pointed to the view of Salisbury Crags from her back window. "A body can thole a wheen o'troubles when ilka morn she can look at a bonny view like that in the licht o' God's sun." The state of that woman's existence between squalid street and open sky became a symbol for Archie of all our tension in living between distress and glory.

About the same time as he was wondering whether his future lay in such a slum parish, he seems also to have been debating with himself about foreign mission service, no surprising thing in the aftermath of the 1910 Missionary

Conference which had fired so many with its sense that mission was the *raison d'etre* of the church. Madge writes to him with characteristic affection and gentleness, on 19th February, 1920:

> "The great decision that you are called upon to make has seldom been out of my mind. My first feeling was a pang at the possibility of your going far away from us — we had always pictured you in a manse with a garden! The next feeling was one of great joy that you are one of the Master's loyal servants, just waiting for his word. Christ has a plan for our lives, and will unfold it as we follow. I feel sure, my dear, dear laddie that the guiding light will not fail you at this time."

How precisely the light came is not clear, but by late March, Mrs Craig is writing that if he had decided for the foreign field she would not have stood in his way, but that she is personally glad that he is staying in Scotland. She actually draws his attention to charges vacant in the vicinity of Troon:

> "We notice in the *British Weekly* that your friend Mr Cameron has had a unanimous call to Leslie, and the Morebattle minister is called somewhere else. How would you like either of these churches?"

In the event, Archie's interest in Morebattle is complicated by the fact that one of his friends, Laurence, is interested also, and he wonders whether he should refrain from becoming a candidate there in case he pips Laurence to the post. His mother points out that it would be a pity if, on his withdrawal, Laurence also failed to get it, and whether this affects his decision is undocumented, but in the end Laurence is unanimously called to Morebattle, and Archie successfully applies for Galston, near Kilmarnock, where his congregation is "an average muster of some 160 souls in an ex-U.P. congregation of the U.F. church, and comprising in its membership weavers of lace curtains, shopkeepers and tradesmen, some farmers of Ayrshire dissenting stock and a few miners."

One of Archie's graces, both as minister and human being, was to be genuinely interested in whoever he was talking to, with no ulterior motive. And it is no polite reference that makes him say that he learned as much about God and the things of faith from his people as he ever taught them, and more than he found even in his valued theological training. Over the years pastoral anecdotes accumulate, giving colour and concreteness to his overall vision and understanding of what faith is all about.

He was increasingly impressed by the fact that ordinary, modest people could be so rich in insight and expression which left his theological sophistication far behind. He loved the pungency of vernacular Scots, and mentally collected particular treasure —. "She wis fair trachled wi' a squatter o' weans" [really burdened and held back by a litter of children]; "If his taxt hid had the scarlit fevvir, his sermon widnae hae catched it." "Onything but Paul!" (on offering to read a passage of scripture at the bedside of an old woman) "I canna bide Paul! He's aye blaw-blaw-blawin' aboot himsel."

His ordination and induction took place on October 12th, 1921, and was celebrated by his siblings — at least those of them who were around — by a mock proclamation:

"Dearly beloved brother,
      we your bretheren and sisters in the confraternity of US . . . do hereby pledge ourselves, collectively and separately, individually and corporately, to, by all means and devices, by candour and brutality, by false alarms and annual excursions and all other means, whatsoever, stand by and protect you from your worst self . . ."

Sursum corda   Cave Canem
                                        (particularly the collar)

Erskine Church is now the halls of the parish church, but in the 1920's it was a smallish and fairly intimate church building, holding about two hundred people comfortably, and lying at the edge of the town which was dominated by the parish church on the hill.

Archie took very seriously the warning of H.A.A. Kennedy that the tone of a man's entire ministry was set in his first year. His first priority was to preach well and systematically, not text-hopping in a way which he regarded as self-indulgent. Indeed, he wrote at the onset to his dearest theological mentor, George S. Stewart ("the best man I ever knew") asking his help and advice in planning a 40-year scheme of sermons! Stewart wrote back gently that he had never himself contemplated more than five years at a time, and on subsequent occasions would tease Archie with comments like, "The heather this week would inspire many of your forty years' preaching."

His preaching sequence was not, in fact, obtrusively schematic, though he did preach regularly in series through key books or passages, like the Sermon on the Mount or 1st Corinthians. The sermons are most often focused round a single short phrase or sentence of the New Testament, as his father's had been, and while the background scholarship is there, it is not heavily presented, and the use of homely illustration and anecdote is natural and unforced. Occasionally, he indulges in somewhat fanciful elaboration, as when, preaching on Acts 20.38, "And they accompanied him to the ship", he has a long section on the risks to youth of setting out on an unseaworthy vessel, heading for the far country on a ship named *Youthful Enterprise*, whose master is Captain Self-will, the first mate Mr Careless, a near relative of Captain's, and the crew are the impulses of the flesh.

On the whole, however, the four closely-typed quarto sides which seem to have met the Scottish standard of "Twa peppermints, a' sookin' an' nae crunchin" were less rhetorically extravagant, and consist of diligent exegesis combined with pertinent application to his people's situation. They are demanding sermons, not because they are intellectually difficult, though they are lean and marrowy, but because they invite recognition of the life of Jesus as the authentic, final and attainable standard of human life.

The nuclear core of the Gospel for Archie was the Sermon on the Mount, and it is in relation to that passage that he finds both the primary elation and the chief disappointment of his first pastorate. Though his faith was already mature enough to have won the trust of a number of questing spirits who could risk expressing doubts to him, something happened early in his Galston ministry which was, to the end of his days, a kind of Damascus Road, "the nearest thing to a revelation I have known in the course of personal study of the Bible". His account of it, though much later, is borne out by the events of the time, and presumably catches the quality of the feel of it.

He is reminded of the moment by a passage where Thomas Carlyle describes how the Lord's Prayer once began to lay hold on his spirit as though written for him alone,

"Something akin to that happened to me as I reflected one night on the tremendous passage at the end of Matthew five, "Ye have heard that it hath been said . . . But I say unto you, Love your enemies, bless them that curse you, . . . That ye may be the children of your father which is in heaven: for he maketh his sun to rise on the evil and the good, and sendeth rain on the just and on the unjust."

These tremendous words laid hold on me so piercingly, so luminously that I felt impelled to put them to one particular practical test, namely in the context of a personal relationship with a very difficult man in that community — a seasoned and saturated tippler, an exquisite liar, a perpetual nuisance in the community, a terror under drink to a very patient wife and family of small children. Under the influence of a Scripture becoming incandescent and commanding, I dedicated myself to this man. I could easily spend the next half hour describing the kind of dance he led me, and the new vistas of truth that opened out for me in the course of it. . . . My congregation was not much in sympathy with what was considered to be a mistaken use of time and energy. It didn't fit into a recognised and accepted pattern of the life of the Christian community."

This whole episode was central to Archie's sense of ministry, though he never in his lifetime disclosed the extent of the pastoral cost involved to anyone, even to the grandson of the man in question, who was named Craig after him. He did, however, keep among his papers all the letters written to him by this man, Harry Galloway, which at times were coming at a frequency of three a week, and from those it is clear what expense of time and psychic energy was involved. For about twelve years, Archie kept steadily in touch with this man, an unemployed miner, long after he himself had moved from Galston to Gilmorehill in Glasgow, and then into University chaplaincy. The correspondence, mostly of course Galloway's side of it, (though there is one batch of Archie's letters which he had demanded be sent back when he found they were being used to cadge money from other people) reads like something out of Bunyan's spiritual dramas. The entire register of emotional resources is involved, from tender entreaty to stern rebuke, and the intensity of the wrestling, as Archie saw it, for this man's soul leaps off the pages. For long stretches they were in touch, in person or by letter, several times a week, and Archie found the whole encounter a deep earthing of the theoretical teaching on atonement he had had from H.R. Mackintosh, as he engaged with the cost of battling for this man in a quadrilateral of forces whose points seems to him to be God and the devil, Galloway and himself.

A smattering of extracts from the correspondence may give the flavour of it, though the entire episode would stand full chronicling.

"God is rounding you up like a collie rounding up a strayed sheep."

"You are doing a wrong thing, i.e. defying God Almighty by proposing to run away like a miserable mouse, instead of facing up to the situation like a two-legged man."

"You must know by this time that I intend to stick by you through thick and thin (this to the wife). Meanwhile I must also go down with him into all the dark bitter places that he chooses to go into, and take me into."

"Can't you see, man, that you are dirtying me as well as yourself, and make people laugh at me and say "Craig is a fool to trust that man". Don't come to see me. Learn to stand on your own legs."

"My dear Harry, What is up? I am wearying to hear from you."

"The truth is I wrote you a long letter and then I tore it up. It was too much of a sermon! And it is too bad to inflict sermons through the post."

At times Archie is in despair and declares a final crisis in the relationship. At one point he forbids Harry to see him for a year, until he has put himself in order, but for nine or ten years the friendship goes on with extraordinary spiritual intensity. Harry's replies vary from rather maudlin and mawkish sentimentality to sober and stricken remorse and self-scrutiny, the differing moods and frames of mind correlated to deterioration or improvement in his handwriting. He passes through innumerable ups and downs of work and dismissal, minor sentences for petty offences, domestic violence and periods of relative tranquility when he settles down and enjoys exchanging gardening tips or seeds with Archie. It is increasingly clear as the correspondence proceeds that Archie refuses to treat him either as a moral degenerate or as a hapless victim of circumstances, but appeals to his dignity as a free and equal friend. He refuses to let Harry grovel, with the fairly tart injunction:

> "I don't want you ever again in your letters to me to speak of my "goodness". I am a poor, weak creature like yourself. . . . It is to Christ you are to be grateful. And he has to go with you if you choose to go into the public house. We drag *Him* down with us when we sin, so that He is crucified afresh. And still he has faith in us and waits . . ."

Repeatedly he insists that the relationship is one of mutuality, in which he needs Harry's prayers as much as the other way round, and in which he too has to struggle for self-mastery over the temptations of pride, vanity and self-indulgence; and he will not let him off any kind of hook by allowing the relationship to be one of one-way dependence.

The conviction that people were responsible before God was always a feature of Archie's pastoral judgment, however much he acknowledged psychological or social pressures which were extenuating circumstances. It was, for him, gospel not law that we are able, with God's help, to be better than we are. The severity of the demand that we should not be resigned to failure in the moral sphere, whether private or public, seemed to him to be an implication of the gracious severity of God. It must, however, have taken remarkable spiritual confidence to sustain for so many years, against the odds, the hope of Harry Galloway's rehabilitation, especially if his congregation disapproved. In addition he occasionally crossed swords with other ministers who deplored his supportive stance. One fellow-minister, having had Archie's name cited by Galloway as guarantor of his good faith as a debtor wrote at once to the Galston manse:

> "It is your responsibility that a sponger of this sort should be able to walk the land and parade his hypothetical wounds with histrionic power."

What became of Harry in the years after 1933 is unclear, and the regular communication between them seems to have ceased (or else Archie did not keep the later letters). There is however, occasional correspondence with Galloway's son, Sammy, whose response to his father's misdemeanours is to be almost savagely protective of his mother, and to become a resolute opponent of his ever returning home. He becomes the substitute breadwinner of the family, and is a model of responsible citizenship, graduating from Sunday-school teaching to training for ordination as a minister to the deaf in Ayrshire. He writes to Archie in impeccable script, on tidy paper; but gratified as Archie must have been by his community spirit and decency, it is the wayward Galloway, writing from prison or lodging-house in stubby pencil on scraps of torn paper who engages Archie heart and soul.

In 1956, Sammy writes to Archie an account of his father's death in Law Hospital, Carluke, where, after a sudden collapse, he has been unsuccessfully operated on. He tells how his father had, on his deathbed, been reading Studdert-Kennedy, one of Archie's favourite sources of quotation, to which he had introduced Harry.

"Peace does not mean the end of all our striving,
Joy does not mean the drying of our tears
Peace is the power that comes to souls arriving
Up to the light where God himself appears."

In thanking Archie for all he has meant to the family, and especially to his father, Sammy recalls the latter's comment: "I've rummelt aboot amang a' kin o' fowk, an' Airchie Craig's the maist Christ-like man I've ever encooteret."

While Archie was testing his revelation on the pulse, so to speak, he was also trying to convey to his congregation something of the power of the Sermon on the Mount which had so moved him. His sense of failing to do that, indeed of the near impossibility of doing it, was the primary frustration of a ministry which he nevertheless remembered with great love. He writes of it later without rancour, but with a recollection of his dawning alarm.

"These sermons, laboured over with scholarly conscience and delivered with hopeful zeal, sank without trace beneath the inscrutable, and on the whole, lacklustre surface of that little pool which was my first covenanted congregation. Among its built-in pillars was a certain unmarried lady of middle-age, neither neurotic nor acidulated, as churchly spinsters sometimes show signs of being, kindly and actively helpful to all and sundry, a fail-me-never twicer. Her comment, made kindly and indulgently, as an affectionate aunt might speak to a high-spirited and headstrong nephew, was this: "You know, Mr Craig, you really *do* have some original ideas." Rendered speechless by this devastating testimonial, I could only flee and try to understand its spiritual background and provenance. In the last analysis, it seemed to me to be the persuasion that the normal run of church life, as she had known it long and intimately and honourably, needed no kind of innovation or renovation, whether in thought or practice, had absorbed the teachings of the New Testament up to the limit of toleration, and ought not to be disturbed by what she called – I had better say stigmatised "original ideas", even if they at least purported to be derived from the fountainhead of all ecclesiastical authority.

What alarmed me about this little incident was that this lady was really so admirable and serviceable a person, and at the same time as it seemed to me, muffled up and insulated by her far from ignoble standards against any "terror of the Lord", against the monstrous suggestion that in the merciless light of St. Matthew's Gospel, chs. 5-7, an ex U.P. congregation of the United Free Church might conceivably be revealed to be "wretched and miserable and blind and poor and naked." "

To this sense of the very respectability of the church handicapping it, Archie returned again and again, though more often in retrospective reflection or in correspondence to intimate mentors like George Stewart than to the people themselves. He did preach on occasions making explicit what he thought the claim of the Gospel entailed by way of discipleship, but he did it without scolding or nagging; and if he was disappointed at the corporate respectable decency of his people as less than evangelical fire, he nonetheless genuinely treasured, through his entire ministry, many encounters of his Galston days, which he would recall to people by way of edification or warning.

Some of his tales are to do with the gap between his theories and congregational response, like the time when he asked the organist not to play any gathering voluntary before a communion service, in order to generate a devout and meditative silence. The organist's accurate comment afterwards, "Mr Craig, the suspense was fair hellish!" persuaded him that this was one experiment not to re-try. [Archie thought this such a good line that he either transferred it to or from another context recounted to Lesslie Newbigin, where the minister tried having silent prayer in church. Gospel criticism does not provide the tools to determine which narrative is primary!] Or again, twenty years later, during the 1940 *Religion and Life* week in Bristol, he recalls how one of his elders, an old weatherbeaten farmer, Mr Drummond, gently took him to task.

"Mr Craig, I hope ye'll no mind if I make a wee criticism."
"Not at all."

"Weel, it's thae children's addresses o' yours. Mind I like them weel enough whiles, but I've a wee thing to urge against thaim, and I hope ye winna tak it ill, gin I juist put it into words."

"Not at all."

"Weel, it's this — they're no aye anchored in the Scriptures."

Archie took this as penetrating criticism, and acted on it.

Most of his recollections are of folk who quite unselfconsciously put their finger on the point, or express in their own untechnical way lived religious conviction. Old Mistress Baird in Kilmarnock Infirmary, terrified before an operation and giving the nurses hell, who suddenly felt calmed by prayer, and later confided to Archie, "I coudn'a say wha was wi' me." Or another elderly woman with a reputation for shrewishness, whose comment, after a requested reading from John's Gospel, was, "Is it no wunnerful that the Son o' God should come doon in sic like manner that an auld unlettered buddy like me could grup him?"

Another conversation which seemed to chime in with his own growing sense of a Laodicean church took place with the local manager of the Co-operative Society.

"One evening he came round to the manse, intent on making a co-operator of me. He described the aims of the co-operative movement, its value to the national economy, the advantages accruing to its members, and then he said, point-blank, "Will you join us?" Being a borderer, my native caution induced me to reply thus: "You have told me all these fine things about your movement. If it is so good, why hasn't the whole nation flocked into your ranks long before this? Tell me the worst thing you know about your movement." He was a bit taken aback by this, but after a moment's reflection he made a reply which greatly increased my esteem for him. He said, "The worst thing about us is that we have ceased to be apostolic: the fire of our original founders has died out of us.""

Archie's apostolic fire seems to have been tempered by enough geniality and good humour not to scorch his parishioners, who held him in immense affection. The daughter of one of them remembers how her mother would be cooking in the scullery of their ground floor tenement, which looked onto the street, when Mr Craig would stick his head over the window-sill and ask, "What are you cooking today, Jessie?" Her mother described him as "Just like a big miner", that being an accolade rather than an insult!

His routine week seems to have been strenuous enough. In addition to the diligently prepared services, and steady parish visiting, he held each week a Thursday preparation class for Sunday-school teachers, to which, remarkably, teachers from other denominations also came; and a Sunday night congregational hymn practice, since he had from the outset of his ministry the concern for good hymnology which put him onto both the Hymnary revisions subsequently undertaken by the Church of Scotland. He was involved, (whether as instigator or supporter is not clear), in the first local Council of Churches in Scotland, comprising "an ex- United Presbyterian congregation, an ex-Free church one, the Old Parish, and a little Evangelical Union flock." And he was responsible for starting and supporting the first Boys' Brigade company in Galston.

One now elderly lady, Miss Jenny Maclellan, who was the primary schoolteacher when Archie was minister, remembers him being able to charm into co-operation even the fairly stiff and unyielding Mr Hogg, the parish minister of the time, — "He was as different as night from day, but he would have let Mr Craig walk over him" — and still recalls the atmosphere of cheerfulness and naturalness which made Archie so attractive to the children and young people of the town. The mention of his name was enough to rouse her, against all the predictions of her carers, from the silent torpor of a nursing-home armchair to forty minutes of eye-twinkling reminiscence.

It was, of course, a time of acute industrial depression in that part of the country, and of consequent labour unrest, culminating in the miners' strikes of the twenties and the General strike of 1926. The tone of much church comment was entirely hostile, as for example George Reith's scene-setting account of the 1921 Free Church Assembly: "Trade was paralysed, and much inconvenience and hardship inflicted on the community, by one of those foolish, vexatious and suicidal miners' strikes which seem to have become chronic."

Archie's political stance seems to have been more sympathetic. He rarely made direct reference to the strike from the pulpit, but he speaks several times in sermons of the need for humane industrial relations and the cost of them. In 1924, for instance, about the time of Temple's COPEC conference on Politics, Economics and Citizenship, he says bluntly from the pulpit:

"It is a sin to obstruct changes which might, in making the industrial system more just, reduce the sum of our own possessions."

He suggests on another occasion that the rise of the labour movement is the most significant feature of the 20th century up to that point, and speaks against the "oil-kings, cotton-kings and other kings of commerce who create and accept the social evils which oppress so many." Yet, while he expressed the hope that "no word will be spoken from this pulpit which will ease the pressure upon the Christian conscience which these notorious evils rightly exercise", he seems to have been dubious about striking as the way to achieve desirable ends. His only extant pulpit reference to the issue comes in a sermon of June, 1925, on the text "For every man shall bear his own burden", where he says:

> "By God's appointment we live in a world where life can only be supported by a variety of work. If the Canadian wheatfields are left untilled, there is a bread famine in London. If colliers strike, factories must close, and household fires go out."

Even if, in context, this is more to do with mapping the interconnectedness of human action and mutual dependence, it has about it an implied recommendation against striking. Further, one of Harry Galloway's letters gives an account of him breaking a picket to go to work, and he reports this to Archie as if expecting him to find it a matter of Christian commendation.

At the same time, however, Miss Maclellan recalls that he inaugurated a Poor Fund in the church to alleviate the suffering of miners' families, and remembers him organising and leading, with her help, an outing to the seaside a few miles away with miners' children who had never been away from Galston. So he was clearly not dismissing the miners' case as unworthy of support, but may already have been feeling his way towards the position which he later articulated, that the only legitimate modes of *Christian* action must be non-coercive. Certainly, his concern for peace, and his support for the League of Nations as a vehicle of it was already being expressed in public, though much later he was to recognise the naïveté of trusting a settlement which left Germany licking its wounds while calling for the reconciliation of the nations.

Much as he loved this, his first parish, the sense that it was somehow insulated against the sting of the Gospel made him restless; and even with his strenuous agenda of activities and his pastoral care of Harry Galloway, he actually seems to have felt understretched. As early as 1923, he writes to George Stewart about an invitation he has had to be Youth Secretary for some unspecified body [for whom is not indicated]. And many years later he recalled confiding in this dearest of his spiritual fathers that he was finding his ministry intolerably dull and tame. Stewart, with characteristic gentleness, reminds him of the various relevant factors to be considered, what the effect will be on his mother, whether he has a sufficiently schematose mind for an adminstrative job, whether he wants to get untangled [from whom or what], whether he doesn't find the thrillingness of prayer a sufficient consolation for the tameness, and above all whether he is moved by a compulsion of God to remove so soon from his first charge.

If as Norman Porteous suggests, Archie was already a legend in New College by 1924, it is not perhaps surprising that he was at the receiving end of many invitations to move. When, a year or two later, George Stewart replies to Archie's letter intimating his eventual decision to go to Hillhead, he pleads inattentiveness to the common rumour of that invitation on the grounds that "Calls gather round your head like doves — a halo of calls".

Certainly, Archie considered very seriously a call to Regent Square, then the cathedral church of English Presbyterianism, and actually preached as sole nominee there in 1925, before deciding to decline, to the immense disappointment of the Vacancy Committee and of the many members of the congregation who had written pleading with him to come. He was also approached by Newlands U.F. Church, by Bearsden South and by Woodlands, all in or around Glasgow. He seems to have wrestled with the sense that he would be capable of doing more elsewhere, for a friend writes to him in the middle of his Regent Square deliberations:

"Are you going to be more useful to your profession in London or in Galston? For which milieu are you better fitted by temperament and gifts if you feel that Galston fails to provide the stimulus essential to working all your powers?"

Whether it was this sense that he was not being stretched enough, or whether, as the Newlands vacancy committee speculates, he was disappointed at the failure of negotiations for union between the two Galston U.F. churches late in 1925; or whether he felt that his mother's death in January, 1926, freed him in a way to move elsewhere, he preached his farewell sermon in Galston on July 11th, 1926, thanking his people for all the kindness they had shown him over the past five years, and asking forgiveness "from all whom I have wronged by act or by defect according to the standards of Jesus Christ."

His second charge, by contrast with Galston, was Hillhead U.F. later called Gilmorehill, Glasgow, in the middle of the *quartier universitaire*, at the bottom of University Avenue, a charge which in some ways gave more scope to his range of theological interests, and challenged him to address the burning questions of the student world which made up a large percentage of his parishioners.

In fact, his first reaction to the change was one of homesickness, as he found the more than doubled sick-list and the quadrupled number of beggars taxing his pastoral strength. On his first Christmas in Glasgow he composed a verse for his Christmas cards — (not, presumably, for members of his new congregation) — which ran:

O Gawston is a couthy toun, a hartsome toun, a couthy toun,
O Erskine Kirk's a canty kirk,

A cosy kirk, a canty kirk.
O Gawston is a couthy toun
Aft my hart sighs Gawston O.

O Glesca is a fearsome city, a reeky city, a fearsome city
It frichts the flo'ers and chills the marrow
O' ilka blackie, tit an' sparrow
O Glesca is a fearsome city:
Aft ma hart groans Glesca O.

By this time the impending union between the Free Church and the Church of Scotland was the dominating ecclesiastical issue, and Archie was by now definitely in favour of the move. In the run-up, he preaches to his congregation on John 17, 20-21 in extremely strong terms, affirming that organised segregation is incompatible with the Unity of Christendom, that schism is a grave offence against the Spirit, and that the handicapping of missionary activity is too heavy a price to pay for the recognising of minor differences. To resist union between U.F. and Church of Scotland traditions is, he urges, like refusing to let an engagement ripen into marriage because the parties can't agree about the colour of the dining-room wallpaper. He continues in a characteristically generous passage:

"We on our side have become aware that the Church of Scotland possesses gifts and graces which we would do well to emulate. That Church, for instance, has paid great attention to the beauty and dignity of the House of God, and to the reverent preservation of the historic shrines of our land. It has a splendid record of pastoral fidelity in the rural parts of Scotland. Its Men's Guild is an organisation which has no parallel in our church, and it has a sense of mission to the whole nation.
    We bring our special gifts too, ... and it is not our place to be too conscious of them."

Barely had he seen his congregation through the union than he was called in a new direction, one which was trail-blazing in the Scottish context and highly challenging to him. This took the form of an invitation to put himself forward as the first ever chaplain of Glasgow University, a position which he was to hold with great delight for the next ten years.

5 University chaplaincy

"A university will cease to be a university, and will lose its very soul, if at any time it says it has discovered the truth."

*Copied in Archie's Commonplace Book from
the 1951 Conference of University Teachers*

The initiative of asking for a University Chaplain came, in 1929, from the Students' Representative Council, who put the request to the University authorities and were delighted to have it accepted. As Professor James Christian Fordyce of Humanity was pleased to point out later, the University had had a chaplain for most of its history, being "officially pagan" only between 1848 and 1876, when the holding of services presided over by a college chaplain was suspended. But the job had been, up till then, an honorary one, involving the conducting of occasional services, originally in the College church belonging to the Dominican Blackfriars, and then in the College Hall, by men whose main activity was outwith the University. What the students were asking for now was a full-time person to devote himself to the day-to-day religious life of the students and to their pastoral care.

It was a quite new kind of job in Scotland, and Archie was warned against taking it by Principal W. M. MacGregor of Glasgow U.F. College, who tartly remarked that he could not recommend anyone undertaking the "curacy of a fog". But his advocates and supporters were from wide and diverse contexts, and the job offered intellectual excitement, and a real challenge to show faith's compatibility with the other fields of knowledge popularly thought to undermine it. Glasgow Presbytery agreed that the holder was entitled to a seat in Presbytery without there being any jurisdiction, and it seems not to have been a very difficult decision for Archie to move up the hill to the University's own territory.

The references which the University Court sought before inviting him to consider taking up the post were from Dr Donald Fraser, the distinguished missionary and youngest ever Moderator of the United Free Church, Dr Harry Miller, with whom Archie had worked so closely in the Pleasance, and Archibald Main, the professor of Ecclesiastical History in Glasgow. Their testimonials indicate the esteem in which he was already widely held. Harry Miller writes:

"He has the qualities needed – youth, with maturity of experience; seriousness, with a boyish sense of humour; mental power (he was

Professor Kemp-Smith's assistant), with power of simple statement of truth; geniality with the gift of leadership."

Professor Main, who had apparently met him during his Intelligence Corps work at Cologne, endorses this recommendation, and testifies to Archie's merits as speaker, debater and friend, adding that he would rate him not second even to Dr Miller himself, and that there is none of the younger men of the two Presbyterian churches in Scotland in whom he should place so much trust, – no small tribute since Harry Miller was a household name in Free Church circles.

With such testimonies encouraging him, Principal MacAlister, with the Court's backing, approached Archie in September, 1929. His reply ran:

228 Wilton Street,
Glasgow N.W.
29 Sept. 1929

My Dear Principal,

I find myself ready, after thorough consideration, to accept nomination for the chaplaincy, provided the appointment does not take effect and is not made public before Easter, and provided it is made in this first instance a five-years' appointment.

I could then leave my present charge with a minimum of inconvenience to its interests, and at the same time lay myself open to work among the students during the winter in preference to any other extra-congregational work. The second proviso would safeguard both parties to the appointment, should the experimental period be unsatisfactory to either.

The Court accepted the starting date and the proposed duration, but demurred at the request for keeping the matter out of public knowledge for six months, on the grounds that students and other interested parties were pressing for information. So on 30th October, the *Glasgow Herald*, the *Scotsman* and the *British Weekly* carried the news. Within twenty-four hours, scores of letters were being despatched to Archie, from members of both congregations in Galston and Gilmorehill, from former classmates and teachers, and from family and colleagues. To a man they expressed delight at the creation of the job, though the Gilmorehill parishioners were at the same time dismayed to lose him. His brother John found it necessary to say, as a rider to his good wishes, "Don't let the environment make you too starchy and academic", and one friend wrote, 'You will have your own diffident thoughts and misgivings about it, I know." But whatever misgivings Archie may have had must have been very nearly quietened by the tumults of acclamation which greeted the announcement.

Among the most cordial was one from George MacLeod, then associate minister of St. Cuthbert's in Edinburgh. It included the comment,

> "It remains one of the ironies of life that you, who are always so firm in the placid waters of Parish life and unmoved to go swimming in unknown seas should thus have been given a shove, while Ian and I, who thought we saw a light though we saw no wicket-gate, remain firmly embedded in the slough."

So, on 1st April, 1930, Archie began the curacy of his fog, at an annual salary of £600, which came out of an endowment from the industrial magnate Lord Maclay. About the same time, he bought the house at 16 Bank Street, where he was to live with his two unmarried sisters, Madge and Minnie, until 1939, and to return to in the mid-forties. The presumption that a single man could not feed, wash and clean himself had already been made when he went to Galston, since which time Minnie had acted housekeeper, leaving Madge with their mother in Troon. After the latter's death in 1926, both sisters lived with Archie until he went to London, Minnie, his eldest unmarried sister being a kind of capable Martha, and Madge a happy Mary to his ensuing ministries.

The *Glasgow University Magazine* of 1930-31 carried a pen-portrait of the new chaplain as number VIII in its series of "Gilmorehill Gallery", and the writer seems to share the University administration's feeling that they have done well in making this appointment:

> "One of the greatest merits of the man, our "official padre", is that he is so much man that one never thinks of him as official."

So says the author, and goes on to commend Archie as a "friendly, brotherly man". Students of the time remember his open approach to new people, whether it was coming up to someone standing in the quad, and saying, "Hello, I'm Craig," or in the coffee bar of the Students' Union, where he could be found sitting on the floor with the best of them!

Apart from the chapel preaching, which he himself did two or three times a term, he inaugurated a series of evening meetings on the theme, "Questions students are asking." In preparation for this, he sent out a letter to several scores of students, covering a wide cross-section of the university clubs and organisations, with the following introduction:

> "A friend of mine gave a course of sermons under the title, "Questions people are asking". When the last of them had been preached, and he was taking off his gown in the vestry, his beadle said, "Weel, sir, that's the

hinner end o' the questions. They went brawly; it's juist a peety these are na the things the folk are spiering aboot."

Archie's conclusion from the three-score odd replies he got was that students were not much interested in doctrinal issues, though a few voiced the apologetical question of the proof of God's reality. What bothered them was a range of ethical questions, about war and peace, about business ethics, gambling, sex, and about remedying the unattractiveness of the church, all of which Archie himself recognised as serious issues, and tackled with energy in his Sunday evening discussions.

He was particularly sensitive to the needs of overseas students, several of whom wrote to him years after, remembering the hospitality of 16 Bank Street, and he proposed to the Chapel Committee the inauguration of a practice which has since become standard, namely the welcoming of overseas students on their arrival in Glasgow.

Among the many ventures with which the Chaplain was involved, one was to grow into a matter of national importance. This was the pioneering of a series of "Religion and Life" weeks in the University. According to Archie, the title was the brain-child of Robert Mackie, with whom he had become a close friend through his S.C.M. commitment at Swanwick and elsewhere. The first experimental week was held in 1928, co-sponsored by S.C.M., the Students' Representative Council, the Union, the Catholic Society and the Athletic Club, and was so successful that it was repeated in 1931 and again in 1936, and had, by the mid-thirties, been exported to Edinburgh. (As minister of Gilmorehill, Archie had already been deeply involved in the 1928 week, and his achievements during it as expositor of intellectually honest faith were actually cited by Archibald Main in support of his candidature.)

The format was a week of meetings, the main ones at lunch-time, when conspicuously good and lively speakers addressed a large open gathering. Then, in the evenings, there were options for Roman Catholic and Protestant groups, again involving local or visiting speakers of repute. It was of the essence of these events that they were not sponsored by a religious huddle, but had the backing of the University's secular organs, and their central concern was to integrate faith and everyday life, to reconcile religious belief with other modes of knowledge, scientific, historical and so on. The toughness of intellectual fibre and the spiritual resilience assumed among the hearers was considerable: A. A. Bowman, for instance, the Professor of Moral Philosophy at Glasgow, delivered a series of addresses later published as "The Absurdity of Christianity", which would make any easy religious complacency buckle, and he was flanked by other giants such as Charles Raven, H. H. Farmer, George MacLeod and Russell Maltby, who among them presented the cutting edge of contemporary thought on faith and churchmanship in their day.

On the pastoral front, the main thing which Archie was taking on board was the "New Psychology", the popularising of Freudian insights and how they related to ethical and theological issues. About this, he seems to have felt somewhat ambivalent. On the one hand, his retrospective reckoning was that about 70% of his pastoral counselling was dealing with problems which had at least a sexual component, and from this period on he stresses the importance of ministers to be aware of psychological insights; but at the same time he is somewhat rueful about how "Vienna has become a suburb of Jerusalem", and brooks no slackening of what he takes to be the moral absolutes of right conduct in this area. While the sex-instinct is "God's gift, and therefore good and sacred", he can categorise masturbation and homosexual practices as perversions, which are "clearly unnatural", in that they divorce the instinct from its biological purpose, and are therefore rebellions against God. The corollary of this judgement is the recommendation of a "real element of renunciation and denial of the immediate physical satisfactions of sex", which, in the case of one who has been committing sexual excesses, become "absolute and rigid asceticism until he is sure that he is his own master in the realm of sex and not the slave of passion."

While some of this is clearly derived from the dominant, and at the time standard traditions of Christian Moral Theology on the matter, it looks as if Archie had a particular distaste for those sins which indicated loss of control; and while he believed in, and earthed pastorally the wholesale forgiveness of God, there is a note almost of natural scorn in his comments on such sins as sexual licence or drunkenness, as when he speaks of "That miserable soddenness of body and mind which is called alcoholism", or remarks sharply that "Many men think they are over-sexed because they are underemployed." It is perhaps the case also that his feeling and vocabulary were coloured at this period by his involvement with the Buchmanite Oxford Group movement, about which he had some reservations, but which he commended for its moral earnestness. Certainly, in the twenties, Harry Galloway had said in at least one letter that he "wondered how Craig could do without women", to which Archie replied that, like anyone else, he had to do battle in this area. The battle, characteristically, seems to have been fought and won unobtrusively; for the young Lesslie Newbigin, who had shared Archie's home in Bank Street when he arrived to be Glasgow S.C.M. Secretary, wrote to tell Archie about his engagement and impending marriage, with no trace of suspicion that his brimming happiness would cause pain. It must have done, however, and Archie must have trusted him enough to say so, for the subsequent letter from the younger man expresses contrite surprise that, in all their conversations about celibacy and the struggle against resentment, he had never realised that Archie's position was achieved at such personal cost.

Whatever his interior wrestlings, the impact of his pastoral ministry in the university was appreciated by every level of its membership. Hector Hetherington, who became principal in 1936, became one of his firmest friends, and Archie kept a photo of him on his study mantelpiece for the rest of his life. He regarded Archie's job in the University as being the most difficult and the most worthwhile of all, and told him so. Among the staff, he had some sterling friendships, particularly with Bowman and Donald Lamont in philosophy, and letters of gratitude from many former undergraduates indicate how much it meant to that generation of students to have someone who nourished them with a robust intelligent version of Christian faith, while at the same time letting them explore without censure the questions which troubled them. His own range of reading combined with a sharpness of personal acumen, so that he was able to find with precision the thing that was likely to help people over their next intellectual or spiritual hurdle, and he sustained the contact with many students long beyond their university days, often with quite extended letter-writing on matters of theological concern.

His own theology at this point was still ripening. He was firmly committed to ideals of Christian Socialism, and to the kind of internationalism represented by the League of Nations, and equally convinced of the need for a rational apologetic of the sort he found in theologians like Oman, Farmer, David S Cairns and John Baillie on the Protestant side, and von Hugel on the Roman Catholic.

The mid-30s seem to have introduced him to Barth, whose face he admired when he saw a photograph brought back by Norman Porteous from a period of study in Basel. At first he seems to have been completely won over by the massiveness of Barth's evangelical affirmations, and in his correspondence with George Stewart, still his deepest and dearest theological mentor, he tries pleading the Barthian case. Stewart, however, is unimpressed, and replies that Barth strikes him as a sort of intellectual Hitler — a view which some of Archie's other friends, like Charles Raven must have endorsed. In the end, looking back at the thirties from the sixties, Archie's final theological diagnosis was that Barth was rather like Worcester Sauce, a marvellous spicing of a jaded theological palate, but not the substance of a meal and inedible neat! It took the mellowing of some years, however, to alert him to the backfiring of Barth's theological position, which was misused to undergird a dogmatic positivism, to renounce any attempt at rational apologetic and to legitimate a cheap theological triumphalism. In the end, he saw the damage done to questers for intelligent faith by what he called "Barthian cockerels crowing in front of every theological barn door."

It is no accident that the two most sustained blocks of work Archie undertook in one place were both in the university context, between 1930 and 1939, and again from 1947 to 1957 as Lecturer in Biblical Studies. For, while he in no way resembled the caricature of academic life – sometimes grounded in awful reality – as desiccated and bloodless intellectual posturing, he had the deepest respect for what he believed to be the characteristic virtues of a University. What these seemed to him to be is indicated by an extract from one of the commonplace books he kept for many years: von Hugel's list of the intellectual and moral values implied in the pursuit of truth:

"candour, moral courage, intellectual honesty, scrupulous accuracy, chivalrous fairness, endless docility to facts, disinterested collaboration, unconquerable hopefulness, perseverance, manly renunciation of popularity and easy honours, love of bracing labour and strengthening solitude."

While one might find such criteria rather remote from those by which academic excellence is measured in Britain in the eighties, there were, it seems, in the thirties, people enough around to make such words ring convincingly. And certainly they articulate a vision with which Archie was at home, though he might have put some of the ideals into more vernacular form, such as "Facts are chiels that winna ding," a favourite response of his to religious obscurantism.

At any rate, it seems that he found in this context the stretching and stimulus whose lack he had uneasily felt in routine parish work, and he later described this period as an immensely happy and satisfying one.

As the thirties progressed, his reputation became widely spread, though in Scotland it hardly needed to be. As a *quid pro quo* for Charles Raven's involvement in the Glasgow "Religion and Life" weeks, Archie gave a series of open lectures in Cambridge in 1933. He was already in constant demand as a speaker at the Swanwick conferences of S.C.M. and at the Scottish regional equivalent at Dalhousie Castle, which in those days meant that he was known to countless people in all the churches and ecumenical organisations of Britain. And he had already demonstrated his ability as a radio preacher, drawing scores of appreciative letters from every corner of the land and some from overseas, whenever his University chapel services were broadcast.

His only minor mishap was the chapel acoustics, which proved a cause of concern to subsequent chapel committees until an effective loudspeaking system was employed. This was a problem for others beside him; and the chapel committee had in fact vetoed the participation of women as readers of lessons at services, not, it seems, on ideological grounds, but for fear that their voices would not carry. [In compensation they were allowed to take the collection!] Archie's own voice, which had a certain tendency to swallow his vowels, and was not naturally declamatory so much as conversational, was sometimes difficult to hear from the back of a long high building (which perhaps explains the comment in one of his obituary notices that he was handicapped by his voice from being one of the church's greatest preachers.)

His sermons, some of which were published as "University Sermons" in 1938, are sinewy and rich, and were greeted by his friends as something to be treasured. (It is a sign of the Archie's own modesty that out of all the acres of paper he produced for lectures and sermons over the years, he published so little. See Appendix 2.) They show an unevasive awareness of the kinds of difficulties for belief which students faced in the '30s, and tackle them with both intellectual integrity and linguistic finesse. Divided into three sections, Repentance, Faith and Duty, the sermons explore first the human phenomenon, with an analysis of the deep failure of the various manifestations of "*worldliness*", then the core of the Christological challenge, and finally the implications in terms of moral demand and the consecration of the secular.

Conspicuously memorable among his other sermons are those he preached on successive Armistice Day services, when of course the O.T.C. were present, as well as many who shared the pacifist convictions which were Archie's own by this time. It is a measure of the man, and of his sense of the catholicity of the Gospel that he managed to handle the potential dynamite of this situation with delicacy and candour. His pacifism was not Utopian, in that he had spent at least three summers in Vienna in the thirties, and was well aware both of German resentment at the Treaty of Versailles, and of the sinister character of Hitler's rise to power. He recalled meeting young Nazis in the late '30s, and realising how their youthful energy and exuberance was entirely drawn into the blasphemous idolatry which allowed a picture of a Hitler rally to be captioned with the words, *The Word Made Flesh*. And above all he realised the implications of a conversation overheard in a Berlin cafe, where one student was advising another that, if he wanted to have any chance of his doctorate seeing the light of day, he must revise his biology thesis.

It was not then any naïveté about the state of Germany which made him endorse the pacifist cause, but the growing sense that in this context too, the simple and costly demand of the gospels, as they challenged him, particularly in the Sermon on the Mount, summoned the church to the conspicuous gallantry of turning the other cheek to the assailant. His 1935 Armistice sermon on "What do ye more than others" is perhaps his most direct exposition of this stance. It contains these words:

"I believe that the teaching of Jesus does apply to state-morality. The world is resuming the old fatal way of competitive armament . . . . because the so-called Christian states were too rich in prudence and fear and too poor in penitence and faith.

"I believe that a new era will be ushered in, when and only when the

50

Christian state ventures out in obedience to the word of Jesus and in the image of his death."

Somehow, while being as explicit as this, Archie managed to avoid any overtones of "holier than thou" in relation to the non-pacifist community, mainly because he did not *feel* holier than thou. In his 1937 Armistice Day sermon he begins:

"We are met as followers of Jesus Christ. We probably belong to different political parties; make different judgments on Franco; are pacifist and non-pacifist. But the division between believers and non-believers is deeper."

By this time, the debate about peace was the dominant issue in student politics, and focussed round the Rectorial election campaign, in which one of the main contenders was Dick Sheppard, a conspicuous pacifist and founder of the Peace Pledge Union. Archie's public support of Sheppard's campaign certainly caused offence to some within the Church of Scotland. Throughout the thirties he had been a member of a group of Church of Scotland ministers committed to peace, but as the decade advanced, many of those reluctantly found themselves unable to see in pacifism a sane and responsible Christian response to Hitler's threatening aggression. Archie, however, along with others, most conspicuously George MacLeod and Garth MacGregor, felt that nothing but pacifism properly expressed the church's commitment to take the way of the cross seriously.

Though he was immensely involved in a job which gave much outlet to his native geniality and gregariousness, it was in some ways quite a lonely position, in that he had neither students nor teaching staff as peers. He was old enough to feel some benign amusement at student fashions, whether it was their convention of studied unconventionality of dress or their habits of speech and idiom. ("Vidler was wizard. He gave us half an hour of concentrated despair. The church is absolutely mouldy!") Also, his character was not by any means one-sidedly extrovert, and some of the letters he kept from this period indicate that interior wrestlings did not cease. His beloved George Stewart writes to him, for instance, in the mid-thirties, after some period of sick-leave, "I hope you are back in the saddle again and riding, despite the spectres of the mind." And another of the friends who gave him the sense of belonging to a family, in which he had access to quasi-parental wisdoms, wrote to him in October 1933, that he was available "if you feel that a good blow-off would reduce the pressure in the boiler."

This latter was Dr John Coutts, then minister of St. Luke's, Milngavie, whose family provided at this period a real haven for Archie, shared holidays with him, and provided space in which he could be off-duty, free of his University role and playful. With the sport-loving sons of the manse he enjoyed rugby in the large manse garden, braving the wrath of the non-churchgoing neighbour who objected to rugby balls landing in his garden. On one occasion, when both Coutts brothers were hestitating over the recovery of yet another ball, Archie volunteered to go, affirming with confidence that the man couldn't be as bad as all that. Some time later he re-emerged, commenting indignantly, "I see what you mean. The man's a pagan!" and bearing in his hand the corpse of the rugby ball, which the neighbour had deliberately put a knife through.

It is one of the most significant indications of Archie's breadth of character that, at this point in his career when he was most celebrating the fusion of intellect and faith which was offered by his chaplaincy job, these young secondary schoolboys felt him to be more a mate of theirs than of their father and had no sense of him as, horror of horrors, *an intellectual*. There may have been an element of holding back on some of the issues which were his daily concern, for Jack Coutts had also written:

> "I sometimes fear that passing contacts with younger and more brilliant people at conferences, schools etc. may make you impatient of the slower, harder, though perhaps more life-disciplined utterances of a middle-aged buffer like me."

But this was obviously a context in which he could be himself and enjoy genuine relaxation, whether it was helping to dig the manse garden, or, as the sons remember, more often than not *failing* to dig the garden because of the allure of joining Mrs Coutts at the piano to play duets from the *Meistersinger*. Music was, as Lesslie Newbigin remembered from his time in Archie's home, "the only indulgence you allow yourself."

Two milestones within the emerging history of Archie's career took place in 1938. The first was the awarding of a D.D. from Edinburgh University, which one or two friends had predicted at the time of his appointment as chaplain. Once again, the announcement of this honour in March, 1938, was acclaimed across the land, provoking within days a hundred and nine letters and cards of congratulation. They came from all quarters, from Galston, from students and student bodies like the Student Representative Council and the International Club and from brother ministers, university colleagues and family friends. Some express almost indignation at the thought that this distinction distances Archie from common mortals, when his common mortality is what they treasure, and say things like, "You will always be plain Mr Craig to me." His nephew Alick writes, "I am considerably astonished .... Knowing and admiring your efforts for sanity and peace in this lunatic world I would have thought all your ideas were suspect .... "

and others do a little gentle teasing: "I suppose what it really means is that you can put D.D. on your tombstone" and "If the King were doing his duty he would present you with the Dukedom of Bank St. and Gilmorehill at the next issue of an honours list." D.M. Baillie writes, "It is with quite unusual pleasure that I write to congratulate you . . . . the only thing that could have pleased me more would be your getting it from St Andrews."

The other big event of 1938 was that Archie was enabled, by the generosity of Lord Maclay, to go to the huge missionary conference at Tambaram. He sailed out from Marseilles via Port Said, following the route of his student journey to the Far East, and, to the excitement of his sisters, flew back. In all, he had three months leave from university which he used to visit various places of significance and to follow up some other personal contacts. Among them were a visit to James Graham at Kalimpong, whose face struck Archie as a "love letter to the human race"; to the Punjab mission and to the son of Professor Bowman, who was working as a civil servant in Agra. From this trip lifelong impressions were created. One thing which struck him was the vitality and exuberance of Christianity when it was not expressed in Scottish douceness [decency], and in particular he was impressed by hearing the Apostles' Creed shouted as if it were a song of triumph at Sambrial by an Indian congregation. On the same occasion he chortled at a village poet whose recitation of the life of Christ had only reached the Annunciation after seventeen verses, so that the presiding minister had to intervene with the suggestion that the rest be postponed to a later occasion.

Above all, what impressed him from the conference was that the outgoing missionary nature of the church made nonsense of partisan national pride and could transcend all denominational boundaries. Twenty-seven years later he still carried about with him a paper signed by several of those with whom he had shared communion, a Chinese, a Japanese, a Belgian, a Brazilian, a German, two Indians, a South African Boer, a Kenyan, a native of the U.S.A. and two fellow-Scots. As Europe began to break up into opposing forces, the sense of catholicity which he carried home from Tambaram was a potent counter-vision.

Back in Glasgow he was much missed by his sisters, it being the first Christmas since the war when he had been absent from the festive table. Other friends at the University who had come to know him during his chaplaincy, including the Hetheringtons pursued him halfway round the world with sketches, cards and notes of affection. Clearly what had begun as an experimental and exploratory ministry had now, ten years on, established a precedent of chaplaincy which the whole range of the University community found of immense value, and which others were beginning to copy. It could have been a congenial niche, and Archie could no doubt have won Hetherington's approval for staying in it longer, since he had clearly not run out of zest or communicative power.

Nevertheless, as the European skies darkened towards war, Archie made yet another move which took him into the middle of national and international affairs, and shifted his operational base from Glasgow to London for the next seven years. In the ten years which had passed, for all his gifts as a Christian pastor and preacher, he had witnessed, he believed, a loosening of the ties which many intelligent young people had with the institutional church. The desire to give Christian faith a convincing visible form by renewing the commitment of the churches to their common central purpose was now to be tested in a wider sphere.

6 The London years

"There came back to me a story that I once heard Harry Miller tell. He had been waiting for a train at Perth railway station and there he saw a porter being hauled along the platform by a pair of powerful dogs. A voice from behind him shouted to the porter, "Whaur are thae dugs gaun, Jimmie?" And Jimmie replied, "I dinna ken: they've swallowed their labels." "

Since his student days, Archie had been steadily growing in ecumenical experience. The Student Christian Movement had introduced him in his late teens to a wider spectrum of Christian belonging than his United Free Church upbringing had let him encounter, and he had come to appreciate the arrogant parochialism of saying, or meaning, "You do Christ's work in your way, and I'll do it in His." George Stewart, his pre-eminent model of ministry, had introduced him to the spirituality of Roman Catholic tradition, being himself so unself-consciously inside it that he could write to Archie on more than one occasion that he would say Mass for him. Through his influence, Archie had himself come to appreciate such writers as Father Congreve of the Cowley Fathers, or the French Père Grou, and had the deepest resonance in his own spirituality with much Catholic writing and devotional practice. He had registered the irrelevance of denominationalism to many of his army comrades and university students, and he had, with exhilaration, glimpsed the widest horizons of the church at Tambaram.

Within Britain, various channels of ecumenical water had been cutting deeper and deeper in the consciousness of the churches, and the beginning of the Second World War seemed to coincide with an increased sense of urgency about the need for a unified voice of Christian witness.

One day in July, 1939, Archie met in an A.B.C. shop in London a triumvirate consisting of the Anglican H.W. Fox, Secretary of the British Christian Council, Willie Elmslie, the General Secretary of the Presbyterian Church of England, (who had already participated in the Glasgow *Religion and Life weeks*), and the then Secretary of the Methodist Conference, E.C. Unwin, who declared that Archie could count on their all-in support if he would consider coming to be Secretary of a proposed body called *The Commission of the Churches for International Friendship and Social Responsibility*.

This was intended to bring together many strands of the ecumenical movement which had been reinvigorated by the *Life and Work* conference in Oxford in 1937, and the *Faith and Order* one in Edinburgh in the same year. It merged the *English Christian Social Council* and the *British Christian Council* which had been formed in 1929 after the celebrated conference on Politics, Economics and Citizenship chaired in 1924 by William Temple, and was to work in association with the British section of the World Alliance for Promoting International Friendship through the Churches, which had been formed in 1912, and re-formed in 1919 after the war. (In effect this latter was soon elided into the new C.C.I.F.S.R.)

Archie had already been involved in the Scottish Committee of the World Alliance, of which he wrote, "It has always been a matter of wonder to me that the latter body managed to raise any money. For it must have taken men and women with equal elevation of aim and sheer doggedness of character to inscribe a cheque to a body with a length of name like that." The new commission, while no less cumbersome as to nomenclature, did have the merit of bringing together in a more interlocking way the resources of intelligence and energy which had hitherto been working in somewhat haphazard parallel both on British and international questions. Its chairman was William Temple, then Archbishop of York, who in the opening issue of the Commission's Bulletin, *The Church in the World*, described its purpose as being "To bring into fuller consciousness among Christian people the meaning of their fellowship in the Church." This, however was not interpreted in any narrow ecclesiastical sense, but as enabling Christians to "take an effective part in remedying the conditions liable to result in wars, ... and to take our share in shaping a stable peace."

To begin with the Commission shared the premises at 20 Balcombe Street which were already the workbase of Joe Oldham's *Christian News-Letter* and of the *Council on the Christian Faith and the Common Life* which had been the outcome of the Oxford conference. Archie was thus at the geographical and administrative centre of those circles in British church life during the years of the Second World War which were most involved in national and international ecumenism, and which led directly into the setting up of the British Council of Churches and the World Council of Churches. In a way, these war years were to give an institutional form to the links between the mainstream Christian bodies on the British scene and the global ecumenical structures which had been evolving ever since 1910.

The enterprise was an ambitious one, especially since the new Commission inherited from the British Christian Council an overdraft of £205.19.4d, (which was 20% of their entire running budget for their first year) and cash in hand of £2.13.6d; and had to begin their work on a bank loan of nearly five hundred pounds, which was one-and-a-half times the amount that had hitherto been raised from all the supporting churches.

In his account of the Commission's first wartime meeting, Archie outlines the scope of their agenda. The Department of Social Responsibility has as its main goal a vigorous education campaign in the churches which will allow the growth of "that kind of Christianly tinctured public opinion which can exercise a profound influence when statesmen meet round a conference table, and in defect of which treaties may only mortgage the future to the devil."

The primary areas of concern identified are youth, unemployment and the special problems relating to mass evacuation. Archie writes of this:

"Evacuation has resembled a sudden geological convulsion breaking forcibly through the crusts of convention and habit, jumbling up our social strata, and thrusting into prominence aspects of national life which could be blinked as long as they lay in a familiar shadow. What are the main facts, or groups of facts, of which the church must here take notice? What lasting lessons derivable from this upheaval must be brought home to the Christian mind and conscience? How does the Church itself figure in this unusual landscape? Does it look well in it, or ill?"

To enable these questions to have a sharp cutting edge with specific local reference, the Commission planned to undertake a survey of the areas covered by the dioceses of Southwark and Chichester, in co-operation with other interested bodies such as the National Council of Social Service, and the Emergency Committee of the Council for Social Education. To enable a wider spread of data to be gathered, local Christian Social Councils were invited to undertake and communicate the results of similar enquiries.

The International Department was, simultaneously, to explore the character of a just peace, looking at the social and economic aspects of what such a peace might mean, and trying to specify a British response to the World Council of Churches study document on *"The Churches and the International Situation"*. It also had responsibility for the welfare of internees and prisoners of war. Significantly, the two aspects of the Commission's work were seen as so mutually dependent that they agreed at the first meeting *not* to work as separate departments, but as one executive committee. There was, in addition, a Youth Committee, constituted for the first year by the co-option of those who had planned the World Christian Youth Conference in Amsterdam the year before. The interaction of local, national and international agents of mission was seen as essential for the well-being of any part of the ecumenical enterprise.

The short term intention of the Commission was the mounting of a series of what were initially called "Ecumenical Demonstrations", in which:

"the agents will be such teams of speakers (interdenominational certainly, and including, if possible, churchmen from overseas) as war conditions may permit us to assemble."

Meetings were planned to last a week or ten days, through which it was hoped to make an impact on the whole life of the selected communities and to bring home to them the "Ecumenical Message". One member of the Commission had apparently expressed doubts about the intelligibility of the word "ecumenical" in the minds of its hearers, but already at this stage Archie was willing to defend the word as one well rooted in the language of the church, on the grounds that "It has been born of a real movement and is no invention of the study."

Fortunately perhaps, by the time the first demonstration took place in Bristol in September, 1940, the title had changed to *Religion and Life*, borrowed from the series of events which had worked so well in the Scottish universities in the time of Archie's Glasgow chaplaincy. The next was in Bolton the following May, and the third in St. Albans. By July, 1941, Archie was writing to a friend, "the *Religion and Life Week* idea is beginning to catch on, and needs only wise and zealous fostering to grow into a real movement." Only a year later he was writing apologetically to the organiser of the Worcester week, "My diary for September is already so crowded that I do not think I can add a visit to Worcester, much as I should wish to come."

The *Religion and Life* weeks seem, indeed, to have exploded beyond all expectation, with the Commission having a vital co-ordinating role, suggesting speakers, corresponding with or briefing in person local organisers, receiving feedback on programmes and disseminating information about the success of events through the country. Archie himself was a speaker at many, and in demand for more, and travelled the length and breadth of England and Wales. On at least one occasion the journey provided him with the sort of story he so much relished and loved to retell. He was sitting in a compartment, wearing "civvies", and reading a theological book when a lady sitting opposite remarked on this and asked why. "I am ordained as a minister," he replied, "but I am not now in a parish." The lady nodded her head kindly and asked sympathetically, "Was it the drink?"

It must have been a matter of some pain to him that the two weeks which were planned in Scotland had to be dropped when the Home Board of the Church of Scotland expressed its opposition, expressing its opposition in an official letter which suggested that "such campaigns are not suited to Scotland" and advocated instead outreach campaigns organised by the Church of Scotland presbyteries. Perhaps what was most remarkable about the venture was that, on a fairly shoestring budget, and with very rudimentary secretarial equipment, — the first issues of the Bulletin were produced by stapling hand-duplicated sheets — there was really an extremely careful and competent operation in adult education. All the weeks were prepared for thoroughly, and usually followed up by some kind of local formation of an ecumenical group, the origin in fact of what were to grow into local councils of churches. Very often, as in Bristol and St. Albans, there were a number of subsequent meetings to explore further issues which had been touched on without adequate development in the original week, or which dealt with a particular constituency like young people, or people in business. Advertisement in the local community was thorough, involving public notices, house to house visitation and the insertion of announcements in the weekly pay packets of workers, by courtesy of the local firms. Follow-up involved simultaneous weeks of teaching in all the churches, with the formation of small groups to pursue more specifically the felt needs of the people who had attended the larger public events. These groups were set within the responsibility of each local church, rather than being trans-denominational, but there was also recognition of the need to find a meeting-place for those who did not yet feel able to commit themselves to any church affiliation. Beyond this phase, and dependent on its outcome, a further campaign of "challenge and witness" was planned for the subsequent summer.

Some indication of the range of concerns which speakers covered may be found in the list of recommended literature which was printed in *The Church in the World*, much of it in pamphlet form and costing only a penny or two. There was a whole range of pamphlets in a series called "Towards a Christian Britain", which included topics like "*Chaos or Order in Industry and Commerce*" and "*Foundations of Peace*" as well as "*Advice to Christian Fellowship Groups*" and "*The Universal Church*". Slightly more expensive, in the 3d to 6d range, were reprints of papers from the 1937 Oxford conference on "*The Church and the Economic Order*" as well as newly produced pamphlets such as "*Social Justice and Economic Reconstruction*" and "*A Criticism of our Secondary Education.*"

Although the Ecumenical Movement was, in its origins, predominantly an enterprise of the non-Roman churches, the *Religion and Life* weeks were happily marked by shared planning and preparation with Roman Catholic Christians, encouraged in their collaboration by Cardinal Hinsley and his *Sword of the Spirit* movement. A joint statement on co-operation was produced, which at the same time recognised their shared Christian heritage and yet resisted any blurring of the serious theological differences between the Roman and Reformed positions. Archie was never willing to let organisers of *Religion and Life* weeks avoid grasping real nettles. In a statement ratified by the British Council of Churches at its first formal meeting on 26th September, 1942, three days after its inauguration, he writes that "Principles regarding doctrine and worship are not to be sacrificed in order to secure Roman Catholic co-operation". The weeks, that is, are to be intellectually responsible, "deriving their power from their doctrinal content" and not to degenerate into a sentimental fuzz of togetherness. It is perhaps the same fear which makes him, the following year, decline official B.C.C. involvement in a proposed ecumenical music service in Tottenham. He replies to the invitation with courteously serpentine wisdom:

> "The idea of a musical service is attractive, but we have no experience of any such experiments, nor access to the kind of music which would be every man's meat and no man's poison.
> My own unofficial judgment would be that it is a delicate problem to set before a committee of choirmasters and organists from within Tottenham. It is project worthy of their orchestration."

The transition from the Commission of International Friendship and Social Responsibility to the British Council of Churches was first mooted in the spring of 1941, and was therefore effected with what, in Archie's words, was "smooth speed, ecclesiastically speaking." (This was in contrast with his later sad recounting of a friend's comment that the Ecumenical Movement must share the quality of eternity, since a thousand years were, in its sight, but as a day.) His appraisal of the ripeness of the time was that the shift

> "put inter-church co-operation in this country on a new level by unifying and strengthening its central machinery, setting a fresh official seal on its practice and, not least, simplifying titles which bemuse the public."

In practice, the move meant the further amalgamation of the Commission with the *Council on the Christian Faith and Common Life* and the British section of the *World Conference on Faith and Order*. In Archie's judgment, this safeguarded valuable traditions and existing work against interruption, and had the unhesitating approval of the churches.

It was not, however, a move without tensions, and he must certainly have been aware of these, being the very point where quite a lot of crossfire landed. Dr Eleanor Jackson, in her massively-documented biography of William Paton, uncovers, with the dexterity of a whodunit writer, something of the plurality and complexity of interests and elements which were involved in the process. In particular, she indicates the tension between Joe Oldham, who feared and despised the mediocrity of establishment structures, and those who saw the B.C.C. as the mandated organ of the churches. To reproduce her research would be mere plagiarism, but it is one of the most interesting silences in her work that Archie Craig is unplaced in the polemical aspects of that early ecumenical conflict. By 1944, Oldham was willing to take on a position as vice-president of the Council, so his early anxieties must have been either assuaged or diminished in relation to his hopes of the new body. But, insofar as the tensions remained, Archie must, certainly, have felt the pull in both directions, on the one hand from Paton, who wanted the B.C.C. to be answerable to the churches and bound to act on their behalf, and on the other from Oldham, who had been his ecumenical mentor, and thought that the way forward was to create a vanguard of creative visionaries who would probably leave the churches a long way behind.

Archie's commitment on this issue seems to have been on the anti-elitist side, and he spoke afterwards about how he used to tease Joe Oldham about enlisting "first-class minds in the service of the Ecumenical Movement". At the time, however, it must have cost him rather more to resist Oldham's pressure to improve the quality of those invited to ecumenical gatherings. Among the General Secretary's files at Selly Oak is a copy of one letter from Archie to Oldham. The precise context is not clear, but Archie is evidently responding to a request of Oldham that the lower limit of qualification for some conference or gathering should be upped. Archie replies,

> "One of our functions is to mediate for the average minister, and I am never quite happy when he is excluded from gatherings on the ground that he is not above the average."

This sense of the right of democratic access to the best ecumenical experience remained with Archie throughout his lifelong concern with theological education. He was enough of an intellectual aristocrat to regret the phenomenon which he ruefully called in the fifties, "Getting, on the whole, the 'c's into the church"; but there is quite a difference between being saddened that the church is losing most first-, and even second-class minds, and thinking that it should be for them alone. Archie probably shared many of Oldham's specific judgments on ability, but disagreed with his political strategy for the furtherance of the ecumenical cause, in spite of being one of those who had passed Oldham's stringent criteria of excellence. Instead he preferred Principal Rainy's dictum that it was of the essence of good ecclesiastical leadership to be in the van in such a way that you did not alienate the centre, though he liked even better the response of an American train conductor who was asked by an irate lady if he could not go faster: "Sure, madam, but ah must not lose ma train."

While the disagreement with Oldham seems to have been, on Archie's side at least, a matter of good-humoured policy difference, there seems to have been a more serious clash between him and Oldham's right hand woman, Eleanora Iredale, who seems to have achieved the rare distinction of being a person about whom Archie could find no good thing to say. Both Lesslie Newbigin, who was, at a distance, party to confidential explosions from him, and Alistair Forrester-Paton, who was a junior member of the B.C.C. Executive, testify that she made his life wretched at times, and at one point even managed to defer the payment of his salary for several months. Her gift for entrepreneurial success in fundraising was considerable, but Archie seems to have found her a manipulative and dangerous person. The only point in his career when one suspects he enjoyed thwarting someone's hopes was when he wrote to her, intimating that if she raised the question of being seconded from the B.C.C. to work for the Rockefeller Trustees on a project about American church life, he would feel bound to speak against it. His written notice to her of this intent is prefaced by a rather tart sentence to the effect that "I don't think it helps right-thinking people to get painful answers wrapped up in tissue paper."

The job of General Secretary was, of course, being worked out in the doing of it, and the amount of paper which flowed across Archie's desk was immense, both in bulk and scope. He wrote to Visser't Hooft in March, 1942, while still working for the Commission,

> "I have taken on this administrative job pretty late in life and am only learning by experience the tricks of the trade, and how important it is to keep a network of contact alive."

On the domestic front the B.C.C. had taken over into its Social Responsibility department the *Churches' Committee on Gambling* which produced massive amounts of paper detailing the horrors of footracing bets being placed at the Workington August Bank Holiday Gala, and like corruptions of the national morals. Archie was, in his Commission days, appointed reader of all their proposed publications, and as late as 1945 led the opening devotions of their Conference. This seems to have been something he conscientiously undertook as a serious commitment, though he had more humour about it than some of the Committee's protagonists, relishing the misprint which produced a document called "*Defeating the Dogs*" as "*Defending the Dogs*", and gently resisting the hyperbole he found in some of the committee's earnest pamphlets. About this he advised restraint in terms of "my steadfast objection to anything that savours of overstatement, which, in my view, always defeats its own end."

At the same time he was personally supportive, both in money and in encouragement to the committee's campaign against the introduction of football pools, and it is probably the case that he mentally classed gambling along with excesses in alcohol or sex as one of the more squalid and degenerate sins, a loss of control which was ignoble as well as wasteful of resources which could be better used.

Simultaneously, on the international front, he was handling massive questions about the healing of Europe, the Jewish/Palestine situation, and the responsibility of the churches to create a new international order. This involved regular contact with people of immense theological and political stature. He was, in addition to the B.C.C. work, a member of Paton's *Peace*

Aims group, which was officially under the aegis of the emergent World Council of Churches. This group, which included Temple, Bell, Henry Carter, Reinhold Niebuhr, and Pitney van Dusen among others, had contacts in the German Confessing Church, and the ear of senior statesmen both in Britain and the U.S.A. such as John Foster Dulles and the British Foreign Office. Both in terms of publications, addressing to the British public unhysterical information about the German church struggle and the need for post-war reconstruction, and in terms of keeping a watching-brief on British foreign policy decisions the group was remarkable for its ability to keep its finger on the pulse of European affairs in a trans-national way, while many secular institutions like the press and the radio were committed to mere morale-boosting nationalism.

The work of the group is well-documented in Eleanor Jackson's biography, though Archie's role in it merits no special mention. In the minutes of discussions in which he was participant, his interventions seem to have been rare, but pointed, as when he interjects in a conversation on post-war Europe that the conversation seems to have been entirely pragmatic, whereas the distinctive contribution of the churches should be more prophetic and visionary.

What this meant is perhaps shown most clearly in the little symposium which appeared, under Archie's editorial guidance, in 1946. This was not an official B.C.C. document, though all its contributors were active in the B.C.C. and four of the chapters had been worked over in the relevant B.C.C. departments. Rather it was an attempt to express the significance of the *Religion and Life* weeks for the churches and for British society as a whole. The book had been assembled with some difficulty; as Archie put it in a letter to the Bishop of Sheffield, "I am afraid I did not foresee the immense difficulty of getting seven chapters written from different points of view which would 'compluther', as my grandmother used to say." When it did appear as *The Christian Witness in the Post-War World*, it was a trenchant and lucid handling of key issues for the British ecumenical movement. Archie's introductory chapter is crisp, not fudging the kinds of criticism which were (and still are) levelled at ecumenical structures. For a popular paperback, produced by S.C.M. press for 3/6d, the language is stretching!

"On all the branches of the Church the fruits of the Spirit appear, and on all there is also an unsightly clutter of barren and dead wood, so that by the dominical test of identification by fruits none can vindicate claims to hegemony. The only reasonable inference from the facts is that the separate stems of the Church spring from a common root-system and convey the vital saps of the faith. A practical corollary for the critical situation in which Christians stand today is that they can and must make a common witness to Christ and salvation through him."

This urgent need of common witness was what lay behind another of Archie's wartime involvements, the Cloister Group, which was a meeting of Christians who stood on both sides of the pacifist/non-pacifist divide, with all the serious differences that that involved in an actual war situation, and yet were committed to manifesting that the gospel of reconciliation transcended even that difficult division. It had been the brainchild of a group which spanned the divide, Charles Raven and Percy Bartlett, who were absolute pacifists, and Bill Paton and William Temple who were not. They met every few months, normally at Christ's College, Cambridge, where Raven acted as host, and by 1943 the group had produced a little Penguin Special called *Is Christ Divided?* which was edited by Temple and contained essays by many of the Cloister Group members, Temple and Raven themselves, Leonard Hodgson, Paton, George Bell and Franz Hildebrandt. Though Archie does not contribute to the volume, he seems to have been involved in the negotiations with Penguin Books, and he was deeply committed to the stance voiced by Raven:

"The fact is that one who is a pacifist on the basis of his Christian faith finds that this faith unites him more closely with those who share it, even if in the matter of war they oppose him, than with those who share his pacifism, but for whom pacifism is differently grounded."

This sense of overarching loyalty grounded in the shared faith in Christ was very much at the heart of Archie's ecumenical vision, and he had no time for prudential ecclesiastical joinery. The fact that his deeply felt pacifism could engage, without compromise, in dialogue with the equally committed non-pacifism of Paton and Temple, was a tribute to the experience of solidarity across real and profound differences of understanding or ideology. It must also have been true that these weekends in Cambridge were a welcome break from the strictures of an organisational job, giving him the chance to share in deep theological exploration with friends who were dear to him intellectually and spiritually. Not, by his own admission, a temperamental administrator, he deliberately adopted in the B.C.C. job the disciplined persona of a senior ecclesiastical civil servant.

Whatever the internal stresses of being caught up in a complex administrative job, Archie seems to have communicated to those around him a massive sense of being the right man for the task. In a letter to Temple, written in April, 1943, Paton says:

"It is already obvious to everybody that Craig's own gifts, his keen churchmanship, his evangelistic zeal and his power of speech are, on the secretarial side, far and away the greatest asset that the Council has."

In addition to these undoubted qualities, the sheer geniality of the man was an immense asset. Mabel Small, who was appointed as the Press Officer of the Council shortly before Archie resigned, remembers coming into an office where the practice was that at tea-time, everyone who was in the building, senior, junior, beggarman, thief, would come to Archie's room for tea, and business talk would be outlawed. Clearly as the scale enlarged, such a meeting became logistically impossible, but for the duration of Archie's secretaryship, the relaxation of that tea-break was one of the human events of the day.

From 1942-1944, his secretary was a Miss Dorothy Crumpler, who worried protectively about the amount he did. Years later, in a letter of thanks for the series of radio talks on the Beatitudes, she recalled the years in the office:

"I thought of the little black book you once told me contained the only sermon you ever wrote, and wondered if it still existed. How well I remember that sermon and the amazing number of purposes it served. Often when I was concerned because you had no time to prepare an address, you would confidently pat your pocket as you departed and say cheerfully, "Don't worry, the little black book is here." If you have it still, please give it my most grateful remembrances."

From such merry human recollections, it is difficult to remember that the context of all this activity was a London at war, with all the stress and difficulty that involved. When Archie began the job with the Commission, he worked from Oldham's office, and when that arrangement had to end, he appears to have done half the work from his home address, which was Burlingham's house in Letchworth, Hertfordshire, and to have gone up to London only once or twice a week to meetings held in a room lent to the Council by the English Presbyterian Church. Every so often, a letter about Commission or Council business makes reference to the current state of bombing, or to how hard it must be to work in such conditions. There were also restrictions on paper use and availability, which meant for example that when *The Church in the World* reached Bulletin no.7, its size was reduced and its typeface was much smaller than before. In addition the *Towards a Christian Britain* leaflets were forced to undergo a sharp price rise to one penny each!

Apart from the common pressures and limitations imposed by the war, and in part, perhaps because of them, the British ecumenical scene suffered a number of specific casualties. In the spring of 1943, Charles Raven had a massive heart attack, which effectively brought the Cloister Group to an end, though Raven recovered. In the August of the same year, William Paton died after being operated on for a perforated ulcer, and only weeks later, Archbishop Temple had a fatal heart attack. These were not only professional, but personal losses to Archie, who had counted both as friends, and who was strengthened by their supportive energy and commitment. As Henry Leiper of the American office of the W.C.C. wrote in November 1943,

> "the staggering sense of loss which we all feel as the result of the unexpected passing of W. T. must be extremely heavy on you and your colleagues . . . . To have him go so shortly after Bill Paton is to increase by an incalculable amount the load that rests upon those who must try to carry on."

Much later, Archie comments on the sense of calamitous loss, both at these deaths and at others, notably those of Theodore Hume, the recently appointed director of Inter-Church Aid, whose plane was shot down on the way to a meeting in Sweden about European Reconstruction; and of Denzil Patrick, a fellow-Scot of immense promise who worked for the World Student Christian Federation in Geneva.

Further blows followed. In November, 1943, Kathleen Bliss resigned from her half-time position as officer of the General Council, on the grounds that she needed all her time to work on the *Christian Newsletter* and the *Christian Frontier Council*. H.W. Fox, who had first invited him to take on the Commission job had to withdraw from his B.C.C. role as Press Officer because of heart trouble. From the time of Paton's dath, Archie's workload had immensely increased, since he was then acting not only as B.C.C. General Secretary, but holding the fort for the British desk of the W.C.C. (in process of formation), and enjoying the collaboration of Oliver Tomkins. The *Religion and Life* weeks were still in full spate, with much of the planning and some of the speaking devolving on Archie, though his colleague, George Grieve, had specific responsibility for that area of the work. The job involved considerable travelling, mostly within Britain, but occasionally abroad, as when he visited the States just after Pearl Harbour to make official contact with the U.S. Federal Council of Churches.

The extra pressures must have been colossal, and, ironically, Paton had written a few months before he died to Temple, specifically to suggest looking around for a co-secretary to share Archie's workload, which Paton, himself a workaholic, considered excessive. At any rate, by early in 1944, Archie was himself quite ill. The specific nature of the illness is undocumented and unremembered by those who knew him at the time, but it was serious and prolonged enough to provoke solicitations from many of his correspondents. On 23rd February, Burlingham informs Geoffrey Fisher that "Craig seems to be making good progress . . . . he will not be back before the second week in April." And as late as 22nd May Nathaniel Micklem is writing, "I have heard disquieting rumours about your serious illness", though a week later he is reassured by a letter from Archie that he is really better.

66

As if all this were not enough to cope with, on 9th February, 1945, a flying bomb hit the offices of the Presbyterian Church of England where a B.C.C. meeting had just finished. The gentle Willie Elmslie, who was one of the mainstays of the European contact network, and Father Reginald Tribe, a Mirfield Father on the B.C.C. Executive were killed outright, Leonard Hodgson was very seriously injured, along with a secretary typist and a lay member, Mr Kenneth Parry of Bristol. Archie should have been at the meeting, if Oldham's note of a few days later was accurate. Along with his condolences, he wrote, "I am glad to think that by a merciful Providence you were prevented from attending that meeting."

Whether Archie's own deep sense of Providence as the keystone of Christian faith was rocked by this train of calamity and by his own exemption from it is not recorded. His immediate response to Elmslie's death was, in his own words, one of numbness, but it would not have been hard for an opponent of ecumenism to reconstruct the data of those twelve months as divine providence bumping off the chief architects of ecumenical advance with superlative efficiency. The following July, Hugh Herklots, the Field Secretary for the service of Youth resigned regretfully to take up a pastoral charge, apologising to Archie for making his task yet more difficult. Burlingham, who had also been ill with overwork, announced privately to Archie his wish to retire within the next few months (though in the event he stayed on as Acting General Secretary till 1947, and as International Secretary till 1949).

Archie's announcement of his intention to resign came like a bolt from the blue, when he made it, apparently without warning, to the Council meeting in May, 1946. Even Burlingham, with whom Archie had been billeted and with whom he travelled regularly from Letchworth to Bloomsbury St., was stunned by the news, and Mabel Small, the newly appointed Press Officer who replaced Fox, recalls the sense of shock at what was almost her first meeting. No one cause seems to explain the abruptness of the timing, or the uncharacteristic lack of preparation of friends and colleagues for a departure which was to give the Council a real headache in finding a successor. (It was eighteen months before Archie's successor, David Say, was appointed.) A whole range of factors must have made him decide: the sense of loss of so many of his fellow-pioneers; the state of his own health; a measure of homesickness for Scotland, where his sisters and closest friends still lived, and where he went for all his holidays, with instructions that no mail was to be forwarded while he was there; the sense that an organisational job, with all its administrative demands and necessary impersonality of sorts was not his permanent metier; all these in combination seem to have tipped the balance in favour of moving back north. In addition, there may have been others than D.S. Cairns who had been writing to him in terms of his being needed in Scotland.

As the news broke, letters of regret poured in. The Bishop of Worcester wrote,

"We in the British Council feel very deeply the loss we are sustaining through your resignation. We do not doubt the rightness of the decision you have made, but we do feel rather like orphans."

Speaking at the spring meeting of the Council after Archie's resignation was announced, Geoffrey Fisher, who had succeeded Temple as President, named Archie as a chief architect of the Council, a role which Archie had, characteristically disclaimed by attributing it to Paton. Fisher went on:

"He had borne an immense burden, without doubt greatly increased by the deaths of William Paton and William Temple. It was not however because the burden was intolerable that he had resigned. I cannot but feel that his decision was right . . . . We have not a proper claim on more than a certain amount of the life service of such a man as Dr Craig, who has given us seven years of unrestrained and devoted service . . . . All through these years, nothing could have surpassed the wisdom, the courage, judgment, coolness and catholicity of mind with which he has served this Council."

Archie's own appraisal of what had been achieved and not achieved was contained in a short memorandum written about the time of his departure. The outstandingly successful Department was, in his judgment, the Youth Department, which, under the leadership of its Scottish Secretary, Jean Fraser and of Hugh Herklots had achieved an evenness and homogeneity of work in the educational and publication fields; whereas he felt that other departments, partly because they took on unfinished agendas and existing staff from the earlier ecumenical organisations, were more pragmatic and haphazard (in Archie's eyes, "*typically English*"). The *Religion and Life* Movement seemed to him another major achievement, though he thought it needed, like the Youth Department, a properly equipped Field Section. Also as positives he rated the level of communication with Government departments [the B.C.C. contribution to the 1944 Education Act, for instance was considerable]; the fruitful relationship with other ecumenical bodies, which kept the B.C.C. from becoming insular or parochial in its concerns; and the output of publications, which had made the foremost ecumenical thinking of the day available to a large readership. (Some of the pamphlets had initial sales of over 22,000.)

On the debit side, he thought too much had been undertaken, with the ensuing risk of the B.C.C. becoming a body of incompetent omnicompetence, or, as he alternatively phrased it, omnicompetent mediocrity. The very success of the *Religion and Life* weeks had been a problem for the overall balance of the Council's work, in that they had, for the first two years "run away with it". The pressure of making *ad hoc* administrative arrangements for them meant there had been too little coherent policy-making. Too little, he thought, had been done on the Faith and Order side, which needed better representation at the staff level. And finally, there needed to be better lines of communication with the governing bodies of the Churches. This was necessary for two reasons, first to prevent the Council from being abused as a platform for "the Bishop of X's latest enthusiasm or Dr Y's brighter ideas", and secondly to feed through to parish level a real awareness of the Council's work and goals. He was, however, scathing about those who claimed that the central problem was about self-publication:

> "Some people seem to think that the chief of these (problems which face the Council) is to "get itself known". Unless this means "to get itself known for doing its job effectively, and in particular known and trusted by the governing bodies of the Churches in that sense" it is great nonsense. Advertisement in advance of achievement is a deadly danger in that it brings so many others in its train."

His sense that the Council was vulnerable to theological axes being ground was a major worry of Archie's. He was scrupulous about not putting his name to public causes of which he personally approved, like the campaign against football pools, or the National Peace Council, in case his support in an individual capacity could not be separated in people's minds from his B.C.C. role.

The debate about answerability was clearly a hot issue in these early years. Apart from the Oldham-Iredale-Bliss axis, with its conspicuous commitment to an anti-clerical, anti-Establishment pioneering stance, some of the Church leaders who were involved were themselves worried that the B.C.C. might become merely "an inter-church office with efficient colourless staff" manifesting "staid assembliness". Leslie Hunter, the then Bishop of Sheffield, who voiced this fear to Archie, shared Oldham's fear that it would lead in the end to a second-rate output by "a not unuseful organ of the decaying ecclesiastical set-up."

Certainly, in those first years of the Council, Archie Craig was vital in managing to hold together, in his own person and in organisational terms, deeply-rooted churchmanship with the ability to nurture and harvest the most adventurous patches of Christian engagement with the concerns of a largely secular post-war world. It was a measure of his own hope for the churches that he did not accept that there was any necessary polarisation between creativity and institutional allegiance, or at least none which better education could not solve. That theological elasticity which marked the founders of the B.C.C., their sense of the mission of the church resting largely on the laity, and on their embeddedness in the concrete complexities of the working world, is hard to recapture in a time when the laity have been theologically pauperised, and the equation of leadership with clerical status has become commonplace.

The robustness with which the early B.C.C. assumed that "the Churches" did not mean "the clergy" meant a commitment to listen to the best analysis of secular affairs which could be given, not usually by those who were professional churchmen. Thus, the original Council included men and women of the professional stature of Walter Moberley, John Maud, Marjorie Reeves and John Trevelyan, and a host of others who would have been accredited in any appraisal as immensely capable within their own fields. Archie's strictures against omnicompetent mediocrity were shared by others, and even more sharply expressed by a Methodist civil servant called W.G. Symons, one of the contributors to *Christian Witness in a Post-war World* He submitted a memorandum on the work of the B.C.C. in relation to Christian social judgment, which was fairly scathing about the recurrent confusion in B.C.C. documents which came, in his judgment, from the mixing of "half-digested technicalities with opinionated value-judgments which in no way prove their Christian authorisation."

From a vantage-point of some fifty years later, however, it is hard not to be impressed by the accuracy and political anticipation of those involved in the Council and in the overlapping Peace Aims group. Within one conversation, for instance, which took place on November 7th, 1944, when there was an extensive discussion of the shape of post-war Europe, those present identified the risk of Russia becoming the effective political master in Hungary, Yugoslavia, Romania, Bulgaria and Finland; foresaw the Middle East becoming an arena of conflict between Jews and Arabs; and predicted the possibility of imperialist wars in the Far East if America and Russia grew into superpowers.

It is also noteworthy that the massive attempts at outreach achieved by the *Religion and Life* movement made the B.C.C. particularly sensitive to problems which have come home to roost in the second half of the 20th century, and which the denominations, catering mainly for gathered believers, have still hardly begun to take seriously. It was, of course, Oldham's reiterated warning that even a document like *Christian Witness in a Post-war World* was sheer Greek to many people who were neither stupid nor hostile to Christian faith. But the sense of how deep the alienation from standard religious language was for great tracts of people was documented over and over again from less predictable quarters. There is, for instance, in the files of the B.C.C. an account by the then Bishop of Hull of a carefully planned week for the British Forces in his diocese. There was a considered decision not to have hymns or prayers for the first two nights, and the men were allowed to smoke as they listened! In spite of this, the bishop sadly reports that Archbishop Temple, aware of a communication gap, was translating ahead into words of two syllables, as if using a foreign language. Even worse, "Bill Paton was speaking in a foreign language the whole time." The fact that two of the brightest stars in the ecumenical firmament, with an indisputable concern to address the contemporary secular world, could be perceived as speaking a foreign language might have warned the churches of the immensity of their task.

Certainly, the warning became part of Archie Craig's consciousness, and his own report of the Bolton *Religion and Life* week presents the challenge in characteristically tough prose:

"There is a need of deep wrestling with the Gospel, on the hypothesis (difficult for us parsons) that it is a foreign language in which we are only smatterers: a new sensitiveness to voices speaking not from the pulpit but to the pulpit, on the hypothesis (positively repugnant to parsons) that the matrix of the new world need not be the organised church as we know and manage it: since the wind bloweth as it listeth, demanding an elastic and continually revised adjustment of methods and techniques."

For a man with so bold a sense of what *semper reformanda* meant to wait without shrillness upon the mandate of the actual churches was a stance of near-dominical patience, all the more so because of the exhilaration and freshness of the ecumenical vision shared by that pioneering generation. The patience was to be even further tested when Archie returned north of the border, but for all that he felt in the last few days in London "the wrench of actual severance from the Council's work", he was clear that it was in Scotland that he now wanted to be.

71

7 Return to Scotland

"It takes a long long time for a lead given in Geneva to penetrate to Auchtermuchty or Acharacle."

Preaching in a Scientific Age, 1953

Retrospectively, Archie Craig described his acceptance of the invitation to become Deputy Leader of the Iona Community as something of a *mariage de convenance* , entered upon because he wanted to get back to Scotland, while George MacLeod wanted an assistant so that he could travel in pursuit of finance for the growing community.

The two had been friends since George's days as Associate Minister with Norman Maclean in St. Cuthbert's, Edinburgh, when Archie had been struck by the *sparkle* of the man, and by the feel of poetry in his personality, eloquence and diction, a quality, as he drily remarked, not overcommon in the Presbyterian ministry. They had shared the experience of Tambaram, at which George gave an address, and had been prominent in their pacifist stance in the thirties, but Archie expressed some surprise at having been invited to be a sponsor when the Iona Project was first mooted. The venture appealed to him, combining as it did the symbolic act of rebuilding Iona abbey with an extremely practical concern to reverse the progressive divorce between organised religion and organised labour. In addition, it aimed to create a microcosm of Christian community where ministers and laymen would work together in actual and not just theoretical parity, and it was based on a core commitment of structured devotion which was highly sympathetic to him.

By 1945, the Community had emerged, as Archie put it, from vociferous infancy to maturing teenage-dom. Its main lineaments, ecumenical, socially and politically aware, liturgically adventurous and spiritually centred, offered the kind of challenge to the whole man which the young Archie had so wanted to be able to claim for Christianity, in the face of friends who accused it of being a pallid kind of half-life.

In view of the options, curiously enough, in spite of all that, he remained as Deputy Leader for only a year, though he retained responsibility for Associates and Minister members groups beyond that time, and was a lifelong defender of the vision which undergirded the whole venture. The writer of the *Times* obituary for Archie went as far as to claim, "This was not a happy time," but without substantiating the allegation in any way. Certainly, no patent unhappiness registered with those who spent time on Iona in the summer of 1947, nor with Bob Craig who succeeded him as Deputy Leader. Indeed men like Douglas Alexander remember it as a heady mixture to hear George and Archie vying with each other in wit and anecdote.

Archie himself at the time wrote for *The Coracle* his impressions of the long hot summer, when dishes had to be washed in rationed water, and the watchword was "*stink or swim*". Those are entirely positive, celebrating not just the quality of visitors and participants in activities on the island, but the quality of his experience there. Above all he registers "A feeling of dynamism in the air, of released force, which reminded me of the change from trench warfare to open campaigning in 1918". This emerged, in his judgment, from the reality of "conversion" which Iona invited, not any stereotyped scheme of salvation associated with one definition of dogmatic articles, or marked by convulsive emotion, but a decisive avowal of commitment to Christ and his church. The signals of this were an imagination-empowering revival of worship, and renewed dedication to the needy world, both transcending the categories of shared human common purpose and belonging to what Archie repeatedly called "*the vertical plan of reality*".

While his summing-up of the Iona phenomenon was of a "powerful new religious force unleashed in Scotland, channelled through the spirit of a man of genius", there was, somehow, a sense in Archie that he could not remain permanently at the epicentre of the movement. Without elaboration, he puts his giving up of the deputy leadership as if it were almost a matter of *his* unsuitability for the job: "I had little difficulty in accepting an invitation to go to Glasgow University. George needed someone as much younger than himself as I was older."

This may be an utterance of genuine self-deprecation, or a characteristic courtesy in refusing to "file his ain nest". But there are some indications, both in Archie's own writing and in the memory-impressions of others, that he was at some subliminal distance from the direction the Community was to take. In an undated paper on the future of the Association he warns against a kind of Messianism which would turn the movement into a sectarian camp, dissociated from the Church of Scotland. In his view, loyalty to the larger church was needed, both as a safeguard against heresy, and as a safeguard against party spirit. What was welcome as an *emphasis* was sinister if it became an *obsession*.

Several of those who saw him work in tandem with George MacLeod testify not only to an immense mutuality of respect and affection, but also to divergences of style, which might have become explicitly disruptive if two such giants were in constant proximity. Both were convinced pacifists, but George was a crusading pacifist, whereas Archie was reticent except under what he took to be evangelical constraint. George would go on protest marches, Archie never did, a fact about which he had some misgivings, according to Nelson Gray. Whether it was due to his intimate working with non-pacifist Christians in the Cloister Group, or to his native distaste for anything remotely smacking of propaganda, he had more desire to let people come to their own conclusions than to have them agree with his. (For instance, he hever discussed pacifism with his professional soldier nephew-by-marriage, in spite of their close and fairly regular contact at various stages.) Both were commanding speakers, but George's rhetoric was almost incantatory, whereas Archie's style was drier and cooler, depending more on rational appeal than on inflamed passion. (He once said to Robin Barbour that George had a very *feminine* mind, in that he went off on an instinct!)

It is probably true that what most attracted him in the early days of the Community were its mystical, liturgical and ecumenical aspects, and that, while he appreciated too the social and political commitment, he was quite unwilling to *equate* socialism with the gospel. (The Community, of course, would not formally have endorsed the equation either, but it was often perceived to do so, as when, in recent years a layman who was interested in joining was informally advised that there would be no place for someone who was a member of the Tory Reform Group.)

At any rate, the approach by Hector Hetherington on behalf of the Glasgow University Court opened a door through which he was happy to step, and took him, for the second time, into a ten-year stretch of employment by the University.

It is a matter of fairly common repute among senior Scottish churchmen that he might well have been appointed instead to the Chair of Practical Theology and Christian Ethics in Edinburgh, which fell vacant in 1946. There was a unanimous sense that he was academically and experientially an outstanding man to succeed Professor Lamont, not only among many of the Faculty, but also among the students of the year, who got up a petition on his behalf, having become wise to the rumours of discrimination against him on political grounds. Certainly Hugh Walker records in the Greater St. Mary's news of 1948 that, at the dinner in his honour after the Cunningham Lectures in New College, "regret was expressed that Archie was not a full-time colleague on the professorial staff". The resistance to his appointment was led by a senior layman on the Appointments Committee who deplored the possibility of the Chair being given to a pacifist. Archie was wont to say that he had never really had to suffer for his pacifism, as did those whose profession gave them no exemption from military service. But his rejection for a position he would certainly have relished, in favour of Willie Tindal, must have taken a bit of swallowing.

Though it was less prestigious than a chair, and less directly in the ambience of the church, the new job at Glasgow was a challenging one, and, yet again, a first in University annals. The Lecturership in Biblical Studies was not initially a graduating course for Glasgow University students, though they were welcome to take it as a non-graduating class, and many did. The request had come from the Church of Scotland's Education Committee for a course that would count towards the *Article 39* teaching qualification, taught partly in the University and partly in Jordanhill Training College. This request had been processed by the Arts Faculty — significantly not by the Divinity one — and the Senate and Court had subsequently agreed to make an appointment. It seems, reading between the lines of Court minutes, that there were enough people around who knew Archie's record as Chaplain in the '30s to endorse Sir Hector's suggestion that he be directly approached as the right man for the job.

So began a fruitful partnership with J.W.D. Smith, the head of Religious Education at Jordanhill, and a man very much on Archie's wavelength in the exploration of intelligent and life-enhancing faith. It is, perhaps, worth underlining the fact that Archie spent twenty of his professional years in the university context as his mode of fulfilling his vocation as an ordained minister, more than twice as long as he spent either in parish work or at his ecumenical desk. Though he was versatile enough to do well in whatever sphere he worked, it seems that the most congenial to him was the particular fusion of intelligent quest and faithful response to which the university world challenged Christian men and women. Nor was this merely a matter of temperamental self-indulgence. From his boyhood on, he was clear that the church would lapse into sentimental pietism or offensive dogmatism unless it wrestled with the toughest of questions thrown up by fields of adjacent secular knowledge. His commitment to the engagement was one of principle as well as of taste.

Though he refused any dissociation between faith and scientific knowledge of any sort, he did believe that there was a difference of role between preaching on the one hand and teaching on the other. This he enlarges on in various contexts, particularly in a paper he gave in mid-office on his vision of the objectives of a Biblical Studies course.

His first aim was to make the Bible interesting, or, as he put it, "less presumptuously, to exhibit the many-sided fascination of the Biblical literature." This was not the same as persuading them of its truth, though he was candid with classes that he himself saw Scripture as belonging at the intersection of two planes, one of human history and enterprise, the other of divine self-revelation. It was rather a matter of seizing the imagination, awakening the appetite of the student to learn more and fascinating his spirit.

Secondly, he wanted "to set the Bible as a whole in a comprehensible perspective, to exhibit the Scriptures as the literary deposit of a uniquely gifted people along a thousand years of its chequered history, to show when and why and in what circumstances and to meet what situations and exigencies its various parts were written." This he saw as a contribution to rescuing those who would be teaching the young from dangerous and fantastic readings of the

Bible, like the reading of Ezekiel's prophecies as predictions of Soviet destruction by the West.

Thirdly, he wanted to show "that scientific spirit and scientific method, so far from being an improper tool of Biblical study, is essential to it, and is in fact productive of immense rewards." Here too his primary concern was to rescue the young from the sense that their religious convictions had to be held in a watertight compartment, sealed off from every other sphere of school learning. Speaking with feeling of a fifteen-year old who had attacked him at an S.C.M. schools' conference for using the phrase, "the profound *myth* of the Garden of Eden", he elaborates on this point with sturdy and forthright conviction:

> "In my view it is little short of a tragedy when the best results of Biblical Criticism, reached by the immense labours of the last century, are not laid open, of course in suitably graded disciplines, of course with all the arts of pedagogy which are applied to all other subjects, but in the end laid fully open to the young generation, so that they may be saved on the one hand from the tragedy of a religion that is sealed off from all their other mental and spiritual experiences, and, on the other hand, from an unnecessarily exaggerated conflict within their spirits between faith and reason."

Occasionally, it seems from his lecture-notes, Archie confronted classes explicitly with his vision of the teaching and learning process, in which there was no room for furtiveness or lack of candour. In his opening lecture on "Miracle in the Old and New Testaments", for instance, he writes:

> "But one of the startling and even terrifying things about teaching or preaching is that whether it is bad or good, there is still a *communicatio vitae* or *communicatio mortis* taking place. A teacher does in fact communicate what he is living by or dying of. He may think that he is communicating bare propositions, but what he is living by or dying of in fact percolates through the propositions. If he is in fact embarrassed by the propositions he communicates, his embarrassment will percolate through his teaching. If he is holding only defiantly to the propositions, and in inner tension against another witness in his spirit, the atmosphere of defiance and lack of inner integrity will slip through and penetrate."

More often, the nature of a teacher's integrity is implicit, though no less manifest, in the way Archie himself deals with the material to hand. One of his earliest students on the Biblical Studies course recalls the impact he made, even on a generation of students which included some mature ex-servicemen not prepared to take anything lying down. On the whole his lectures were carefully prepared in typescript, with a full text pointed by red underlinings. Occasionally there are pages done in more of a hurry, mere handwritten headings, even in one or two instances scribbled on the back of torn up University notices, as if time to find fresh paper had not been available. [Or perhaps it was the waste of good paper which offended his sense of economy!] The odd cigarette burn on the page confirms the memory of friends that he smoked quite heavily as he worked!

In today's university climate, anyone producing lectures of such sustained lucidity and liveliness would be rushing to print with them, but Archie was genuinely diffident about his own scholarship, and reluctant, for example, to disagree with Peake, whom he regarded as a really learned commentator (though he did risk it on at least one occasion). He joked against himself that he found it very easy to avoid the risk of being overspecialised with his classes, since he was not a specialist in any particular realm of Biblical study and couldn't over-specialise if he tried.

He seems to have felt most at home with the Old Testament teaching: and indeed for New Testament studies invoked the help of Professor Willie Barclay, and later of his assistant, David Gourlay. Lecture-notes of his own, however, survive on Mark, Acts, 1st Corinthians, Hebrews, James, 1st Peter and Revelation, as well as a general introduction of great polish and pungency to the Pauline Epistles. Students must have appreciated the range of contemporary reference he could make to bring books alive. To get inside the affront of Amos to the religious professionals of his day, for instance, he asked them to think what kind of man would be needed to proclaim in modern Britain, "Your social iniquities are so intolerable ... that it is an awful certainty that the barbarous powers of totalitarian communism will overwhelm, and it will be the Almighty who directs the operation." And he explored the message of Ezekiel in terms of the merits and demerits of ritual in religion, and of the risk of insulating the sacred from the ordinary life of mankind in the contemporary world.

They must also have enjoyed the humour of his presentation, which spiced the hard data which had to be mastered, his account of Isaac as "the colourless man who is known for the first half of his life as the son of his father, and for the second as the father of his son"; or, on the book of Job:

> "It is possible to regard Job under the image of a sandwich, a sandwich with the bread cut very thin and the filling very thick, and a rather thin coating of butter between bread and filling, so that the bread can be easily detached, but the parts are meant to be eaten together, and it is the interaction of them which constitutes the virtue and the glory of the sandwich."

or, to the assertion that the first century disciples were more credulous than twentieth century ones about the miraculous:

> "People sometimes write as though Simon Peter wouldn't have turned a hair if a cod he had just taken out of lake of Galilee started to reproach him in forcible Aramaic."

His empathy with the students was palpable. "Now I imagine that like most other people, you find the narratives of the period during which there were two bordering states in Palestine proper — the kingdom of Israel and the Kingdom of Judah — immensely confusing." "Even after the figure of Samuel has been dehydrated as Wardle dehydrates him on pp56-57, a great man remains." "You won't find in this book (George Adam Smith on Isaiah) the kind of niggling verse-by-verse treatment which is all very well in its way and necessary for a minute knowledge of any book, but tends to be exhausting to the reader." And he had the natural grace to temper the seriousness of the subject with occasional hilarious stories worthy of student magazines, like that of the Welsh Primitive Methodist who was letting his remote cottage for a month, and was asked by prospective hirers if the remote cottage had a W.C. attached. To which he, thinking they meant Wesleyan Chapel, replied that the nearest one was nine miles away and capable of seating two hundred and fifty persons. His reply went on, "This is unfortunate for you if you are in the habit of going regularly, but no doubt you will be glad to know that many people take their lunch with them and make a day of it." Or he would share his glee at having just heard the other day about an undergraduate who "among her other names, has been distinguished by her loving parents for weal or woe with the name of Devorgilla. Can you deduce anything from her parents about that — beyond the fact, I mean, that at least one of them was unusually strong-minded?"

For all the humour and lightness of touch with which he could approach the material, he had high standards of what it meant to be a university student, and could make these clear with no little crispness. Introducing a class to their exam requirements, he warned them that they would be tested on

        a) actual knowledge of the contents of the chapters, (which needed to excel that of the prospective divinity student who, asked for a note on Emmaus, replied, "One of the minor prophets");
        b) imaginative grasp of the situation with which passages deal;
        c) reading round the subject;
and   d) power of shapely presentation of the results.

He so much wanted the classes he took to be actively responsive to the issues that he was tempted to ban notetaking, as one of his old University professors had done, but instead contented himself with warning them that even if they could listen with the nib of their biro, and even graduate on it, he did not want to teach a class of automata. He recounted with palpable scorn having bumped into a student whom he asked what he was reading, to be given the answer, "My notes. I never read books. Books just confuse you." Over against such an attitude he would every so often remind classes of the dictum of Sanderson, erstwhile headmaster of Oundle, that his job was to conduct people to the frontiers of knowledge, where darkness beckoned.

The quality of risk-taking involved in genuine exploration was not for Archie a demand merely for professional academics, but an essential quality of faithful response to the inviting unknownness of a large and complex creation. He loved the location of position given by General Bernard Fergusson during the second Chindwin campaign: "Two miles south of the U in UNSURVEYED"; and the story of the Canadian bushman who was asked if he'd ever been lost and answered, "No, I never bin lost; but once, for about three weeks, I was kinda puzzled." Any obscurantist clinging to safe certainties against the pressure of facing new questions therefore seemed to him an unworthy *human* response as well as a defect of scholarship and a lack of faith.

On the whole, the members of the first Biblical Studies courses were firmly inside the Christian world of discourse, and perhaps even too securely inside it. As a result, the general thrust of many of the lecture courses is to loosen students up to the possibility of appreciating the range of auxiliary tools available to them as teachers: archaeology, geography, lower and higher criticism. He handles miracle stories, for instance, in a way which resists both the dogma that they *must* describe actual events and the dogma that they *cannot possibly* do so. Rather he suggests that they must find more sophisticated criteria, such as whether the event in question is compatible with the general thrust of biblical disclosure about God as revealed in Christ. This allows him to cast doubt, for instance on the historicity of some of the Elijah narratives, or on the authenticity of the Acts account of Sapphira's punishment, as standing in sharp contrast to the mood and feel of the story of the life of Jesus. Even here, however, his agnosticism is tempered by the recognition that the story is told straightforwardly in what purports to be plain history by a man who is a careful, reliable historian, and that, to many, scepticism at such a point seems to be the thin edge of a very dangerous wedge.

He thus seems to have combined fairly candid statement of his own position with the equipping of students to reach their own, albeit different, conclusions, provided only that these reflect wrestling with the full complexity of the issue. His own judgment, that the bulk of the gospel narratives purport to be historical in the technical sense, manifesting the kind of truthfulness we expect in a court of law, would nowadays seem to many New Testament scholars implausible, and the idea that many narratives are *constructs* and not *grounds* for it could

79

not be so disparagingly dismissed as a marginal liberal extreme. But he does not properly put the ball back in the liberal court by asking how much of their rejection of miracle narrative as literal is in fact the outcome of an unduly restrictive view of God's freedom in relation to nature. The debate is not in fact one about exegesis, or not about that alone, but about accounts of God and his *modus vivendi* in the kind of world we know, about what congruity we properly expect between past and present, what special impact on natural process might be reasonably expected if Jesus was indeed the Christ of God, and how far we understand our Christian faith to be dependent on the privileged experience of the first disciples.

Considering that "most Church of Scotland ministers of the time regarded any tampering with the Authorised Version as almost heretical," Archie's lively freedom of paraphrase, his commending of Moffatt, and his willingness in principle to criticise the behaviour or insight of biblical personnel alarmed some students, but most were stimulated by his palpable enthusiasm. The direct relationship that is possible within a small class was further consolidated by his extra-mural contacts with students, whom he regularly invited to participate in a summer-school in St. Andrews, and had round to the house in Bank Street with their partners for an annual party. (As an ice-breaker at one of these he produced a quantity of scissors, paste and various materials and asked everyone to construct an effigy of Tiglath-Pileser III.)

Apart from his gregarious dealings with students, Archie participated with gusto in other aspects of university life. He was quickly involved again with the Chaplaincy, both as an occasional preacher, and, from 1949 as a member of the Chaplaincy Committee, responsible for fabric and policy decisions. He inaugurated a group which ran throughout the fifties, whose *raison d'etre* was to invite new Professors to a handsome dinner, and then to spend an hour or more putting the case for and being cross-questioned as to the propriety of appointing a successor in their field of study. This, apparently, was a source of genuine enjoyment as well as of inter-faculty communication, and Sir James Howie, a former colleague who frequently enjoyed such occasions remembers Archie's verve and flair on such occasions, [which had none of the sinister ring as a university appraisal game that they might have in the more competitive eighties].

On Michaelmas Day, September 29th, 1950, just before the start of his fourth year of lecturing at Glasgow, Archie Craig, at the age of sixty-one, married May Laidlaw, whom he had met forty-four autumns before, and according to live legend, loved for nearly as long. Almost none of their personal correspondence was included in the material which Archie left for public scrutiny, so the interiority of these long years of apparent renunciation remains private and inscrutable. They are accounted for in the lore of family and friends by May's filial devotion to her parents, who needed her to care for them, particularly as her father was severely invalid after an operation in the '20s. Those who belong to the second half of the twentieth century find it hard to credit that even the most loving and dutiful daughter would sacrifice all possibility of marriage for so long, especially in an age when manses had ample room, when extended families were more normal than now, and when the Laidlaw household could easily have afforded domestic staff to help with household or nursing duties. It seems, however, that May simply accepted as her God-given responsibility the task of caring for her parents, a job unshared by siblings, since her only brother, Leslie, had been killed in the Great War.

Whatever the private struggle to accept the apparent destiny of their singleness for so long, May and Archie expressed no bitterness or recrimination of it, and Archie hinted to close friends like Lesslie Newbigin that he was willing to accept celibacy as God's vocation to him, though not easily. In the event however, when May's parents both died in the early months of 1950, late marriage became for her and Archie a happy possibility, and they were quietly married in St. Andrew's Church, Peebles, with Hugh Walker acting as best man. From then on, for thirty-five years, they shared a partnership in which merriment, zest, considerateness and devotion were palpable, and which expressed in a rich variety of idioms what "cherishing" means. Though he was almost uniformly genial and outgoing, Archie was in some ways a very unknown and private person, rarely disclosing his deepest personal feelings, partly because he genuinely saw conversation as a chance to find out about the person he was talking to, and their affairs! For a man who had learned loneliness as one pole of experiencing God, the sharing of such constant partnership must have been an immense bounty, and his utterances about "my May", while not effusive, are consistently delicate and tender.

As well as inhabiting the worlds of home and university, Archie was able, by returning to Scotland, to use his ecumenical energy and experience on his home territory.

Scottish participation in the Ecumenical Movement had been vigorous since the World Missionary Conference in 1910. By 1924 the Missionary Continuation Committee had set up a Scottish Churches Council, which included the Church of Scotland, the United Free Church, the Episcopal Church in Scotland, Methodist, Baptist, Congregational, Original Secession and Free Presbyterian churches. This met every three months for the next twenty-four years, and was a kind of clearing-house through which the different levels of inter-church activity, local, Scottish, British and international were kept informed of one another's activities.

Apart from Archie himself, whose freechurchmanship had been an important counterpoise in the infant B.C.C. to the Presidency of the Archbishop of Canterbury, the first years of that enterprise had involved a significant number of Scots in key positions: Jean Fraser and Denis Taylor in the Youth Department and Mabel Small as Press Officer. Hugh Martin, meanwhile, was powerfully influential at S.C.M. Press, the omnipresent Joe Oldham, though becoming an Anglican, had Scottish U.F. origins and a Scottish cast of theological mind, and Robert Mackie was in Geneva masterminding ecumenical work in the international student world.

The official nomenclature of the Scottish ecumenical body changed in 1948, when the Scottish Churches Ecumenical Committee was set up, incorporating both the former Council and the Scottish Committee of the World Alliance for International Friendship through the Churches. This Committee was the official, overarching body to which decision-making on ecumenical questions affecting member churches was referred, though of course it had no executive power beyond that mandated to it by the member churches. Around this relatively small body was a larger group, a kind of ecumenical aureole, consisting of groups and individuals who were interested in and supportive of the ecumenical endeavour, without being official representatives of their churches. This Scottish Churches Ecumenical Association was less concerned with inter-church business than with the shared grappling with problems and issues thrown up for all the churches by the "outside world". Its nucleus was a group called the Dollarbeg Group, (named after their meeting-place at Isobel Forrester's home in Clackmannanshire) and Archie was a significant participant in this context and immensely influential on many younger church people.

It was characteristic of this ecumenical ginger-group that it took a major area of study each year and then mounted an annual conference with speakers of considerable expertise. Details of this pioneering group, which had its finger very accurately on the pulse of social change, are accessible through Mabel Small's detailed account of the forty years from 1924 to 1964, "Growing Together" [produced, though not commercially published by the Scottish Churches Council]. It is hard not to feel, on reading of the work done in those years, that we spend much ecclesiastical time re-inventing the wheel. In their first year the group tackled the place of women in church and society. (Archie is minuted as emphasising that the church was failing to recruit the most capable and well-trained women because of its "stuffy attitude", while Nevile Davidson urged caution in relation to any step that might hinder church unity! [plus ça change])

In the subsequent years they tackled "Christian Witness in a Revolutionary World", "The Christian Challenge to Communism", "The Work and Witness of the Laity" and "The Christian Doctrine of Work". The subtlety and intellectual openness of their discussions and conclusions, like that of the Religion and Life weeks, easily generate envy of such articulate theological confidence and buoyancy. They address to the churches, for instance, pointed questions about their failure to live convincingly the insight which Marxism

Archie Craig as University Chaplain at Glasgow, sketched by a student, Betty Bartholomew, 1930.

Walking and talking with Glasgow University students in the thirties.

In the garden at Doune, with John Campbell, his gardener.

Preaching at the centenary celebrations of St. John's, Edenside and Ednam, Kelso 1966.

now claims as its own, that social relationships affect and determine the very being of man. They urge that congregations be helped to "shed trivial and outworn activities" in "artificially segregated groups" in order to enter the conflicts and struggles of the new world that is coming to birth. They warn the churches that only "a spiritually intelligent and active laity" can enable the church to meet the modern world, and all their recorded conversations have a ring of robust and undefensive confidence that they belong together in shaping the future agenda of the church in Scotland.

Had the various denominations been able to take on board the insights of this group, which was always aware of the global horizon (communism not posing much of a threat in Auchtermuchty!) the marginality of the churches to much of Scottish urban life at least might not have been so dramatically accelerated as it has become. However, as Miss Small's discreet comment puts it, "The Scottish Churches supported the British Council of Churches with more enthusiasm than they evinced for the Ecumenical Movement nearer home." The Home Board of the Church of Scotland, having argued that *Religion and Life* weeks were not approporiate in Scotland, began in 1952 to plan a campaign of nationwide evangelism called "Tell Scotland" in which Melville Dinwiddie, B.B.C. Controller, Scotland and Dr Ronnie Falconer, Head of Religious Broadcasting were to be key auxiliaries. Though in time there were representatives from other denominations involved in the planning, and the agents of local mission were meant to be all the Christians in a given area (at least all the Reformed Christians), the vastly dominant group in terms of media exposure and publications was from the Church of Scotland, a fact which may have made the other denominations feel that they were not really regarded as partners of any real stature. Certainly, by 1956, beneath the surface courtesies, the Presbytery of Glasgow so much regarded itself as territorial lord of all ecclesiastical affairs that it intervened through its Youth Convenor in the Church Offices at 121 George Street, and then through the Archbishop of Canterbury(!) and the Youth Department of the B.C.C. to block a World Council of Churches youth workcamp which had been initiated by the Churches of Christ in the New Town of East Kilbride.

The tangled politics of how the Ecumenical Committee related to the Ecumenical Association, and how both related to the committee structure of the Church of Scotland, to "Tell Scotland" and to the subsequent "Kirk Weeks" which ran from 1957-1964 would make an absorbing research subject for a historian of Scottish Ecumenism, for it is in this period that the underlying *tone* of Church of Scotland participation in ecumenical affairs seems to change into a more defensive and guarded one, wary of alien intrusions from those unlucky enough not to be Presbyterian. What is conspicuous in relation to Archie is that he was seen as the one man big enough to straddle the various subterranean fault lines under the ecumenical crust. Thus, for instance, when

Kenneth Slack, visiting as B.C.C. Secretary in 1958, wanted to meet officials of the Association, the Committee, the Scottish Inter-Church Aid Committee, and Scottish Representatives on B.C.C. and W.C.C. committees, it was Archie who chaired the meeting. (One suspects that he was also responsible for the vocabulary of the forthcoming resolution that a small group of people be asked to look at "the fissiparous nature of Scottish Inter-Church relations".) In spite of the fact that he was Convenor of the Church of Scotland's Inter-Church Relations Committee by this time, the members of other denominations seem to have felt confident that he would see that justice was done to their interests also, and not merely view the field from a Church of Scotland vantage-point. An even more telling instance is that when the Ecumenical Committee had to find a new chairman in 1962, after the resignation of Nevile Davidson, trouble was brewing at the Church of Scotland's assumption that chairmanship should *naturally* continue under the Church of Scotland. The conciliatory initiative taken by the concerted non-Church of Scotland members was that Archie should be at least interim chairman, a decision which spoke volumes for their confidence that he would never exploit the " *we, the National Church*" line, as some others would certainly have done.

He spanned also, during these years, the subliminal gulf which threatened to widen between those concerned with mission and those concerned with unity. The effective apartheid and subliminal distrust between those mainly involved with "*Tell Scotland*" and those mainly involved with the Ecumenical Association was vigorously contested by Archie, sometimes verbally, but more significantly by his supportive and constructive presence in both. He loved to quote the words of Jim Maitland who was to become one of the original ecumenical ministry team in Livingston New Town: "Mission is the love of Christ flowing into the life of the world along the channels of his Church's life." At the same time it seemed to him axiomatic that the effective flow of that love demanded a *united* church. Another of his favourite images, delivered magisterially in several contexts, was that "the very idea of inter-church relations, implying the existence of separated churches, not separated just spatially but by doctrine or determinative structure — by faith and order — would have been as astounding to him [Paul] as to have seen the four legs of a horse hobbling round the four sides of a city square unconnected with an equine body."

To have come from the intimate collaboration with those who set in place the structures of B.C.C. and W.C.C. to the barely concealed ecclesiastical chauvinism of the Church of Scotland must have sorely tried Archie's human patience. Even the Lund World Conference on Faith and Order, at which he was a Church of Scotland delegate seemed to him a relatively time-marking exercise, recollection of which provoked from him the limerick

"There was once a young bear at the zoo
Who never had nothing to do:
When he found it too slow
To walk to and fro
He reversed it and walked fro and to."

Yet the Lund declaration, that the churches should commit themselves to "act together in all matters except those in which deep differences of conviction compel them to act separately" was itself a revolutionary one in a Scotland where the norm was still a Church of Scotland parish which felt itself self-sufficient, and smatterings of other denominations which had roughly the status of an ethnic minority in Henley. (The Roman Catholic church, of course, was more than a smattering, but in a Scotland which still had Orange Lodge marches on the 12th of July; where one housewife could say to another of a neighbour she *liked*, "She's a Catholic, but she's very nice"; and where the five-year olds in segregated schools on opposite sides of a road got their winter fun by hurling snowballs over the school railings at one another, to shouts of "Dirty Protestant!" and "Dirty Catholic!", rapprochement across that frontier seemed high fantasy.)

It is perhaps the key instance of Archie Craig's confidence in the slow molecular forces of God for the renewal of his one Church that he never became nagging or despairing, though there are signs that his vision of the time-scale altered. He retained, through the Dollarbeg Group, the Ecumenical Association and, latterly, through Scottish Churches' House, a lively sense of the world, and the world-church as the true context of his local commitment. But for all that, within the ranks of his own denomination, he had to weather a storm which rocked him, and which severely holed the ecumenical barque in Scotland for many a year to come.

8   The clatter of arms

Alastair Haggart: "This is ludicrous. The Church of Scotland being afraid of the Episcopal Church is like an elephant being afraid of a mouse, when it could swallow it up with one swoop of its trunk and not know that it had swallowed anything."

Archie Craig: "No, No, Alastair, you've got it all wrong. This elephant knows that the day it swallows that particular mouse it will become an elephant that is fond of cheese and afraid of cats."

Verbatim from Anglican-Presbyterian conversations

As long as the Church remained divided, Archie never saw ecumenical activity as an *alternative* to denominational loyalty, *but as an implication* of it. His hope was that from the cross-fertilising of denominations a new unified structure would in time emerge, in which each of the old structures would make a distinctive contribution, but which would flourish as a single fruiting organism. He worried, for example in the follow-up to *Religion and Life* weeks, that young people, reluctant to root themselves in the life of a given local church, wanted to carry on with a kind of mushy denominationless Christianity in which it seemed to him impossible for proper nurture and discipline to be sustained.

His commitment to work happily within the structures of the Church of Scotland was manifest at many levels, and his diary for the decade of 1947-57 belies any suggestion that he came back from the South with an ecumenical bias against his own denomination's life and work. Quite apart from his university work, he was in constant demand as a speaker, and seems to have been able to take on an immense amount of engagements, conducting retreats, being a visiting preacher, opening church halls, addressing student conferences, broadcasting, all with a verve and sparkiness which never failed to address itself at the same time to the key issue in whatever context he was working. Some of it was related closely either to his ecumenical experience or to his teaching, but he never came across as a heavy expert, and was indeed a master of disarming openings, as when he spoke to Edinburgh's S.C.M. on Amos, beginning "You really ought to have got some specialist." He had the facility of adjusting to very diverse situations, whether it were a Glasgow Dons' Discussion Group or a local country Women's Guild, but he was never trivial or patronising about what people could take, and loved to quote Russell Maltby's counsel to preachers, "Do not talk down to your people, they are not there." Even for something as light-hearted as an after-lunch speech at Trinity College, Glasgow, he gave a scintillatingly sharp few minutes on the theme

"On saying a few words" in which he deflated all would-be clerical pretensions to permanent on-tap verbosity, and urged the careful preparation of even the smallest public utterance. This was in part, no doubt, due to his temperamental affinity with language well-used, and his personal distaste for the slack or slovenly. It was also his professional concern as a minister who was well enough aware of his profession's temptation to speak on the cheap, until people became so unexpectant of freshness or colour that they effectively stopped listening.

Two major honours in this decade were invitations to give the 1948 Cunningham Lectures in Edinburgh University, and five years later, the Warrack lectures on preaching, a rare double in so short a timespan. His theme for the former was *The Church's Impact on the World*, and in those he explored the dual nature of the Church, as human institution sometimes almost unbearably repulsive, and at the same time, in the dimension of faith, the *Una Sancta*, the mystical Body of Christ, destined to stand unblemished and consecrated before God. How, in this complex and sometimes contradictory way of being, the Church could and should address the contemporary world was the main thrust of the lectures. The demand of the young man who had insisted that faith must not exclude the faithful from the glories of European humanism was still loud and clear: "Unless faith can integrate the whole man and his whole experience it is too small." At the same time, the intervening years had confirmed his confidence that such integration *was* to be found in Christianity, so that he could use language which sounds astonishingly bold to the internalised pluralist hearing of late twentieth century culture. Thus, without embarrassment, he could speak of "A Christ unswervingly bent on world-dominion", and of Christianity as "a totalitarian faith" which must intend to be world-conquering.

This of course, needs to be qualified by his reiterated theme that the mode which distinctively characterises the Christian Church's proper outreach is the paradoxical one of suffering love in the image of God. He had no enthusiasm for tub-thumping, nor for intellectual or emotional bullying. Furthermore, he was assuming as the penumbra of the Christian Church in Britain a world of secular materialism, rather than one of diverse faiths sustained in ethnic communities. Nonetheless, from the references in his sermons and talks to other cultures and the Christian missionary presence among them, he seems to have been unambiguously clear that there could be no rest for the Church until the whole earth owned the Lordship of Christ. His direct and indirect experience of foreign mission was that people were visibly rescued from superstition, ignorance and sin by the preaching of the gospel. The characteristic concern of modern social anthropology that Christian missions have often disorientated and destabilised whole cultures, as, say, with aboriginal Australian or American Indian peoples, seems not to have begun to threaten his confidence as to the missionary mandate, though he would have taken it as a *sine qua non* that the method and the style of evangelism must be courteous and unbelligerent, listening and serving.

There appears to have been some contract, or at least some preliminary arrangement that the S.C.M. Press would publish these Cunningham lectures, and there is, among Archie's papers, a letter from Professor Gregor Smith in which he suggests a few emendations which might be made before they are printed. The matter, however, seems to have been taken no further, and there is no indication of what caused their regrettable non-appearance in print.

The Warrack lectures, on the other hand, were produced by S.C.M. within a year as *"Preaching in a Scientific Age"* (1954) and dealt in more detail with some of the specific nettles which the truthful preacher must grasp in a contemporary world conditioned to think scientifically. He looks in particular at the way one can preach about miracle, about the Resurrection and about the Last Things. In each case he argues a sophisticated theological case against the preacher capitulating to the so-called common sense of scientific humanism, and explores the implications of a text he has never ventured to preach on, ("because its flight is too high"), namely, "For all things are yours, whether Paul or Apollos or Cephas, or the world, or life, or death, or things present, or things to come; all are yours; and ye are Christ's; and Christ is God's". Thirty years later, enclosing a second-hand copy of the book to Nelson Gray, the head of Scottish Television's Religion Department, he was to comment that his basic position on these issues had not really altered in any significant way.

Though the pre-war phase of pacifist activity had obviously moved into a new key with the end of the Second World War and the beginning of the nuclear threat, Archie retained his involvement with peace issues. In 1952 he was actually invited by Charles Raven to consider taking on a job with the International Fellowship of Reconciliation, but as Raven had rather expected, he was not attracted by another administrative job, though Raven had thought it worth asking since he "did so long to see a man of virility and intelligence doing it."

Two years later, however, Raven did involve Archie in a visit to Russia by a group of pacifists, which included also Donald Soper. They were in no way official representatives of their denominations and were told that they must make it plain that their respective churches were not committed to pacifism. Yet the visit was a small attempt to cross boundaries not often crossed at the time, both as an act of peacemaking across the Iron Curtain, and as a way of strengthening contact with the Orthodox church, whose participation in the ecumenical venture of the World Council of Churches was so important.

May was highly alarmed that Archie might be detained, and had to be reassured by Raven that there was little risk of Moscow being interested in keeping them. She was also worried that food might be in short supply and along with recommended warm clothes and overshoes, made him pack several tins of sardines as emergency rations. In fact the party ate like kings, with batteries of cutlery at every meal, and returned laden with gifts, accompanied, for the purpose of customs clearance, by an official note saying: "The carpets, books and other things in the Rev. A.C. Craig's luggage are Christmas presents from His Holiness Alexy, the Patriarch of Moscow and all Russia."

Archie found the visit fascinating and was genuinely amazed by his own reactions to the elaborate ritual of the Orthodox Liturgy. He subsequently put the ambivalence of his response in these terms:

> "It might be thought that one born and bred a Scots Presbyterian would be repelled, and even nauseated by the elaborate ritualism of Orthodox worship, so much like those Roman modes which the Scottish Reformation taught the nation to abhor than the forms of service to which it led, in which reliance is placed on abstract intellection rather than on any sensual aids to devotion. But . . . . I found there was much to learn in Russia."

What he learned, more vividly than it had struck him before, was what the doctrine of the Communion of Saints meant across time as well as across space, when the Liturgy involved the worshippers in a fellowship extending back to John the Baptist. This became, as the fortnight advanced, stronger than the immediate sense of "baffling archaism" which oppressed him, even as he admired the physical impact of beauty in the worship. This richer awareness of an authentic tradition, continuous through the centuries, gave him a sense of the "thinness" of the Presbyterian apprehension of the Communion of Saints, and his conclusion at the end of the visit was,

> "At all events, I felt that we had something to learn from our Orthodox brethren in this realm of things, and might learn less suspiciously from them, if only we could get to know them intimately, than from any other branch of the Church Catholic."

One of his treasured ecumenical possessions, along with a British Council of Churches scarf and his Tambaram notebook, was a loaf of bread that he was given by the Patriarch as a gesture of fellowship, and which now sits, having resisted mould and corruption for almost forty years, on the bookshelf of the Church of Scotland's Principal Clerk!

Of all Archie's activities in the fifties, however, the one which brought him most prominently to public attention was his work with the Inter-Church Relations Committee. The General Assembly had, in May, 1953, instructed the Committee to renew conversations in which the Church of Scotland, the Church of England, the Scottish Episcopal Church and the English

Presbyterian Church would participate. The original Chairman nominated to the Church of Scotland panel was Donald Baillie, but for the bulk of the conversations, after his death in October, 1954, the chairmanship was held in rotation by John Baillie, William Manson and Archie himself. The weight of the presentation of the ensuing report, however, and the public personification of its intentions lay with Archie.

Conversations between the Church of England and the Church of Scotland had already taken place from 1932—1934 and again from 1949—1951, with the Presbyterian Church of England and the Episcopal Church in Scotland as observers. The earlier conference had already anticipated Lund in drawing up a list of *Things that might be undertaken in common*, which included exchange of pulpits; occasional mutual eucharistic hospitality; fraternal recognition through Assembly greetings and shared information; occasional joint pronouncements, when appropriate, on public, national or international questions; the setting up of a Joint Advisory Council to deal, (without prejudice to Church Committees) with practical matters affecting local relations between the churches; and encouragement at every level of moves to foster better understanding between the two.

In setting up the third round of talks, and including in them the two smaller denominations which had earlier been observers, the Church of Scotland had officially committed itself to work towards both "a long-term policy looking to the ultimate fullness of the Church's life" and a "short-term policy looking to the establishment of such closer relations between the two churches as may be immediately practical", the latter being so pursued "as neither to include nor to lose sight of the former."

From this, the appointed Panel believed it had a mandate to grasp the central nettle, which was to reconcile the diverse forms of ministerial stewardship entrusted to the churches involved, given that they already acknowledged immense tracts of common theology in relation to the being and nature of God, to Christology and atonement, to the Holy Spirit, the authority of Scripture and most of the other articles of the common classical creeds of the church.

Even on ministry there were massive areas of more than preliminary consensus. At least on paper, the participants agreed that the whole church exercised ministry, and that all specific ministries in the chuch must be exercised within the context of that corporate priesthood. All agreed, further, that there was a particular ministry of Word and Sacrament for which some were set apart by ordination, and that the unity and continuity of the church included the unity and continuity of the whole body through its baptismal incorporation, and the unity and continuity of the ministration of Word and Sacrament through ordination. This latter ordination included responsibility for oversight or *episcope* in the following areas:

a) Apostolic mission and authority;
b) The pastoral office;
c) The continuance of the Ministry of Word and Sacrament through ordination;
d) Guardianship of truth and exclusion of error;
e) Representation of the Church in its unity and universality.

The crunch came on the question of *how* this function of oversight was to be exercised. In Presbyterian tradition it was exercised corporately by Presbytery, and by the higher courts of the church. In Anglican tradition, the same functions coalesced in a single person, the bishop, who represented the whole community of the Church.

The basic recommendation of the Joint Report, hammered out in four years of hard conversation, was that all the participating churches should recognise this diversity of practice as compatible with the continuity and catholicity of the Church, and should show that recognition by incorporating in their structure the modes of participation which were cherished by both. Thus, the Presbyterian churches would modify their structure in the direction of adopting a form of episcopacy which was acceptable to both, while the Anglicans would develop a form of order in which ordained ministry and laity would be more closely linked in decisions concerning government and doctrine.

That this decision was reached in good faith after much wrestling with the theological issues is the testimony of those who were members of the panel, and the evidence of the minuted discussions. It was certainly Archie's perspective on the matter. It was clear that Anglo-Catholics would be dismayed by the refusal to define episcopacy in *hierarchical* terms, and equally clear that there would be Presbyterians who thought that any form of episcopacy was the thin end of a Papist wedge, but in the four years of the conversation's life the panel actually arrived at a point of trust where all were willing to sign the report in the conviction that it pointed the way to new possibilities of common witness, and was in no way a selling of the pass either for Presbyterians or for Episcopalians. Archie, speaking later in 1957 to the Presbytery of Dalkeith, was adamant:

> "I could not have signed this document if I had thought that there were necessarily implicit in it the view that, when a Bishop, acting as the principal minister in an ordination, ordained a man to the ministry, the man's ministry would be mysteriously superior or more valid than the ministry of one ordained by the laying on of hands by a Presbytery."

It is impossible to evaluate the response of the Scottish press and public without having a stance towards it, and that stance, of course, is liable to colour one's judgment of the whole episode. What is clear from any perspective is that few church reports have ever got so many people involved in theological debate since the controversy between Arius and Athanasius was hot gossip in the barbers' shops of Antioch!

Archie anticipated a rough passage. Before the report was published in April, 1957, he wrote to the Archbishop of Canterbury,

> "On the whole the omens here would seem to point to a stormy reception of the Report, certainly by our Scottish Nationalists, and perhaps also by middle-of-the-road churchmen who haven't been much affected by ecumenical trends of thought."

In the event, the publications of the report on 30th April, 1957, was as close as possible to the date of the Assembly, so that there might be as short a period as possible between the two events, in Archie's words to Geoffrey Fisher, "so as to limit misguided press comment." The actual effect was to fuel the suspicion that awful deeds were being surreptitiously done, and the intervening month saw a blazing outcry, fanned to permanent flame by the *Daily Express*, in which the main accusation was that the Report was a sell-out to Anglican superiority and a betrayal of the principles of the Reformation. The hostility had two components, sometimes coinciding. On the one hand there were the "conscientious Protestants", such as the members of the National Church Association, who genuinely believed that any move towards episcopacy in any form was a deviation from Scripture, and thus from the supreme standard of faith and life in the church. On the other, there were more ecclesciastically flexible men of cosmopolitan European theology, like Professor Ian Henderson, author in the sixties of *"Power without Glory"*, whose New Testament hermeneutic would have scandalised the Protestant evangelicals and whose anger at the report was rather in terms of a perennial attempt by the English (with Anglicanism as their ecclesiastical arm) to subdue and eliminate the distinctive voice of Scotland (of which the Church of Scotland was a primary custodian). Evangelical and nationalist motives both found a focal-point of resistance in the recommendation that the Church of Scotland accept a form of episcopacy, especially since many Scots were still smarting from the palpable insult of the then Moderator, Pitt-Watson, having been refused communion at the coronation service. The general Scottish cultural scene was also regaining in the fifties, through writers like Hugh McDiarmid, a renewed sense of nationalist pride.

From thirty years' distance, the then editor of the *Daily Express*, Mr Ian McColl, a dedicated Church of Scotland elder, insists that he had the most immense personal respect for Archie, and would never have regarded him either as a knave or a dupe in relation to his ecclesiastical heritage. This is a little hard to reconcile with the paper's editorial policy in the '50s, which never once attempted to put the Panel's case as its members saw and meant it, and which for many months kept up an unflagging hostility to the report. Indeed when the controversy was at its height, Archie had to take to leaving Bank Street by the back lane, so persistently hectoring were the reporters waiting for him outside the front door.

In the weeks before the Assembly, in spite of the committee's desire to keep the matter as low profile as possible, controversy raged up and down the land, correspondence columns burgeoned, provoking Roy Whitehorn, the leader of the English Presbyterian team to write a fornight before the Assembly, "I am disgusted at the way the papers, even the *Times*, have done their best to poke up a row."

What worried people, even some who were by no means fanatical Presbyterians, was the implication they drew from the report that their ministerial orders were somehow held to be invalid, and that at best it was by Anglican condescension that they would be legitimated. Had Geoffrey Fisher been able or willing to say in public what he wrote to Archie just after the presentation of the report to the Assembly, many Presbyterians might have been reassured (though some Anglicans might not!). In a letter dated 31st May, 1957, Fisher wrote, in the course of congratulating Archie on his presentation,

"Validity is a perfectly stupid phrase and means nothing. I have long ago realised that wherever people of God meet together in sincerity and perform Christian rites with conviction in the presence of our Lord, Christ must give Himself wholly to them. He gives all that He can give of Himself, and the worshippers receive all they can receive of Him, and therefore in that sense every sincere worshipful act is valid."

Archie and the other Church of Scotland members of the conversation seem to have been so sure that they were equal partners trying to find a way of expressing the compatibility of their two systems of government as part of the one Catholic church of Christ, that the question of bishops seeming to be brought in as *legitimators* lay far in the past of their discussions. Indeed, when the Rev. T.M. Donn proposed an addendum in the debate "that any other church recognised the Church of Scotland to be a true branch of the universal church and its ministerial orders and sacraments fully valid and in nothing defective spiritually", Archie rejected it, precisely on the grounds that "there was a sense of inferiority in this addendum. I maintain that the Church of Scotland requires no certificate of fitness from any other church."

By this time, Archie had come to feel, partly no doubt through his experience as B.C.C. Secretary, and certainly through his visit to the Russian Orthodox church in 1954, that what the Reformation churches lacked, for reasons which had been in their time perfectly proper, was a sense of the historic continuity of the Church. They took, so to speak, an airborne leap straight from the apostles of the New Testament to John Knox, or at least to Luther and Calvin, whereas the churches which had retained episcopacy had a much stronger sense of their temporal continuity through all the centuries, and of identification with the whole of that history. His diagnosis of the present situation was not that the Church of Scotland needed to be validated by anyone else, and certainly not that episcopacy was the bitter pill to be reluctantly swallowed as the price of Anglican acceptance, but that each system would learn from incorporating and coming to value what was precious to the other. As one of the preliminary Anglican papers put it,

> "Thus for the healing of the Scottish schism, Anglicans must be willing to convey the episcopal succession up to the presbyterial ministry of the Church of Scotland, while themselves accepting such reforms of administration in the threefold ministry as may remove the suspicion of prelacy, as well as receiving the authority of the presbyteries for ministry among the people in their spiritual charge. Presbyterians must be willing to accept reintegration into the old episcopal system as a condition of ministering among those of episcopal tradition."

When the day came for the Report to be presented to the Assembly on 28th May, as Archie put it a week later to a group called *Friends of Reunion*, "Certain sections of the Scottish press confidently and gleefully anticipated an unholy scene in our General Assembly a week ago." The hall was packed, and the atmosphere electric.

Archie's introductory speech emphasised three points, all of them germane to the public controversy. He emphasised that the pursuit of the conversations had been the consistent will of the Assembly for many years and was not just the whim of a few ecumenical enthusiasts. Secondly, he urged that the core of the report from which arose the recommendations of structural changes was essentially theological and not merely pragmatic or prudential. And thirdly, far from being an attempt to bulldoze the church into making a hasty move in the episcopal direction, the committee was clear that all it asked the participating churches to do initially was to accept the Report for prayerful study. This, in the case of the Church of Scotland, meant sending it down to the presbyteries for consideration and comment over the next two years.

After presenting the report, Archie had to sustain three hours of questioning. Press comment varied, of course, depending on the editorial line of the issues, but most agreed that it was, on any account, a *tour de force*. One reporter commented on the impact of Archie's manner:

"Here probably was the greatest speech of the Assembly. It sought no effect beyond the impact of fact presented in proper order, faithfully with transparent sincerity and kindly humour. Here was obviously no Quisling but a lover of the Church longing for its spiritual integrity, believing that the report begins to draw off the poison deeply infused through centuries into certain ecclesiastical terms.

Then Dr Craig had to face his ordeal, a flood and storm of questions on the report . . . How would he stand this? To my mind this was the turning-point of the debate — the knife-edge, a dizzy, slippery path. One slip of evasion, a hint of indignation, dismay, petulance or impatience might have led to a fall. But among all the dangers he walked his simple straightforward way . . . He had nothing to conceal."

When Hector Hetherington attended an Assembly function at Holyrood the next night, he "found the place ringing with your speech and subsequent handling of the questions." Even a stalwart opponent like Alec Shillinglaw, who was firmly opposed to the proposals sent a note of congratulation on the manner in which it had been done. But at the same time, in the flood of mail which arrived in the next few days, much was vituperative. Some was anonymous, or signed simply, "A Kirk Elder", and contained sentiments like, "Shame on you for your most base betrayal of our Church yesterday, for unscriptural practices and dead unity." Or, from a 1954 graduate of Glasgow, "I want you to know how ashamed and distressed I am that you as the representative of the University should be identified with the proposed changes . . . The Church of Rome is spreading its cancerous growth through University and City life. What are you doing about this? Accepting a milder form of Papacy?"

On the whole, however, the impact of Archie's presentation was not to inflame but to persuade the majority of those who heard him in person at the Assembly that the report did deserve to be received for study, and that it was not being offered as a sacrosanct document. Professor Pitt-Watson's comment caught the commonest response to his handling of the matter:

" "Disarm" had a new meaning for me. You rose to face an Assembly that was two thirds against you, the opposition ranging from the moderate and reasonable to the extreme and fanatical. When you sat down, one could almost hear the clatter of their arms as they threw them down."

That the report was accepted at all, then, even for prayful consideration was in some eyes itself miraculous, and for the next two years, after his retirement at the age of sixty-nine from teaching at Glasgow, Archie travelled all over the country, speaking to church groups who wanted to tease out further the implications of the report. The fact that there was opposition neither surprised nor shocked him, and he treated antagonists of union with the same grave courtesy as he showed to sympathisers, refusing to demonise them. What saddened him, however, was the dawning realisation of how little inroads the ecumenical spirit had actually made in the church which commanded his loyalty. He reflected ruefully:

"Doubtless, more and more people have gradually been becoming aware of the Ecumenical Movement, World Council of Churches, British Council of Churches etc. in much the same way as football fans are aware of the test matches, or as elephants presumably are of field-mice. But the Movement and its organs just haven't enjoyed their attention and interest as things requiring to be bothered about in any critical way."

For the next two years the report was vigorously debated up and down the land. It must have saddened Archie in particular, as he kept the mounting score of Presbytery returns, that the *Kelso and Borders Chronicle* reported that Presbytery's judgment that the time was not yet ripe even for joint services, and that there was a risk of moving too fast, and causing the destruction of the Church of Scotland or the possibility of another Disruption. Every time a Presbytery or Synod voted, it made headline news in many papers, and led to a fresh spate of letters, most from Presbyterians supporting rejection, but occasionally, confirming the fears of the ecumenically sympathetic and firing the zeal of the anti-ecumenical Presbyterians, from Scottish Episcopalians dissociating themselves from a church they could not hold to be part of the true church of Christ.

It must have been a particular blow to Archie that Professor Gregor Smith, the Regius Professor of Divinity at Glasgow University, and an esteemed colleague, wrote for the *Manchester Guardian* of 14th and 16th December, 1957, an account of the Report which accused it of being written in a spirit of bland accommodation, and of masking irreconcilable positions by smoothness of style, a comment which reflects rather harshly on the integrity and theological toughness of the protagonists in the Report's making, and the costly readiness to change to which all four sets of denominational representatives felt committed.

In the event, it was clear to the Inter-Church Relations Committee after studying Presbytery returns that they could not hope for the support of the majority of church members. Only one Presbytery wholeheartedly endorsed the Report's recommendations, thirty-nine were clearly opposed and the rest wanted to reserve judgment until further theological issues had been tackled.

Archie's candid 1959 speech to the Assembly in no way disguised this response, though he admitted that it had been a hard task to "scrutinise, analyse and finally skeletonise a body of documents so intractably diverse in respect of format, length, theological depth and lucidity of expression." The central pleading of his speech was that the clear rejection of the Report should be distinguished from rejection of the *intent* of unity. If this distinction were not made, the committee believed that the Church of Scotland would be retreating into a "citadel of spiky presbyteriansm" and turning aside from the mainstream of the ecumenical movement.

Their proposed deliverance to the Assembly, which enshrined this distinction while conceding the Report's rejection, ran:

> "The Assembly judge the proposals in the Joint Report regarding modifications in the polity of the Presbyterian Churches to be unacceptable in their present form".

Had that been accepted, Archie would have been saddened, but willing to go on working for the Inter-Church Relations Committee. What persuaded him that the Church really did not want *any* real move towards structural unity was the form and tone of an amendment proposed by the Rev. George Dryburgh which was carried by 300 votes to 266. This amendment ran:

> "The Assembly are clearly of the opinion that the proposals are unacceptable in that they imply a denial of the Catholicity of the Church of Scotland and of the validity and regularity of its ministry within the Church Catholic."

Archie felt obliged to resign, not out of pique because the report had been rejected, but because he sensed, behind the rejection, a complete abandonment of the Lausanne commitment of the churches to work for that organic unity proper to churches which *did* recognise one another as belonging to the church Catholic. There is an interesting difference between the public text of the resignation letter he sent to Tindal, and the full version which was not for public reading. The letter for the Committee was a fairly formal affair, concluding, "I shall only say that membership of it (the Committee) has been a continuously educative and enriching experience." By contrast, there is a much fuller statement of his grounds for resigning among Archie's papers, though it is not clear whether he actually sent both, or merely drafted the longer one as part of his wrestling with his own reaction to the whole situation.

At any rate, the longer text makes four points. In view of the Presbyteries' response the Committee had already agreed unanimously that it must declare the Church's dissatisfaction with the report, but has disagreed as to whether the formula chosen should assert or imply a repeal of the general policy informing it, or merely of the specific recommendations of the Report. Archie, within the Committee, had already made it clear that he could not continue in the Convenorship unless the long-term policy of working for organic unity were "substantively safeguarded". He had therefore been willing to accept the deliverance in the form of its final draft, finding "the proposals in the Joint Report unacceptable *in their present form*," the main grounds for that acceptance being that the long-term policy was not thereby threatened. The form of the Assembly's rejection, however, as voiced by George Dryburgh, that "We do not want to hear of these proposals ever again, in this or any other form", seemed to him clearly intended to mean a repeal of the long-term policy and a disavowal of Lausanne, as well as a rejection of the specifics, and therefore to be a repudiation of the principle which for thirty years had been the basis of every advance towards organic unity.

He had already intimated to the committee that, if the Assembly voted against the general policy behind the specific recommendations, he would no longer feel that he had a credible mandate as convenor of the Inter-Church Relations Committee. He therefore moved an amendment at the end of the debate that he himself should resign. This led to a public wrangle, under the chairmanship of Professor Pitt Watson, as to whether it was competent business for the Assembly that he should tender his resignation on the spot, or whether the due process was that he should tender it to the committee. Merging in with this technical debate were a number of voiced pleas that he should reconsider resigning, both because of his unparalleled experience on ecumenical matters, and on the grounds that the rejection of the report was less drastic than it seemed at first glance. In the end, being recalled to the rostrum to reply, Archie expressed his sense of the whole discussion as very, very, embarrassing, and re-affirmed his decision to resign by whatever procedure the Assembly thought fit.

Judgment on how his resignation is to be read must also be bound up with the stance of the reader towards the whole ecumenical issue, and with his reading of the Assembly's underlying mood. But for Archie it was an extremely distressing shock to find that his own church seemed not to welcome even the *principle* of moving towards a fuller concrete expression of the unity he believed to be the reality of the Church. To have come back into the direct service of his adopted, if not natal denomination; to have given eight years to being Vice-Convenor and then Convenor of the only Church Committee which had unity as a serious item on its agenda (a task he felt to be one of the great honours of his life); to find that the very mandate which the Committee took as its presuppositional starting-point was rejected by most of the Assembly he so loved and trusted; all that must have felt like a painful and apparently useless expense of time and energy. One divinity student of that year, on the day on which the report had been rejected, remembers seeing him in a tea-room on the Royal Mile, sitting by himself at a table, and having him pointed out as Archie Craig, who had just shocked the Assembly by announcing his intention to resign from the Inter-Church Relations Committee.

It says much for Archie's magnanimity that he was willing to rejoin in the '60s the next set of Anglican-Presbyterian conversations. It says much, too, for the esteem in which he was held even by those who deplored his ecumenical interests that he was, within two years invited to the highest office available in the Church of Scotland and nominated as Moderator for the year 1961 to 1962.

9 Moderator

"I once dreamed a dream, whether in the body or out of the body I know not. I seemed to be in a great court of justice: the tribunal was hidden from view by a projecting wall, but the pleaders were in sight. They were all church dignitaries and the case concerned the adjustment of boundaries of some sort. I had barely discerned thus much when a voice from the hidden bench said: "But what is a Presbyterian?" And then I knew it must be the last judgment, for surely the end of the world must have come if a judge didn't know what a Presbyterian was. One of the pleaders wearing lace ruffles answered at great length and many familiar words fell on my ear — sessions and assemblies and tiends — but finally the voice from the bench sad; "All this is very interesting but not entirely relevant in this court: the only things that count for much here are faith and hope and above all, love. And remember, all of you, these two things: there are no boundaries to faith and hope and love, and Caiaphas was a church leader who defended his church against the terrible effects of these forces."

The news of Archie's nomination as Moderator was greeted with acclaim by his many friends, especially since it came as a kind of vindication of how highly the Church rated him, in spite of their bruising rejection of his ecumenical vision. He himself, according to his own record, was given the news by phone, and responded, with a concise elision of surprise and prayer, "Good Lord!"

Glasgow University, his last place of employment, gave him his moderatorial robes, with Sir Hector Hetherington making a warm and witty speech about how Archie had been predestined to the moderatorial office with a truly Calvinist inevitability. Glasgow also gave him his second D.D. degree, with a degree ceremony being arranged for that single purpose, and the Principal teasingly calling the honour the "second tier of the triple crown he will shortly wear." (Trinity College, Dublin, was to give him yet another D.D. later in the same year.) May was given a handbag and a cheque for the balance of the fund, delivered with the teasing comment that it was "enough anyhow to let her acquire the occasional pair of gloves and even that highest glory of womanly ambition, a new hat."

Whatever movements in Archie's subconscious produced the detail of his Day of Judgment dream, it was not a moderatorial reverie, for he had recounted it in a sermon preached in Glasgow University chapel while he was still on the staff there. It anticipates curiously not only the lace ruffles of his office-to-be, but a passionate controversy for which he was to hold the presbytery jackets as the various Church of Scotland parishes in Alloa fought fiercely over the re-adjustment of their parish boundaries in 1964-65.

It is, however, faithful to his waking vision too, in regarding the institutional structures of the church not as absolutes, but as *relatively* adequate or inadequate vehicles of the gospel, vindicated only by their *relative* capacity to make transparent the love of God. All the activities of his moderator's year were appraised in those terms, whether it was opening a church hall, and disconcertingly asking the congregation what their new hall was really *for*, or reminding office-bearers that numbers were no infallible index of spiritual success. (He loved the story of the elder on door duty who came into the vestry before an evening service and said, "There's an auld wife and a wee laddie pourin' in. Gie them a bummer.").

For a man in his seventy-third year, the physical pace was fairly demanding, but as one Nigerian observer put it, he entered into everything with the zest of a schoolboy. His Presbytery visits ranged from Kirkudbright to the Orkneys and Shetlands, and took in Lochcarron, Perth, Auchterarder, and, happily, Irvine and Kilmarnock, which let him revisit his first pastoral charge in Galston. And his foreign visits were to Nigeria and the Middle East, and, within Europe, to Rome, Genoa, Lausanne and Geneva.

Wherever he went, his cordiality and gift of story commended itself to his hearers, and by the end of a year of what he called "almost continuous locomotion and allocution" he had notched up a further fund of anecdotes, many of them at his own expense. He chortled, for instance, at the not very *sotto voce* remark he overheard as he moved in to address a kind of youth rally in the Waverley Market area, dressed in full moderatorial fig: "Jings, an' they talk about us teddy-boys!" Of the Shetland visit, the memory which most appealed to his sense of humour was meeting one old woman on the Skerries, who described the advantage of living six miles from the nearest house, it being that she found the distance a great antidote to falling out with her neighbours.

Stuart McWilliam of Wellington Church, Glasgow, one of his chaplains, recalls that he was often quite nervous before a big occasion, and concerned that things should be properly done. At least one hilarious moment happened during an evening dinner at Holyrood Palace. The Moderator's party had been advised that it would be their signal to leave when the Lord Lyon rose and left the room. Archie must have kept a corner of an eye and his consciousness on the eminent gentleman, and promptly rose with his entourage at the designated moment — only to discover once they were up and out that they were following him to a nearby lavatory!

The most distant of his visits was the three-week trip to Nigeria, another first for him, in that no Moderator had hitherto been there on an official visit, though there were strong Scottish and Presbyterian links in the mission-field there. The trip is graphically and merrily described by Bob MacDonald of Itu Leper Colony in his small book about the Calabar mission, "A Corner of Africa". The Scottish end of the organisation was negotiated by Sandy Somerville, a missionary on furlough, who returned to Nigeria with dire warnings about the weak state of the Moderator's stomach, which were later followed by lists of taboo foods sent out from 121 George Street. In spite of these instructions being passed on, Bob MacDonald watched with horror as the President's wife, Mrs Azikwe, produced, on the first night, exotically spiced Nigerian dishes containing all the forbidden ingredients, which Archie consumed with gusto. After a night of misery, rehearsing the names of the most capable doctors in Lagos, whom he presumed would be needed to deal with the inevitable awful after-effects, Bob arrived anxiously at the Presidential Palace, to find Archie hale and hearty, and with no trace of a disturbed night.

The overwhelming impression of Bob Macdonald's narrative is of the colossal exuberance of the man, hopping around the country in a variety of vehicles (mostly provided by Shell B.P.) which ranged at the one end from small plane and sleek Pontiac to battered landrover and canoe. He spent his seventy-third birthday at Itu, serenaded by the Leper Colony band, and enchanted by everything he saw, and filled the three weeks of the visit with a wide range of engagements, speaking, preaching, seeing hospitals, schools and colleges. He himself recorded the pleasure he had at hearing a sermon of his delivered in translation by a Nigerian who embellished it as he went with vigorous gesture, the like of which Archie would never have used. It was on this trip too that he met the Burnet family who were to return to Scotland and to become his Doune neighbours in 1965. Tom Burnet remembers his heart sinking as Archie preached, on a Sunday morning in the Trinity College chapel, a sermon of such theological sophistication that he was afraid that the nurses who were to hear him in the hospital chapel later that day would be floundering. To his delighted surprise, Archie's simplicity of style and directness on the later occasion proved again how sensitive he was to the specific context of his preaching, and how flexible he could be in the pitch of his delivery. (The Burnets remember too the immediacey of rapport he created with their children, by accosting them, as he approached the house, with the nicknames he had heard before meeting them: "Now, which one's Boffin and which one's Tufty?")

The episode which won the most prominent press coverage during his Moderator's year was, not surprisingly, his visit to the Pope. Archie was due to preach at the centenary celebrations of St. Andrew's Church, the Scots' Kirk in Rome, and the question arose as to whether he might also make a courtesy visit to the Pope. The Assembly debated the suggestion, which, of course, was opposed by some "conscientious Protestants", still able to use language like, "We should not show any eagerness in running to Rome" and "Is this not a question of the fellowship of light with darkness?" It was characteristic of Archie that when he heard that John R. Gray, minister of Dunblane Cathedral, intended to move against it, he asked him to come to discuss it, and opened the conversation with the words: "I want to thank you, John, for your opposition. It makes us think clearly." John Gray did in the end try to block the visit by suggesting that it constituted a "sudden alteration and innovation of discipline", and must therefore go down to presbyteries under the barrier act. He failed, however, to satisfy the legal counsels of the Assembly that the visit could be so described, and his amendment was ruled out of order. The Assembly agreed that the matter should be referred to the relevant committees, Inter-Church, Administration, and Colonial and Continental, and the outcome of their deliberations was that,

"Since Christian charity could be manifested, goodwill fostered, and no truth safeguarded by the Church of Scotland compromised," the Moderator was free to pay such a courtesy visit.

Among the St. Andrews's congregation in Rome, some were scandalised that Archie could, in the same breath as it were, celebrate their continued existence and visit the historical arch-enemy, but for Archie there was no contradiction. In the Centenary sermon at St. Andrews he spoke directly of what had to be celebrated by them as Presbyterians worshipping together in the heart of Rome. That was, centrally, the fact that, for a century,

"thousands had been enabled to worship God according to the forms in which for them worship may be offered naturally, sincerely, and in good conscience."

This genuine commendation, however, left no room for Protestant triumphalism, for he went on to express the prayerful hope that they would go on being "*evangelically and ecumenically successful*" taking as their yardstick for the latter the inclusion of the whole creation in the inexhaustible love of God. And that had ecclesiastical specification, requiring

"effort at the level at which the separated churches, by opening themselves afresh to God's love, learn as churches to live in love towards each other, lay aside pride and jealousy and suspicion and fear, and move out towards each other in love in the image of Christ's love."

It was in the context of such an understanding of the ecumenical task that Archie arrived at the Vatican on Wednesday, 28th March, 1962, accompanied by Stewart Louden, the Convenor of the Colonial and Continental Committee, Dr Alex King, its Secretary and, the minister of the Scots' Kirk, Rev. A. J. Maclean.

Archie himself said on one or two occasions that he had made it a rule not to "chatter in public" about the encounter, while himself evaluating it as "a historic event, minor but significant." This reticence must, to some extent, have been out of prudential discretion, since the topic was an inflammatory one in many quarters, but it was more than that. By temperament and conviction, Archie clearly believed, and occasionally said that there were areas of personal life which not only *need not* but *should not* be exposed to voyeuristic curiosity, and this in the religious as well as in the domestic sphere. The Vatican encounter seems to have been for him something of spiritual delicacy and trust, which could only be cheapened by publicised detail being noised abroad.

From the memories of Dr Louden and Dr King, however, certain things are clear, either from their first-hand experience after they joined Archie in the Papal apartment, or from his direct narrative.

The group was driven to St. Peter's Square in a gleaming Vatican limousine, and emerged to find huge crowds, among them a vociferously friendly group of Belgian nuns who asked for, and were given, a moderatorial blessing! Cardinal Bea of the Secretariat for Unity, and his secretary, Willebrands, who briefed the Scots, told them that the Pope would be seated on a raised dais, and it had been expressly agreed that Archie's courtesy should not extend to making the customary obeisance, which might be liable to sinister misinterpretation by those on the alert for signals of Protestant betrayal! In the event, the spontaneity of Pope John XXIII undercut the normal protocol, for he came down from the dais with open arms to greet Archie with the words, "Dr Archibald Craig, out of the simplicity of the heart I thank you for your visit." According to Dr King, the two men hit it off instantly, even through the language medium of an interpreter, and so much enjoyed talking to each other that the next papal visitor, Cardinal Spellman of New York, was kept waiting some twenty minutes for his audience. At the point where, according to schedule, they should have left, the Pope beckoned to Archie to resume his seat, and seemed genuinely reluctant to end the conversation.

The apocryphal version of their parting, chortlingly sustained by Archie himself, was, "Arreviderci, Archie." "So long, John." In fact, the encounter ended with an exchange of gifts, in which the Scottish contingent were given Papal medals, while Archie presented to the Pope a bookmarker with an Iona cross, and a stone he had picked up from the Sea of Galilee earlier in his moderatorial perambulations. John XXIII's farewell words were that now they would pray for each other, and at the throne of grace would see each other's faces.

In days when bilateral and multilateral conversations include Roman Catholics, and grass-roots ecumenical activity can often take their participation for granted, it is fairly hard to re-construct the sense of new ground broken which attached to this small exchange of courtesies. One immediate, measurable result of Archie's visit was undoubtedly the strengthening of the case for having Protestant observers at the Second Vatican Council, but less specifically, Archie was delighted to find the *tone* of his own Scots' Kirk sermon of a week earlier so remarkably echoed and confirmed.

Achieving much less media coverage, but in its way as significant, was the fact that in the course of his visit to the Middle East, Archie also visited the three Patriarchs of Jerusalem, Orthodox, Latin and Armenian, another link in the chain of contact which the B.C.C. and W.C.C. were seeking to establish and consolidate to make the range of their ecumenism genuinely catholic. May accompanied him on this visit, and they enjoyed together seeing the actual sites of biblical events and narratives. Among their engagements were a meeting in the home of Mr Ben Zvi, the President, a conversation with the Chief Rabbi on how peoples of faith could stand together against the growing forces of materialism, and a visit to the Hebrew University, where they looked at the Dead Sea Scrolls, and presented the University Library with a 45-volume set of Calvin's Commentaries. (Whether the excess baggage charge was waived is not recorded, but the Professor of Comparative Religion at the University declared them to be the best New Testament commentaries in existence!) It was the official reception in St. Andrew's Hospice which provoked Archie's generic account of such functions:

> "A reception is a kind of sausage-machine. The person or persons receiving go into it with a sense of organic, personal integrity. One comes out at the other end, a couple of hours later, with the sensation of having been chopped up into a hundred very small pieces, and of being held together by only a precarious outer covering of skin."

Among his other direct narratives of moderatorial experience, he disclosed that the Moderator's chair is surprisingly draughty; and that he found chairing the Assembly rather like what he supposed surf-riding to be, especially since "one has to keep reminding those commissioners who address questions to the Convenors of Committees that the purpose of a question is to elicit information and not to impart it."

Under all the jokes, however, or rather, in and through them, Archie had the deepest esteem for the Assembly, while recognising that "No Assembly of any Church could be considered really complete if it considered itself to be self-sufficient." He delighted in poking fun at himself and the proceedings, speaking of joining the ex-Moderators in the range of extinct volcanoes, and relishing the definition of a physicist friend who had told him that "a moderator is a device in an atomic pile to prevent the generation of excessive heat". He could quote laughingly the description of Presbyterianism as "government of the old by the old for the old", yet his sober appraisal of the Assembly was that it was a wonderfully representative gathering, allowing open, free and fair discussion, providing a firm official voice on burning issues of the day and at the same time seeking to pay heed to the word of God and to stand in the dimension of the eternal.

Over and over again he used the image of *intersection* to characterise the church. It was the incarnated intersection of a human and flawed society with the manifestation, providentially sustained and irradiated, of God's new creation. On the human level it often earned the condemnation of Laodicea, and worse, being not merely tepid but repulsive. But it commanded loyalty and love as the bride of Christ, endlessly open to the transformation of his love. It was this synoptic vision which allowed Archie to be refreshingly candid about the failures and defects of the churches while not losing hope; for the two aspects of the Church's reality for him were not merely to be held together in a kind of schizophrenic tension. His interpretative principle was that "We are to judge the church that is seen by the church that is believed, and not vice versa." This seemed to him to be the implication of his divine tribunal dream, of the Hosea story, and ultimately of the costly atonement worked by God in Christ. He frequently related this ultimate forgiving of the church to a pastoral episode which had much impressed him in Galston. One of his members had come to him in great distress, his wife having run away with someone else. The man's words had gone into Archie's bones.

> "I want you to advise me what to do, but I shall be obliged if you would refrain from blackening my wife's character in anything you may say. Please remember that I love her."

This lively sense of the Church as *simul iustus et peccator* freed Archie for sober and untriumphant estimates of the day-to-day achievements of the institutional church. Just after his moderatorial year had finished, he said to a refresher course in Trinity College that for all the country's wealth of spiritual capital, Scotland, and with greater particularity the Church of Scotland, was not afire with the Gospel, that his conclusion, after a year of "moderatorial perambulation and allocution" was that there was *nothing Pentecostal to report*. He referred specifically to the dearth of candidates for the ordained ministry: to "forced and unnatural linkages": and to "the shabby face of our Church's work in Palestine."

Even these shortcomings, or indications of shortcomings, were ambiguous to him in the light of his deep sense of the providence of God. He wondered, in the next breath, whether these things, looking like disasters, might in fact be a blessing in disguise, so that the laity might be awakened to its missionary responsibility, and those training for the ordained ministry might learn what it meant "to be fishers of men and not aquarium keepers."

On the positive side, he found the developments in relation to the Church of Rome one of the two major good things to report, on the grounds that you cannot either speak the truth, far less speak it in love, unless you begin to speak. His conclusion to the Trinity students about the current state of affairs was:

> "I for one deeply believe that this is an answer to prayers from both sides of the gulf, and that it is bound to lead us out into very difficult country that will test us to the depths, country we might well wish to avoid were it not country to which God is calling us."

In his concluding remarks to the Assembly of 1962, as he looked forward to a year of "anchorage and comparative taciturnity", his judgment of the situation was a bold and paradoxical one.

> "The healthiest symptom in the life of our church is not the staunchness of institutional loyalty observable throughout its borders, but rather a deepseated uneasiness — you might almost call it a malaise — which is causing many of our people, and especially many of our office-bearers, to ask the most fundamental questions — questions about the Faith itself, about the nature and mission of the Church, about the unity proper to the Church, about the basic reasons for the continuing shortage in candidates for the ordained ministry."

That such a malaise could be isolated as the most conspicuous positive about the life of the Church of Scotland was a measure of the adventurous trust of the man. It chimed in well with the thrust of the centenary lecture he was so proud to give in tribute to David Cairns, where he commended a characteristic critique which Cairns had made of some eloquent sermon on immortality. "It was very pretty, but for me one steady look into the dark is worth a hundred of your farthing candles." The entire lecture endorsed Cairns's next sentence, "The first necessity for us all is to have courage to look steadily into the dark."

That commitment, catching up all his vision, both of education and of faith, was to be tested on the pulse for the remainder of Archie's life.

10   Retirement and old age

"This purpose of destroying letters is the hesitant forerunner of an activity which May and I must begin seriously to pursue – viz. dismantling our stuffed premises with a view to John Morley's 4th phase of a rightly-ordered conception of human life – be–do–do without–depart."

The years of Archie's retirement were, to begin with, scarcely leisurely. Even before his moderatorial prominence, he had been a kenspeckle figure, and his combination of wit, penetration and human warmth brought him many invitations to speak on all kinds of civic and ecclesiastical occasions. How many he declined is not calculable, but there was a fairly constant stream of public events: dedicating church halls, church windows, church basements ("elevated", as he put it, "to undercrofts"); radio, and latterly television programmes; retreats and conferences for kirk sessions, synods, missionaries on furlough; events and committees related to Scottish Churches' House; preaching at centenary services or other notable landmarks in the life of congregations, particularly those with which he already had some connection of history or affection; leading devotions at preparatory or follow-up meetings for international ecumenical events.

One index of the pace he seemed to be able to cope with in his mid-seventies comes from a letter he wrote to David Cairns in March, 1963, where he says that since the beginning of February he has had speaking engagements in Manchester, Alloa, Paisley, Stirling (*bis*), Dunblane, Clackmannan, Bearsden and Borgue. Apart from apologising that this has been the primary reason for what he was wont to call his *unwriteousness*, the letter is a sprightly epistle, recounting with glee the prayer he had heard tell of from Archie Campbell, the minister at Borgue: "that a gracious providence might shield and deliver us from the acts of God." And all this was from a man only months short of his seventy-fifth birthday.

Though the batting average may have dwindled slightly as the sixties became the seventies, Archie was game for stamina-requiring exploits with undiminished verve. In 1974, for instance, Bill Christman, then minister of Lochwood Parish Church, Easterhouse, one of Glasgow's "ghetto" housing estates, full of multiple deprivation, had tried unsuccessfully to find someone to lead a week of renewal. All the ministers he approached pleaded over-business. Archie, who had never met him or heard of him, on being approached out of the blue, decided, in spite of May's gentle remonstrances that it was too much for him, that this was a God-given challenge. Five nights in a row, he was picked up from Doune, and driven to Easterhouse, where, according to Bill Christman's report, "people hung on his every word", as he spoke for an hour each night, (including pub night), then stayed for tea in the hall and prayers in the church, before being driven home by an elder. The people loved him, and a little later made a special collection and bought him an evergreen conifer shrub which was given pride of place in the centre of his garden like a spire. Archie himself was delighted by the whole encounter, and wrote of it enthusiastically to friends. The whole event cheered him, both in its cordiality and its robustness, and he cherished it as an instance of the living Church in the face of a television programme on the state of the church a few months later, which he found dismal and "without the faintest whiff of the divine dimension." Bill Christman he described with relish as a *rara avis* in the Kirk,

> "a hummingbird among crows, an immediately lovable character, beloved of vandals, gangboys, the godly, the douce, the dropouts; a kind of Protestant miniature of Pope John XXIII, in that faith, hope and love emanate from him as the spiritual ingredients of an irresistible buoyancy."

(He also predicted that such an extraordinarily unconventional ministry was liable to get him into trouble with the Presbytery some day!)

About enroaching age he was witty but not evasive, though he actually doesn't seem to have *felt* very old until somewhere around the mid-eighties. (His neighbour, Tom Burnet, remembers him once asking in church, "Tom, who's that old man over there?" of a seventy-year old, to whom Archie himself was significantly senior.) From about 1974 on, the references to failing faculties and slackened tempo become fairly regular in letters to friends, though usually in a brief last sentence, and often with a near-audible chortle: "We both begin to suffer from *multiple disseminated annodominitis*" was one of his favourite ways of putting it, and there was more glee than self-pity in his announcement to David Gourlay that he had been elected Honorary Chaplain of the Fifty Club "apparently *ad vitam aut gagitudinem*".

The years of their retirement were lived out in the little Perthshire village of Doune, where they had a house built to May's precise design specifications. Late in the fifties, May had had a slight heart attack, and they had come to recuperate for a short while at the Woodside Hotel there. May's family origins were in Perthshire, at Muthil, and both of them seem to have fallen in love with Doune and its environs, and to have decided without much soul-searching that they would settle there. It was an ideal location, with the pleasures of village life, and yet good access by road and rail to the rest of central Scotland. It had also the advantage of being a stonethrow of a mile or two from Dunblane, the historic Cathedral town which had become the home of Scottish Churches' House, and crucial in Scottish ecumenism.

This, with its possibilities of ongoing involvement for Archie, as frequent consultant, occasional speaker, and happy chairman of the Churches' House Garden Committee, helped to clinch the decision in favour of Doune, rather than, say, the Borders, which had been his rooting-ground, or the Ayrshire of his young manhood.

May's design for the house filled Archie with pride, and they were to enjoy twenty-four happy years in it out of thirty-five married, the first and last joint home they made together, for Bank Street was already deeply impregnated with Archie's bachelor past when May joined him there in 1950.

Looking from the outside like a simple cottage/bungalow, the house was deceptively roomy, under a copper roof. The main sitting room had, at the garden end, a wide French window across its whole breadth, giving on to their treasured garden, and allowing in winter vistas of the outside, which, as Archie prided himself, was never without some bloom and colour. There was a study for Archie at the front, a spare room for guests, a central hall which doubled as a dining-room, and held more of the overflowing books, and, with the respect for decent privacy which May thought proper, a shaving room for Archie off their bedroom, and a kitchen window-paned with frosted glass against intrusive eyes.

The garden was equally well set out. A distant compost area at the far corner, hidden by a tall trellis; an ample shelved and pigeon-holed garden shed in which Archie or the gardener could potter; (Archie regarded "potter" as the official word for what men did in gardens, while women *worked* in kitchens); a long conservatory/greenhouse; and overlooked round the side of the house, a discreet area for hanging out washing.

In spite of Archie's earlier history of stomach trouble, and May's heart condition and blood-pressure problems, which could so easily have made them valetudinarian, they enjoyed the next two and a half decades immensely, sustaining zest and immense interest in the world outside, in Archie's case till the very end; and in May's till she was more and more nibbled at by senile dementia. They loved their house, and almost every letter which Archie writes after 1961 alludes to the joy of their garden, which ran from aconites and snowdrops through crocuses and daffodils to its summer glory of roses and delphiniums. Both of them had an immense and detailed knowledge of plants and flowers, and of their proper botanical names, and worked systematically each winter on planning revolutions in the garden for the following year. Archie admitted that the craving inspired in him by seed-catalogues was the nearest he came to lust, and the thing most likely to bankrupt him.

Alick and Margaret Craig had had a gardener in Troom called Old Bell, with whom the family had the most affectionate relationship, and Archie and May were also blessed with two gardeners who were immensely valued by them both, not only for their professional skills, but for their sterling humanity. Of the former, John Campbell, Archie was wont to say that he had dropped from paradise before the Fall, and was "an incarnate mark of interrogation set against any too narrow interpretation of '*extra ecclesiam nulla salus*'". He was a man of few words, but the few were graphic, like his consolation to Archie on hearing him complain about the effects of age: "Mind this, Doctor; a man's no drunk till he's clutchin' the grass."

When John Campbell became too old to do the work, there were a couple of years when the garden went into decline, but it was wonderfully rescued by Mr MacMurtrie, who restored it to its former glory, and is still, five years after Archie's death, "keeping it in the spirit Dr Craig would have wished", Archie having left money explicitly for him to carry on as gardener. "The spirit Dr Craig would have wished" was clumps instead of straight lines, a sore trial to both gardeners, who were brought up straight men; but it says worlds for the affection and loyalty of both that Archie's scandalous heresy prevailed.

"The ultimate slow justice of the earth" was a phrase from Victoria Sackville-West much quoted by Archie, and the depth of his attention to how things grew, to the reticence of maturing seed or root, to the penalties of neglect and the prodigality of blossom was as much a metaphysical passion as a cherished recreation. Many friends spontaneously describe his intimacy with flowers and birds as Franciscan – both May and he being able to bring garden birds to their hands when they stood, holding no food.

When Archie was not away from home, their domestic life was an ordered one. Archie had been very impressed on reading a life of Casals to learn that his first act every morning had been to play two Bach sonatas on the piano as an overture to every day. And his mother described to him, in one of her letters to the trenches, her morning ritual of standing on the front doorstep to smell the air and greet the world.

From the frequency with which Archie reiterates the centrality of prayer to any depth of understanding or growth in Christian faith, one can imagine how constant a discipline he exercised in that sphere, but that would not be the sort of thing he would think it decent to noise abroad. Lesslie Newbigin, however, testifies to the naturalness of shared prayer with Archie and May at the end of their visits to Doune, and to Archie's insistence that they kneel – "the only proper position for prayer". And from the advice he occasionally gives at ministerial retreats, though without citing himself as exemplar, it seems that he thought an hour a day of private devotion an indispensable minimum.

May certainly kept by her bed a small devotional diary with a reading for every day of the year, which she used till its pages were well-thumbed and beginning to curl slightly at the corners. (It was a thing Archie always registered, if someone in home or hospital produced a Bible of the old sort with gilt-edged pages, where the streaks of fingering were most evident, be it at the

Psalms or one of the Gospels, or whatever.) As the years passed, dates in May's book were inscribed with births and deaths and events of significance to close family and friends.

They knew how to work at friendship, and, though Archie was forever apologising for not having answered letters in decent time, he actually kept his spirit poised towards friends by keeping a "friendship book" linked to intercession on a regular basis. This discipline of orderly spiritual contact was, as he confided to one friend, ideally in a monthly rotation, "but actually, σαρξ being σαρξ, and very imperfectly pneumatised," less frequent. In fact, however, he sustained a very high level of fidelity in correspondence where he felt that this might give support, remembering, for instance, a friend who had been widowed eight years to the day after the death of her husband. He also had flair for the small gestures of thoughtfulness, giving neighbours a box of chocolates for a journey, or a rose on their return from holiday.

After breakfast, Archie's first act of the morning would be to walk round the garden, investigating what had happened as the slow molecular forces of nature took their course. As they both began to want a less brisk pace, this ritual came slightly later on in the morning, and breakfast was eaten in bed with *The Times*, *The Glasgow Herald* and *The Scotsman*, Archie relishing the news and May tackling the crosswords first.

Archie often did the shopping, since this provided the opportunity to meet lots of people and hear the local news. He was known by all the village shopkeepers, and loved it when there were long queues, that affording more talking time. May, who was ever so slightly what Scots would call "perjink" [proper, with an edge of genteel self-consciousness], was a proud and provident housekeeper, with the skills of home-making at her fingertips, and unobtrusive devotion to Archie and his well-being. They lived comfortably, with traditionally well-made furniture, and with many pretty and valuable ornaments in the sitting-room where they entertained and where Archie played his grand piano. Yet they were careful, even frugal, about some things. May used to patch or darn old tea-towels, and Archie kept in the garden/workroom any small household items which he could mend in finite time.

May was Archie's regular chauffeur, since he had never learned to drive, and as late as 1975, when she was 82 and he 86, was delighted by their new Triumph Toledo which was significantly lighter to handle than their old car.

The rhythm of ordinary days, apart from house and garden duties, consisted of dealing with some of the unanswered correspondence, often a game of chess played with the neighbours' son, Douglas, and regularly, at 4 p.m., an hour of what Archie called "2 x HB", which, being interpreted, meant horizontal bliss for two. Neighbours knew well that this was not a good time for social calls, so that normally Archie and May could retire to enjoy forty winks or a peaceful hour's reading.

At night the table would be set for breakfast, and windows would be shut and doors carefully locked. They were both actively careful about security, and on one occasion the piano tuner came on a valuable ring of May's which had been hidden in the piano against possible burglary! Finally Archie would play something by way of goodnight to the piano, and they would retire to bed. Archie's favourite mode of reading was lying enjoying a book, with a jar of "soor plums" at hand to satisfy his sweet tooth. He enjoyed anything that was good of its kind, travel narratives, detective stories, biography and autobiography, war memoirs, essays and poetry. By the mid-seventies he was admitting to finding formal theology a bit tough and unrewarding, but he read everything else with a theological ear cocked, and found in most areas suggestive and illuminating data for faith to attend to and appreciate.

Their range of friends was so diverse and so cosmopolitan that it rescued them from what Archie felt, with some ambivalence, to be the dominant Perthshire ethos. He wrote to David Cairns on one occasion:

> "This county and neighbourhood positively bristles with retired army officers, most of them quite delightful people and pillars of the kirk, and all of them rapturous flag-wavers scarcely fledged mentally. I suspect that their private prayers always include the petition, "Lord, save thine Argylls, and bless thy Conservatives." "

As their travelling capacities became more restricted, the house at Doune became a kind of minor pilgrimage centre for people who loved Archie and valued him as listener, counsellor and chuckling sage. At times, much as May and Archie loved conviviality, it sometimes took its toll on May to cater as hospitably as she did with the streams of visitors who came to see them in affection or in need of advice and spiritual recharging. By 1978, Archie was writing, again to David Gourlay, his successor but two in the Glasgow University Chaplaincy, that "visits from friends should be 'mild and reg'lar' like Sarey Gamp's liquor, a perwision which we insert because last summer May began to show signs of wear and tear, as did the road outside, by reason of poppers-in multiplying so unconscionably."

Archie's outgoing correspondence registers with some precision the sequence of the *annodominitis*: in his own case failing eyesight, occasional lumbago and what he called a "leaking memory", though by any standard he had an amazingly lively grasp of the detail of his own and his family's past, of the natural world, especially of the botanical, of novels, poetry, music and anecdote which made for an immense range of animated conversation with all kinds of people. To safeguard against the day when he might not be able to read, he began, about the age of eighty-four, to learn by heart the poetry he wanted to have regular access to. He studied for old age, reading in 1968 Dean

Swift's *"Resolutions when I come to be old"* and measuring himself against them to a friend:

> "I think I've complied with some of them, e.g. "Not to neglect decency or cleanliness for fear of falling into Nastyness", "Not to hearken to Flatteryes, nor conceive I can be beloved by a young woman", "Not to be over severe with young people, but give Allowances for their youthful Follyes and Weaknesses" . . . Ah, but! What about "Not to tell the same story over and over again to the same people", or "Not to talk much, nor of myself"? Dear Dean, you wield a trenchant rapier."

For a couple of years in the early seventies, Archie's elder brother John came to live with them at Doune, a quiet man, whose solitary life as a retired schoolmaster had struck May and Archie as rather depressed when they shared a holiday with him. It was May's suggestion that he should come, Archie having hestitated to propose any such thing, but he appreciated May's generosity, and hoped that it would give John a new lease of life. Sadly it didn't. John tended to keep out of the constant coming and goings of the much-visited Archie, and by 1973 it was clear that he was beginning to fail. In a sense it was a blessing that his decline was not prolonged, for, as Archie confided to close friends, it looked as if May's none too robust health might be endangered by all that was involved in coping with the situation.

From John's death on, the tone of Archie's self-description becomes a bit more subdued, though always brisk enough to resist what he called "the slops of self-pity". In March, '74, for instance, he writes:

> "In the last year we are both more than one year older — radius shortened — tempo slower — memory less reliable and losing its fly-paper stickability for names and things read — LAZIER, oh yes, much lazier and more unresistant to what Bottom called "an exposition of sleep" . . ."

Then, characteristically,

> "Nevertheless, the zest of living upon this planet has not seeped away from us, nor been entirely consumed by what our dear gardener calls "chokit tubes"."

John's death was however, a significant end of an era, for it left Archie the sole survivor of the eleven brothers and sisters. Only one nephew, Stuart, still bore the Craig name, and by 1976 he too was unexpectedly dead, and the patronymic had died out, though fourth and fifth generation descendants by marriage remain. The acceleration of deaths among his friends became striking. His beloved Hugh Walker had died already in 1958, but by the mid-seventies he felt as if it were a weekly event to lose someone or other whom he had known. Glasgow University seemed to him a changed place when he preached his swansong there in 1975, in the absence of immortals like James Christian Fordyce, Professor of Humanity, whom Archie judged the best reader of Scripture in the University. Younger university friends and colleagues turned out in heartening numbers, but he nevertheless had the palpable sense that his generation was gone.

In 1976, he was painfully shocked by the deaths, by suicide pact, of Pit van Dusen, and his wife who, as Betty Bartholomew, had been one of Archie's close friends in the 1920s in Glasgow, and had sketched him as a young man. And he greatly felt the loss of Robert Mackie, who had been his co-adventurer in the global ecumenical vision of the first half of the century, and, probably more than any other Scottish churchman of his vintage, the one with whom he could take blessedly for granted a common vision of the coming church in the world.

Archie never lost ecumenical hope, in spite of the grudgingness of the institutional Church of Scotland to embrace his vision of it. He did think however, that if there was no real shift in momentum at the level of official inter-church conversations, they should be given a decent sabbatical rest! He judged that the real creativity, sadly, might not be at that level at all, where leaders in gaiters and tricorne hats negotiated terms, but rather in the small-scale ventures which touched people in their everyday encounters. Scottish Churches' House and Leighton House in Dunblane thrilled him, and he worked with them in many capacities, finding the openness of the place, its concern with wider than churchy issues and its range of participants a scale model of what he hoped Christian ecumenical encounter should be.

He and May planned what they would do if they became too old to manage the house in Doune, or when one of them died, and had the "reserve plan" of moving into Peebles Hydro. At the beginning of 1978, Archie's 90th year, they set to clearing and disposing of some of their voluminous papers, a task May found much more congenial than Archie, who said of the enterprise that May was given to keeping her possessions slimmed, while he was "addicted to hoardom". But he was appalled to think of how an executor could face the business of dealing with the contents of St John's, and the garageful of papers which he *did* leave were apparently only a fraction of what he could have left.

In mid 1978, Archie hit a bad patch of uncharacteristic lassitude and zestlessness, which turned out in the end to be caused by anaemia, and from which he recovered in time to enjoy a luncheon on the 2nd December, and a tea-party on the 4th, flanking the actual date of his ninetieth birthday. He thanked his hosts by reading some verses he had composed for the occasion, and returned the compliments of more than one friend by citing a favourite passage from Sir Walter Scott's Journal — (Scott being one of his most re-read authors):

> "There was a prodigious shaking of hands, and a flow of compliments such as sober sense prevented me from swallowing and good manners restrained me from spitting out. I could have wished for a little more of the old Scotch causticity."

By 1981, there were traces of May beginning to lose her short-term memory, forgetting who people were, and repeating the same question within minutes, always with the tone of interested gentility which characterised her normal social style. This gradually and steadily worsened into clear senile dementia, and she also became physically less able to manage any household jobs, and eventually even to walk.

As the condition worsened, Archie did everything in his power to minimise May's sense of exclusion from the surrounding world. He would constantly include her in conversations by saying, "Isn't that right, dear?" and touching her arm. He had the steps in the garden converted to a ramp so that she could be wheeled out to enjoy the flowers and the birds, and when visitors came, he made it clear to them that May was to be treated still as mistress of the house, while not able to do any of the actual lifting or fetching. He himself managed things with such imaginative courtesy that even, for example, when a B.B.C. television camera crew visited them in Doune only months before May's death, the entire team responded to his delicate and tender manoeuvring, which maintained her dignity as hostess.

They were wonderfully supported in these latter years, by their devoted housekeeper, Mrs Armstrong, who cooked and cleaned; and by a wonderful district nurse, Margaret Thomson, who was very dear to Archie. They were also blessed in having immensely caring neighbours, who had known Archie since his moderatorial visit to Nigeria, could handle the medical aspects of the situation and also shared their world of faith in a way which let Archie confide in them at a very deep level, and be supported in the process he called "relearning the alphabet of love". That level of spiritual support from them, as well as the practical kindnesses of sitting with May to let him go down to the village, made bearable a situation which must have been at times immeasurably distressing. The Burnets, for instance, remember him coming in one night to tell them that May had just said to him, "Tell me, does the name Archie Craig mean anything to you?" It was with them that he wrestled and prayed through the decision to let May be taken into a nursing home in Callander late in the August of 1985 to give him three weeks rest and the chance to recharge his "depleted batteries".

Events then moved quickly. Though he had found the decision immensely hard to make, Archie was confident once it was made that it was for the best, and enjoyed what he called "leisure and freedom of spirit." He not only had energy enough to take up correspondence with manifest mental vigour, though his handwriting by now had become significantly less formed, but he actually relished the restored possibility of social living, which he had all but given up for May's sake. Most evenings, he would have a group of neighbours in for cocoa at nine o'clock and immensely enjoyed the company.

Meanwhile, May, aged ninety-two, had had a fall in the nursing home and had broken her hip. After some days in hospital in Stirling, she was moved to Bannockburn to convalesce, but on Thursday, 22nd August, she died.

Earlier in the same week, on the Saturday before May's death, Archie had got out of bed at night to shut a window in his bedroom, and fell. He couldn't get back into bed, and lay all night on the floor, having managed to pull a carpet over him for warmth. The following morning Mrs Armstrong couldn't get in − (May and Archie didn't like handing out keys) − and went for Dr Burnet next door. When they got in they found him still on the floor, a bit weak, but otherwise all right.

The next morning, Archie's grand-niece, Shiona Fargus, his eldest sister's grand-daughter, came up with her husband to Doune, and were with Archie for the days that followed.

When the news of May's death came, Archie's first feeling was of intense relief that she had died first, for it was clear that if he had died before her, she could no longer have stayed in St. John's, her haven of safe and familiar people and things. At midnight on the day of her death, he rang the bell for his niece, and they talked through till morning and enjoyed together a beautiful sunrise. On the Friday, he spent the whole day up, sat out in the garden with a blanket round him and said to the Burnets that he was thinking how wonderful it was for May to be talking to her father and mother and brother. The phrase which sticks in the mind of those who were in touch with him during these days was his tribute to *the impeccability of the divine timing.*

He himself had been due to go into hospital the following week for some tests related to suspected throat cancer, but with May safely "happed away", the need to brace himself for the future had gone.

On the Saturday, he held a small summit conference with his lawyer, the parish minister, Kenyon Wright of Scottish Churches' House and David Lyon of the Church of Scotland's World Mission and Unity Department. The house had actually been in May's name, having been built largely out of her family resources, and so technicalities had to be seen to, so that Archie could leave it, as he wanted, for church purposes. His first idea had been to leave it as a furlough house for missionaries, since that was the aspect of the church's life which, after worship, seemed to him most vital. However, since that was not a particular area of need in the Church of Scotland, he settled for a looser commitment, that the house should be used for some purpose furthering the work of mission and unity, and that a small Trust should be set up to administer that use, and to deal with his papers. He discussed also the arrangements for May's funeral, choosing hymns and readings with Mr Dawson, their parish minister; and spoke too about his own funeral with total absence of morbidity, (responding to one suggestion about the proceedings with rich gallows humour: "Over my dead body!").

On the day before, Archie had phoned Nelson Gray, the head of Religion with S.T.V. asking if he too could come on the Saturday. By the time he had phoned to check on the suitability of a time, Mrs Fargus thought that Archie was in a coma, but Nelson decided anyway to drive up to see him, since their friendship over the last few years had been a deep and mature one, and he wanted to honour the request that he should go. When he arrived and was shown into Archie's room, the latter opened his eyes, and recovered sufficiently to ask Nelson's opinion as to whether his papers should be preserved or destroyed. When Nelson insisted that they had immense value, not only as a record of Archie's life, but as a history of twentieth century Scottish history and churchmansip, he asked Nelson to look after them for him and closed his eyes again.

Since the Friday, the doctor had arranged for nurses to come in at night and sit with Archie, so that the Farguses could have a little rest after four days of twenty-four hour attentiveness. On the Friday and Saturday nights, the nurse who came was warm and informal, dressed in ordinary clothes and gentle-mannered. On the Sunday night, after a day which Archie had spent in bed, very weak, not wanting food and sucking ice-cubes, a new nurse came, uniformed this time and more briskly rigid and officious. Mrs Fargus has said that she was to be called at any time, but when Archie called out "Douglas" in the middle of the night, the nurse did not call her. If she had, they would have known that he was asking for the next-door neighbour's son, for whom Archie had a very special quasi-paternal fondness, and would have fetched him. As it was the nurse gave Archie an injection "to settle him"; and he, who thought it shallow that people said, "We want to die with dignity, and so we'll dope you sufficiently that you don't feel anything, and then we'll cover you with flowers", died in his sleep. In a sense, however, apart from the run-in of the last months, when he would tell his friends he had been "preparing for his Finals", he had been living his own death for the four days since May died, and was ready.

PART TWO
11 Of lightning and of music

"Within the realm of religion we come upon this central experience: awareness of the impingement upon the human will of a Will immediately discerned to be unconditional in the demands it makes. The sacred is that which demands unconditional, absolute obedience, even though obedience means the obliteration of the self. It is also experienced as ultimate or final succour."

Lectures on the Religion of the Pentateuch

Archie never lost the conviction that the central category of all religion was the holy. The majesty and glory of God was properly responded to with nothing less than adoration and wonder. He loathed the "cheap familiarity" of some ways of talking about God as if he were a room-mate, and thought ministers should have to read Otto's "The Idea of the Holy" at least once a year to counteract the tendency. He even found it difficult to tolerate the use of "You" rather than "Thou" in public prayer, never himself using it. One of his verses speaks scathingly of

"churchly colleges,
Where earnest students of divinity
Learn to domesticate Infinity.
(One such the other day was glad
He could call God Almighty "Dad"!)"

This holiness had a double aspect, of beneficence and judgment, twin elements which properly provoked a twin response of security and dread. This he identified with Otto's account of the holy as *"tremendum et fascinans"*, and he worked in his study beneath a reproduction of Grunewald's Isenheim Altarpiece, with its telling images of simultaneous pointing to, kneeling before and shrinking back from the cross. He had a particular fondness for the formulation of the same point which was once articulated by Professor Bowman to a group of students, making "innocent eyes gaze and downy jaws drop". That ran: "In religion there are always two moments, simultaneous but antithetic, which we may call respectively the anagogic and the apotropaic."

This holy God was not just inertly numinous, but active in the world's life, where the primary category of his directive presence was providence. Of all

119

Calvin's key themes, this was one that meant most to Archie, and which he constantly used to interpret events both in his personal life, and in the macrocosm. Over and over again it appears in sermons, in letters to friends:

"The Hand of God is in every event that happens. He is the prime mover in whatever comes to pass that is good, and He overrules and exploits for His own ends whatever comes to pass through the evil will of His creatures in their disobedience".

Not only God's general providence, but His ability and willingness to intervene in specific situations, for instance in response to prayer, seemed to Archie to be one of the central nerves of lively faith. "If it be subtracted", he wrote in 1956, after digesting a wide-ranging booklist on the subject provided on request by Tom Torrance, "the result is not simply a reduced or fractional corpus of doctrine, but the corpse of the corpus." He was completely unembarrassed by the idea that a God who intervened in natural processes sometimes, but not always, was capricious or unjustifiably inconsistent. That he *could* intervene was a corollary of his sovereignty in creating; nature being, as it were, the glove of God, pliant to his hand. That he *would* intervene on specific occasions, in our eyes inexplicably; or, even more inexplicably, would *not* intervene to prevent massive woe and pain, was a function of his all-knowing benevolence, which could see uncloudedly what was for our long-term good, even when it remained totally opaque to us.

While he was never facile or glib, and thought such theological talk could only properly come out of "smelting in the image of the Cross" and never from the complacency of "snug doctrinal burrows", Archie could not quite feel in his bones that there was as much of a problem of evil as was sometimes made out. His dealing with the theoretical problem of unjust suffering, like his pastoring of those in pain, was grave and compassionate, but he could never quite identify imaginatively with those who, like Ivan in *The Brothers Karamazov*, saw defiance and active disbelief as the proper responses to a God who could let his world be so blighted.

The heart of his belief about suffering is perhaps most lucidly set out in the Lenten talks he did on radio in 1956, called *Arrows of the Almighty*, but it was a theme to which he returned on many occasions. Much of the world's suffering seemed to him explicable in terms of our own abuse, individual and corporate, of the world we were meant to steward. Poverty, hunger and even much of the world's disease were direct causal consequences of human failure, greed, gluttony, neglect, ambition and so on. Other suffering, not correlated to sin, but to achievement, was disciplinary, suffering to teach us the cost of learning a skill, or of achieving some worthwhile end. This seemed to him one of the structural lines of human living, and one which by temperament and conviction he was happy to accept, the alternative seeming to him to be a kind of decadent lotus-eating. One can feel the scorn in his pen as he writes,

> "Would you really like to live in a world without risks, in an utterly safe world, a kind of rabbit's hutch of a world, with lettuces laid on at regular intervals? Devoid of heroism, that is steadfastness in the teeth of mortal danger?"

He was, in relation to this kind of suffering, robustly opposed to whining.

> "Healthy-minded people of anything like robust moral constitution have little difficulty in accepting the law of sacrifice which experience shows to be deeply engraved upon human life."

Or again,

> "We live in a world which very strongly conveys the suggestion that the Almighty does not intend that men should ever be too safe, in case they should degenerate into an awful insipidity of moral quality."

He regarded it as merely shabby and flabby that people should complain about such strenuous conditions for the achievement of what was important to them, and seems not to have had much feeling that people could be taxed beyond their strength by life, except by whatever stupidities they might inflict on one another.

Finally there was penal suffering, not to be understood as the revenge of a punitive God, but as "the winter ploughing for a future harvest", making clear to us the depths of our past and present sinfulness and the cost of our salvation.

This analysis of sin and its dynamic impact on creation seems at first glance, and even at second, hard to reconcile with the geniality which Archie brought to his natural human encounters. It had nothing to do with misanthropy, even though he could, in certain contexts remind his hearers of such sombre words as "Behold I am vile", or use in his addresses in Oxford such a phrase as "the swampy foetid valley of human beastliness". Not only did the horrors of 20th century history, holocaust and nuclear bomb confirm that it was no over-statement, but the subtler sins, "medullar complacency" and the untroubled life-style of villadom, excluding both horror and glory.

The gravity and pervasiveness of sin was not for him primarily a sociological or psychological datum, nor even the result of truthful introspection, but an inference from the Cross of Christ. If God could, had to, go through Calvary to put right the relationship between Himself and man, the state of alienation must have been colossal beyond computing.

121

What made geniality possible was that the Christian Church existed, for Archie, on the far side of the rift between men and God, recognising the costliness of its healing, but able to put the past behind it and to challenge people to become the sons and daughters of God they were made to be, empowered by the life of the risen Christ in the mystery of faith. That, at least, was the divine reality of the Church, though it co-existed still in terrible tension with the social and political history of Christendom, which seemed so much at odds with its proper insistence that its reality could ultimately only be judged on that "vertical" plane.

Archie never thought that any of this was self-evident, or to be taken for granted as obvious to all people of good faith. His vivid image of the kind of truthful agnosticism which he so much respected, for instance, in some of his academic colleagues like Bowman or McNeile Dixon was that they were honest climbers up the same hill of God as believers were, but had the harder job of climbing faithfully on the sunless side, whereas believers climbed in the sunlight of God's own revelation. At the same time, people climbing on the sunny slope could also dig themselves into snug little burrows, private or institutional. For these forms of evasive belief he had no respect at all, deploring convictions born of mental sluggishness or of the appetite for cheap, escapist certainties. He also warned constantly against belief taken on at second-hand, not entitled to say it saw when it was only honestly looking. He frequently quoted one of his New College teachers who had said that the two chief ministerial sins were laziness, and the habit of saying just a little bit more than they were entitled to say.

Much of his understanding of the relation between theology and living religion — he never accepted the Barthian put-down of "religion" by contrasting it with "faith" — had been wrestled for in arguments he had with George Stewart in the twenties, while he was exploring preaching in his first charge at Galston. He had clearly been suggesting to his loving mentor that to make sense to twentieth century people, the Gospel had to be translated into twentieth century language, and that some of its traditional categories were in fact obsolete. In this context he had sent George an article by one Miss Dougall, which he apparently thought was doing the right kind of job. Stewart's reply is interesting, and very much expresses a position which later became Archie's own.

His letter reads:

"In general, when a belief has long held the church, one must assume that it is based on *experiences* which constitute revelation. Revelations are not bare: they need interpretation. I don't think it will suffice to say, "That belief is all wrong", without giving another interpretation of the experience .... What did holy men of the past see and experience which expressed itself in "damnation"? . . . . There is no use, best beloved, in an article like this, which is purely negative and very shallow . . . . There are great words woven into the literature and classical expression of the Church's faith, which are falling into disuse . . . . partly because of spineless and amorphous thinking. These words need to be de-polarised and redeemed, else they will drop out of use. If they drop out of use, much of the New Testament, and of the religious classics becomes obsolete, and the facts become of less moment."

While Archie remained unaware that religious words *could* come to lose all currency, (a perception which Joe Oldham reaffirmed, and which the *Religion and Life* weeks in many cases confirmed) he seems to have been convinced by Stewart's contention that the real root of classical theological language was people's living experience. Thus, in a paper on "The Authority of Dogma", he urged:

"The theologian has to colonise for the intellect the territory which living religion has opened up; and for this task he has no other instruments at his command but the thought-forms and mental furnishings of the era in which he happens to live."

Or again:

"The theologian as such, is not necessarily a *pioneer* of living religion. He may be that too, of course — to think otherwise would be unduly to limit the scope of grace and the concept of miracle; but in his capacity as theologian his proper business is to follow close in the wake of living religion, and to set in order for the intellect the territory which living religion has opened up."

Though he found Scripture to be the Book of books, he did not believe that it was equal in every part, and felt free in relation to it to register false starts and childlike errors. He was also sensitive to the question of genre, recognising that Scripture's narrative modes were much more diverse than the strictly historical. But he was more confident than many academic biblical scholars would now be about the factual historicity of New Testament, and particularly Gospel stories, on the grounds that critical scepticism about, say, nature miracles or resurrection was due to dogma about "normal experience". That dogma seemed to him unreasonable, since the unique penetration of the world's life which was the life of Christ could *reasonably* be expected to manifest extraordinary powers, even over nature (indeed perhaps *especially* over nature, since it could not offer any resistance, as could free-willed beings, to the creative intent of God). He was convinced that the nature miracles, as well as the healing ones were manifestations of redemption extending to the material cosmos, as it had to do, God's love being towards his whole creation, and not towards gaseously disembodied souls. (He once pointed out to a student advocating the immortality of the soul detached from the body, what unfortunate consequences there might be if anyone lit a match in heaven!)

Archie was clearly *au fait* with what he regarded as the extreme liberal view that much of the New Testament writing is not the documentation of factual occurences, but a narrative construct of faith. Though a colleague of Ronald Gregor Smith and Ian Henderson in Glasgow, both of whom would have argued that much New Testament narrative was "mythological" in the sense used by Rudolf Bultmann, he seems nowhere to have given this position the kind of close, argued attention that he paid to challenges from natural science. He simply avers, on various occasions, that he believes the nerve of the Gospel to be cut if miracle is not affirmed as actual historical event, in the sense in which the orbiting of the moon is historical event. In particular, he regards the denial of Jesus's bodily resurrection as theologically unacceptable, and actually lambasts the view in a sardonic passage of one of his verse epistles, where he links demythologising views of the Resurrection with shallow ethical relativism.

He speaks of theololgians who

> "delete
> Centuries of hard won truth,
> Counting it the worst of crimes
> Not to keep up with the times,
> Dubbing morals 'fashion's see-saw,
> Down goes Jacob, up goes Esau'.
> Simply current taste wherein
> There's no need for discipline
> Since there's no such thing as sin
> And the fleshless bones of God
> Lie six feet beneath the sod."

It is hard to be sure whether he refrained from arguing the toss with the existentialists because he found their position too silly for words, and not worth wasting intellectual time on, or whether it actually got beneath his theological skin in a way which was quite worrying to him. He had considerable respect for Gregor Smith, so it is unlikely that he would simply have written off any position which the latter took seriously. Yet there are no more than a few elusive sentences on the specifics of gospel criticism in all his written papers. Arguments from silence are notoriously unreliable, however, so the absence of comment on this area of theology in the lectures and papers Archie gave during the '50s and '60s, though conspicuous for one of his range of reading, is open only to speculative interpretation. David Cairns, who was in regular telephone contact with Archie during the last decade of the latter's life, judges that he was so convinced of God's direct and lively intervention in time and space, that any position denying that seemed self-evidently to him less than fully-fledged Christianity, and not worth much attention.

Certainly, when he gave his account of Incarnation and Atonement in the course of the 1948 Cunningham lectures, his diagram of God's central saving involvement with our history marks out five phases and four key points in the life of Christ, treated as continuous and congruous elements in one dynamic parabola. The diagram goes like this:

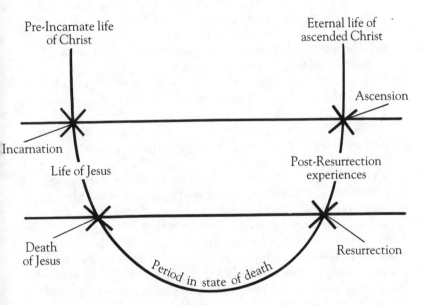

On the other hand, if he suspected he had among his students advocates of anything like Biblical literalism or fundamentalism, he leapt to the defence of the critics' role, pointing out that it was, on the whole, an enterprise carried out by devoted scholars of the church, and necessary if faith was to be seen as able to exist with integrity in the modern world. At the same time, his metaphors of the critical activity have a certain ironic tinge. Critics are "worms that turn the soil for the crops of God", even though he softens the comparison by adding "A practicing domestic gardener must have the highest respect for the worm."

The topic was obviously one which came up constantly in his Biblical Studies courses, and with teachers and would-be teachers he walks a delicate knife-edge between saluting the critics and defusing their sting by the reminder that their conclusions are provisional. One typical passage, from a talk given to the Glasgow Teachers' Conference in 1959, runs thus:

"The impact of textual and historical criticism of the Bible has appeared to set a question mark over against the truth of the Bible, because it has rendered untenable the theory of plenary and verbal inspiration in terms of which the Bible used to be understood and taught. Take as a simple illustration the case of Abraham. Even as short a time ago as the days of my youth, Abraham was still a reliably solid old patriarch who walked the solid earth round about 4,000 years ago, and from whose personal piety many profitable lessons could be reliably drawn. But the Biblical critics put Abraham into their bath of analytic acids, and he emerged at first in the guise of no more than a personalised symbol for a hypothetical migration of enigmatic Semites on a roughly north/south axis in the Middle East. Very upsetting!

Modern scientific criticism . . . . has been applied to the whole continent of the Bible, and has appeared to conjure up a cloud in which it is impossible to distinguish between history and myth, fact and pious fiction; a cloud in which, in particular, the central figure of the New Testament seems to be blurred in a tangle of question marks."

Whatever Archie's deepest personal response to this line of critical scholarship, his public commitment was to defend the critics against the hostility of conservative or fundamentalist approaches. He registered that there was in the churches a significant but inevitable breach in the old homogeneous Bible-centred community, which now consisted of "the horrified, the mystified and the edified." He refused, however, to let people indulge in pious nostalgia for the good old days of pre-critical belief, on the grounds that whatever emerged from the labours of *bona fide* scholars, be they scientists, philosophers, historians, psychiatrists or whatever, was proper grist to the theological mill, and could not be marked off as a no-go area by nervous believers. Wherever issues arose between the alleged truths of any two disciplines, he was clear that there could be no bucking the issue (one of the motives behind his interdisciplinary dinners at Glasgow University) and he wanted no-one, least of all school children, to be kept in compartmentalised ignorance. Indeed he urged, in corroboration of the principles practised by J.W.D. Smith in Jordanhill, that it was the school's responsibility to train the young generation in "that kind of understanding of the Bible which the best modern Biblical study has made available."

This is an area where it is relatively difficult to identify and isolate Archie's inmost soul. Though he would brook no contradiction between reason and faith within the believing community, he occasionally voices the distinction between pulpit and lecture-room in a way which could be abused to feed the furtiveness of preachers about what they know to be the current state of scholarship. So, for instance, when dealing with the Abraham narrative in his Biblical Studies class, and pointing out the discrepancies, cultural parallels and influences, he can say, *en passant*,

> "on the whole the pulpit ignores difficulties of this kind, and rightly so, in the main. The pulpit is content to seize and expound and bring home the main theological truths intended by the writer . . . . but the Biblical scholar must not refrain from asking further questions . . . . He must ask, "How do these difficulties arise?" "

This distinction, in effect making the church the place where the "vertical dimension" is explored, and the schoolroom or lecture-room the place where the "horizontal" is, and relegating the engagement between the two to some not clearly defined zone of encounter is a little surprising, since such a division of labour may provoke precisely the kind of schizophrenic religious allegiance which Archie was concerned to abolish, for he takes it for granted that the preacher will be constantly working through with integrity how the preachable and the teachable will relate, though not necessarily disclosing the workings to the congregation. He draws an analogy with diet, where the important thing is that people are properly nourished, and can recognise good food, but need not themselves know all the technicalities of vitamin or protein content. The dietician, however, must know why some foods are better than others.

Of course, on the assumption that people have access to good religious education in school, or even in Sunday-school, there is not much problem about seeing this as a fair enough division of complementary labours. And Archie was certainly not advocating anything which let separate watertight compartments be constructed for faith and reason. This is clear from many of the letters he received from people, ex-students and others, who had been in touch with him about aspects of belief or doubt. Over and over again he has clearly advised them not to give up on the tough intellectual questions. Though he would never have used so vulgar a word as "cop-out", many of his correspondents express gratitude that he has not counselled them to try blind faith, but has steadily led them along paths of suggestive reading which have "found" them intellectually, and therefore let them move on in some way. He was never shocked by disbelief, only by complacency of disbelief, as when he heard the distinguished scientist being asked, in a radio interview, "Finally Dr. Crick, do you believe in God?" and answering, "Of course not".

With genuine search and genuine doubt he was tender, identifying it with the delicate ambivalence of "Lord, I believe. Help Thou mine unbelief." It was, perhaps, one of the most positive implications of his doctrine of providence that he could bear whatever time it took for people to find their own truthful way. He repeatedly advised people not to rush at faith, but to go slowly, biding the ample time it needed for them really to appropriate any particular doctrine. Indeed, he was even generously confident enough to believe that

> "Now and then,
> A robust well-planted kick
> By a hardy heretic
> In the pants of orthodoxy
> registers heaven's vote by proxy".

These verses end with the note, "To be continued, perhaps and perhaps not".

Even heresy's less creative role seemed to him important, in that he thought it was often no more than an exaggerated concentration on one aspect of the truth, to the virtual obliteration of others.

One key instance of that perspective was how he weighed up people's stances in relation to the doctrine of the Trinity. His Presidential Address to the New College Union in 1969 made his own position clear:

> "So far as theological doctrine is concerned, I draw towards the end of my days in the persuasion, deepened as the years have gone by, that the Christian faith and message, to be balanced, true to human experience and true to the Scriptures, requires a trinitarian formulation."

(It was on this ground that he supported the practice of including the doxology after Psalms or paraphrases in worship.)

It was one of his private mental party-games to work out, beneath formal allegiance to the doctrine of the Trinity, what the *actual* allegiance was. As he put it in the same presidential address,

> "It has been a life-long interest to me to note how, within a Trinitarian theology respectfully saluted, one or another of the six possible *working* unitarian and binitarian theologies have actuated one or another group or school of thought."

Some of his assessments are fascinating. He illustrates his point by reference to his own childhood:

128

"The feel and flavour of the theological atmosphere in which I was reared was in such wise Christo-centric as almost to deserve the name of "second-Person-unitarianism" . . . In restrospect it is easy to see the defects of a theological scenario in which the doctine of the Third Person, if it appeared at all, even on His Sunday, made an embarrassed and apologetic entry, like a distant cousin, invited for form's sake to a wedding-party."

On other occasions, he characterises John Robinson's *Honest to God* as virtually binitarianism of the Second and Third Persons; or questions the Charismatic Movement as Third Person Unitarianism, (as well as thinking it has elements of self-indulgence — "people louping about the floor in supposed ecstasy").

He was quite fond of encouraging conservative evangelicals and deflating self-righteous liberals by insisting that if it came to a bare choice between the simple piety of someone like William Quarrier, with his deep conviction that God would provide two shillings and sixpence on demand by a certain time, and the current Bishop of Birmingham with his sophisticated theology, he would prefer William Quarrier every time. But he was convinced that no such choice was necessary, and sought on most occasions where the issue arose to substitute a "both/and" for an "either/or". Quite how this is compatible with his deep Christological sense of renunciation of magical power in favour of the way of the cross is not clear.

Archie himself could not easily be recognised as belonging to any one theological school. He was, in the '20s and early '30s, much impressed by Barth's recovery of the transcendent otherness of God, mainly as a challenge to the smugness of self-satisfied or self-important preachers of the Word. (He never managed to win over George Stewart, whose response to books enthusiastically lent by Archie was that Barth was an intellectual fascist, but he held his ground.) He never seems to have felt, however, that his appreciation of Barth entailed any blanket denunciation of human reason, or of the kind of Christian apologetics done by theologians like John Oman, John Baillie, H.H. Farmer, D.S. Cairns or Charles Raven, all of whom Archie trusted with his life, theologically speaking, and all of whom were committed to the kind of apologetic activity which Barth seemed to renounce.

As for Barth's theological acolytes, Archie reproached their stridency as

"The raucous crowing of Barthian cockerels in front of many ecclesiastical barn-doors. Barth himself declared that his purpose was only to throw a pinch of spice into the theological pot . . . . but the cockerels took the spice, if I may be allowed somewhat to mix metaphors, and offered it as the whole Gospel."

On another occasion he used the analogy of drinking neat Worcester Sauce. (Brave words to utter within New College walls in the late '60s!)

This discriminating approach to doctrinal absolutes was a matter both of temperament and of theological expectation. It was in part the kind of canniness which he recognised with appreciation as typically Scottish, and particularly strong in Borderers. It was also his conviction that God was "using this clay" to mediate His truth, and that it was a kind of arrogant sacrilege to treat any man as if he could be written off as a mere blot on the landscape of truth.

He also recognised that belief did not always or necessarily manifest itself through the medium of language, certainly not the language of abstract conceptual prose. Frequently he reminded students and ministers that they were much more likely to encounter living truth in the pages of poets or dramatists than in theological textbooks, and he himself clearly found this to be the case. Ralph Hodgson, Studdert-Kennedy, Edwin Muir, Dorothy Sayers, Wordsworth, Tolstoy and many more, were for him, at different levels, explorers of the truth of God and its articulators. He even thought that they might strike home aspects of the Gospel more convincingly than Scripture itself, since the latter was often "rubbed flat by continuous and sometimes clumsy pulpit handling." He treasured the Robert Louis Stevenson comment, "I believe it would startle and move anyone, if they could make a certain effort of imagination and read it (the New Testament, and in particular the Gospel according to St. Matthew) freshy like a book, not droningly and dully like a portion of the Bible."

It was apparent to him that many people, whose faith was deep and steady, had no formal or explicit theology at all, even if their Scots reticence had allowed them to disclose so intimate a part of themselves. It was here that he placed the importance of good hymnology, for he thought the love of certain hymns, the living inside them, their "aroma", was for many their only mode of doing theology. It was that which made important the screening out of the banal, the sentimental, the triumphalist, both in words and music, for these threatened and cheapened the worship of the living God. Archie's long and loving service on both Hymnary Revision Committees (pre-1927 and 1963-73) was as deeply and toughly grounded in theology as in his musicology. He was firmly convinced that the handbook to the Church Hymnary was, next to Scripture, an indispensable tool for the parish minister. Once, when lecturing to some Glasgow Practical Theology students, he set them the task of selecting the ten worst hymns in the book, giving reasons for their choice; and he relished the memory of William Temple's comment on "Hark, hark my soul, angelic songs are swelling" as being a minor but indisputable indication of the existence of evil!

Even more important than the explicit theology of hymns was the implicit theology of action. For Archie, belief in God was not primarily a matter of intelligence but a matter of the will. This did not mean that people could screw themselves up to thinking six impossible things before breakfast. Rather it meant that the response to God, which might not always be self-conscious, was visible in life, not in speech. It was that which constituted in his mind the peculiar danger of a comfortable congregation, with no sense of the irony of the words in their unmenaced situation, singing lustily, "Take my life and let it be"; and of a church which verbally, even credally, affirmed its faith in God alone, and then argued the prudential case for nuclear weapons or laissez-faire capitalism. He was not Utopian about what people could manage, but an ethical position like Niebuhr's, accepting that gospel ideals were in principle impossible, seemed to him to be near-blasphemy, suggesting that God supplied light, but not the power to go with it. What he deplored was the moral shrugging of the shoulders, acceptance of failure, rather than faithful pursuit of the not yet attained, as our metier. For it seemed to him that, whatever the hiccoughs, transformation and strength were promised to faith. What he called "the ethicising of eschatology" was what lay behind both his pacifism and his ecumenism. Or to put it more simply, he believed that when Jesus, the potent healer said, "Go and sin no more", he meant it.

It was here too that he parted company with Barth, finding that his emphasis on the incapacity of the human to aspire to the demand of God cut the ethical nerve of the Gospel. He used to quote to his Biblical Studies students the naughty parody of Barth's position:

> "Sit down, O men of God!
> His Kingdom God will bring.
> Sit down and wait with folded hands;
> You cannot do a thing."

The Shelley quotation from which this chapter title comes was, to Archie, close to the heart of the matter. The shock of the lightning, exposing dark corners of the earth, and signalling God's capacity to search the furthest points of the world's experience; and the harmony of life responsive to the searching light were for him key categories. It was this confidence that the darkness did not have the last word which nerved his conviction that, against the odds, it was possible to earth the values of the Kingdom, and that it was the distinctive vocation of the Church to do precisely that.

12   The risks of establishment

"And for heaven's sake keep it dark
If the guardian of the Ark
Be a Presbytery Clerk
Fired by no exalting vision
Counting it his sacred mission
Just to go as grandpa went
By the light of precedent."

From A Nonogenarian's Rhyming Ruminations

Archie Craig's doctrine of the Church could not, in a sense, have been higher. It existed, he believed, "to be an incarnate word of God to men." Yet he could say, speaking at the Diamond Jubilee of Colinton parish church Women's Guild, "The church is dying of churchliness." Precisely because his vision was of a community through which the love of God would actually be made palpable to the outside world, he was sometimes shocked by the introversion and unadventurousness of the institution to which he belonged. The discrepancy between the words of salvation and the accredited bearer of them reminded him of a procession he had once seen in Sauchiehall Street in Glasgow. There, around the time of the First World War, he had seen a group of men carrying placards which affirmed the Biblical promises of immortal life. Archie's comment was, "I found it hard to attend to the placards. I could not help looking at the sandwichmen, broken down old men who stumbled along like symbols and advertisements of death."

What disturbed him most was not the spectacular evils of church history, the savagery of the Crusades, the ferocity of the Inquisition, the persecution of Jews; these at least were crimes of misguided passion. It was, rather, the contented mediocrity of a church without fire in its belly, a church ruminant instead of militant, and therefore betraying the Gospel.

In his Cunningham Lectures, Archie characterises some of the danger signs:

"Have you never attended a congregational meeting at which the successful tithing of mint and cummin have been jubilantly reported? Have you never sensed through all the life of the church a fear of the infinite, a longing for some enclave of safety from holiness rather than for salvation into it, a longing for some system of collective moral security so roofed in and curtained that no uncomfortable shaft of light from heaven can break into it?"

In a different gear, he could make the same point by gentle teasing. He loved telling the story of the beadle, training his son to take on the job, who ended his catalogue of specific dos and don'ts with the words, "Above all, William, resist a' improvements." And he commended the "impressive daftness" needed the church by comparing it with the petition offered at the installation of a new president of the Woman's Guild: "Lord, give her grace, we beseech Thee, never to do anything unprecedented."

That this was a travesty of the church's mission was the clear implication of Archie's conviction that Christian faith was adventuring, not hugging the shore, but heading out for open sea. From the days of his early preaching in Galston, he sought to appeal to the positive motives of honour and chivalry and heroism in people (for all that he was doctrinally committed with Calvin to believe that human beings were not natively friends with God). He spoke with admiration of those who were "spiritually debonair" (the quality which had first attracted him to George MacLeod), or were mountaineers of the spirit, like George Stewart, whose description of the thrill of prayer reminded Archie of Tensing talking about Everest. His vision was of exciting possibilities, of men made "formidably good, creatively good, good enough to fight for great causes, to labour and struggle and suffer, losing themselves in the task of re-creating the world". He acknowledged that the church was, of course, an asylum too for weak, gentle and tired people, "refugees from the world's life," but went on:

> "but these refugees must not begin to think they are the only pebbles on the church's beach, and that the supreme function of the church is to dispense spiritual cyclobarbitone tablets to chronic invalids, and not also, and more importantly in a sense, to tonic and arm the strong for fighting."

It was not that Archie was opposed to the idea of an established church, and certainly not to the idea of a parish. He was proud of the Christian history of Scotland, which had the vision of the Reformation so enfibred in its corporate soul that it was proper to be scandalised that a Director of Education did not know the First Book of Discipline. He believed that it was the Christian understanding of each created person being valuable in God's sight which undergirded so much of the country's law, as, for example, when a costly enough enquiry was set up to investigate the death of a window-cleaner who had slipped while cleaning windows in Bank Street. It seemed to him a privilege to belong to a nation which could still, with some truth, see the voice of the General Assembly as the voice of the people, and he was proud of a heritage in which, for instance, ordinary workmen in manual trades could have subscribed the publication of an edition of Luther's sermons.

But he saw that it all contained latent dangers. Above all, once the Church was institutionalised it could easily become so fond of hugging to itself its historic traditions that they became a winding-sheet rather than a suit of fighting armour. What should have been stability degenerated into inertia.

> "Establishment, to use the current jargon, will always form the ballast of any society: and by far the most important part of Establishment is the unblazoned, unsensational, submerged two-thirds of it: and a chief criterion by which any social institution is to be judged concerns the balance it holds between conservation and change, between a well-tried and tested past and a beckoning future: between the risk of rusting into archaism and rushing into anarchy."

Quite often, in the aftermath of his Moderatorial year, Archie would ask church groups if they did not think that "our church life sometimes looks, and in fact is, far too rooted and rutted", thus making it difficult to get an alert hearing for new ideas, or a fair trial for experiments. This disease, otherwise known as *encephalitis lethargia ecclesiastica* might or might not prove terminal, but it certainly called for drastic remedial intervention, if the proper level of "supple adaptibility" was to be recovered.

The core of efficacious curative power was, Archie believed, in the return to "feed at the central flame," which meant the Word rightly preached, prayer rightly practised, sacraments rightly administered and the unobtrusive life of faith communicated in the everyday contacts of believers with their neighbours.

On each of these topics, Archie at various times enlarged, though he claimed to know "as little about the niceties of liturgical rectitude as about the fine points of breeding in spaniels or schipperkes". But he had a very delicate nose for what was authentic and what inauthentic worship.

He had seen enough of the gap between rich and poor to find that there was "something closely akin to farce when a prosperous congregation, comfortably poised between a good sermon and a good dinner, rises and sings

> "they met the tyrant's brandished steel,
> the lion's gory mane,
> they bowed their necks the death to feel;
> Who follows in their train?"

If the farce was enacted in the presence of the unchurched the tone changed. It then became "a matter of well-justified anger and disgust when the promise of heavenly mansions is held out to slum dwellers by BOURGEOIS PIETISTS living in fat comfort in the West End." (Even in heaven Archie hoped *not* to find effortless ease in surroundings of absolute comfort!)

At every level and in every aspect of church life, he was sensitive to the mismatch between words and action, and responded to it with tart incisiveness:

> "If the evangelist preaches glowingly about the friendship of Christ, and the fellowship of the local congregation is as warm as an iceberg, there is no occasion for astonishment that evangelism should not prosper."

or

> "It is all very fine to claim illumination in the context of a church service, and then to refuse to sit beside a man in the bus because he smells of fish."

He noticed too, and was concerned about the impact of the church on children and young people. How awful, to come in from a beautiful country road to a dingy, ugly, tawdry building. How awful to have to fidget through a ten-minute prayer by a Sunday-school superintendent, who would have been better "on his knees for half-an-hour before he comes to the school", and who might then have shown, as well as talking about, the mercy of Christ.

Fallibility and actual failure were, of course, to be expected. As Archie ruefully put it, "The old Adam has a habit of turning up to watch his own funeral." What was not to be expected in lives turned over to Christ was *complacency* about the failure, a total absence of the sense that here was something to be confessed, wrestled with and forgiven. For if the contrast between the harmony of word and deed in the master did not shame the discord between them in the servant, the allegiance was questionable.

Archie's greatest anger and dismay was reserved for the corporate failure of those in the ordained ministry, who dared to take the Word of God upon their lips while betraying it by their attitudes and actions. He never expressed this, never felt it probably, as if he were one who was himself free from fault, and was therefore able to voice the concern without seeming superior or dissociated.

Chief among clerical vices he rates a totally false sense of the importance of the ordained ministry. That it *was* important he had not the slightest doubt, since it was, at least in principle, a competent way of providing trained expositors of the Scriptures and pastors of congregations. But its importance was to *service* the 99% of Christian men and women whose vocation lay in the secular world. Without that sense of their role as merely supportive of and auxiliary to the basic outreach and worship of the whole congregation in its community, ministers would, almost inevitably, misrepresent what they stood for. Their specific remit, to order public worship, to preach, to be occupied with the offices of organised religion could so easily be mistaken as the *raison d'être* of the church, whereas it took the whole life of the whole body of Christians in the world to indicate what the church really was. When ministers forgot this, they lapsed into a ore absurd sense of their cosmic significance. God did not love clergymen more dearly than chemists, or find ministers more interesting than miners.

In his Galston days, Archie expressed the wish that the church would ordain its lay people to whatever secular vocation was theirs. (He thought there were some limits to this: distillery workers, for instance, could not in good faith dedicate their lifework to Christ!) One of his favourite stories, which he cited over and over again, was Anatole France's tale of the Virgin and the juggler. In this, the juggler Barnabas decides to join a monastic community, the better to serve God, and promises to renounce his worldly activities as a juggler. The weeks pass, and the poor man finds himself less and less able to offer praise in the terms of the monastic rule. At last, he goes one day and slips back to the monastery chapel, where he begins to juggle in front of the statue of the Virgin. As it happens, the other monks find him there, and are about to drag him from the place for his outrageous sacrilege. Just at that point, however, the Virgin steps down from her plinth, and wipes sweat from the juggler's brow.

Ordination was, in Archie's judgement, marking out for a specific task, but, as he repeatedly said when he took part in ordination services:

> "These ordination vows are neither more stringent nor more sacred than the earlier vows you took when you became a communicant member of the church. What they have done is to define and limit the field of service."

It was a correlate of this limitation that what had to be done should be as well done as possible, and that failure here would have wide repercussions. The sober warning which often accompanied the giving of charges when Archie did it, was:

> "There is hardly anything more tragically damaging to the cause of Christ, or more drearily sapping of the churches' vitality than a shabby or shoddy ministry of the Word and Sacraments."

About the abuse of the Word, Archie could be devastatingly sardonic. He loved to remind people of Oscar Wilde's line, "The Commons said nothing: the Lords Temporal had nothing to say. The Lords Spiritual had nothing to say, and said it." And he began an after-lunch speech to the Glasgow Rotarians with the words, "The most damaging criticism that can be levelled at any speech is that the speaker was aiming at nothing in particular and proved himself an accurate shot." The temptation to empty verbosity as an occupational hazard of being "asked to say a few words" was colossal; and chief among the thirty counsels for preachers which Russell Maltby had gathered together, it was the last which Archie most often cited: "You may never finish, but you can always stop!" Without self-discipline here, the general public would be vindicated in its conviction that a minister was a kind of automatic talking-machine, into which a penny may be dropped at any moment, and out of which a stream of words ought to flow until the mechanism is wound down.

He loved the unselfconscious absurdities of ministers, and would quote them with a deep chortle which took from the situation any sting of malice. Thinking himself that any minute over twenty for a sermon required double justification, he quoted with glee the minister who explained, "I canna possibly preach for less than forty minutes, for it takes me twenty minutes to get the congregation well into hell, an' far mair than twenty to get them weel oot o' it." And having all his life felt he dare not preach from certain texts which were "too high" for him, he found huge pleasure in the opening sentence of a highland divinity student preaching his first sermon: "My subject this morning is the past, the present and the future of the Almighty."

Nothing which smacked of affectation or humbug missed his penetrating appraisal, and he had a treasury of quotations on which to draw. As he saw it, real intimacy with God never paraded or flaunted itself, which was one ground for his distrust of some charismatic testimony. While not in the least doubting that the Holy Spirit was active in the life of the church, he was reluctant to identify the activity with the special phenomena of pentecostalist groups. One of his commonplace book extracts was a passage from Trevor-Roper about a man who, "by the affectation of sustained panting during the sermon, simulated a particular intimacy with the Holy Spirit." Archie distrusted emotion "unballasted by thought nor harnessed to the will."

As he deplored the abuse of the pulpit by longwindedness, triviality, rambling, evasiveness or bombast, so he was quick-eared for the abuse of public prayer. He often led retreats or study days for groups of clergy, and warned them against prayers really addressed to the congregation, with some idea that God may be eavesdropping and highly gratified to hear himself so well spoken of. Similarly, he disapproved of news bulletin prayers: "Lord, Thou knowest that the King and Queen have this morning set sail for India . . . ."

Hymn singing too had its dangers, the more so when the hymns were familiar and well-tuned classics with swelling words of the spiritual life, which could be sung, "much as the old-fashioned hurdy-gurdy, with a monkey sitting on top of it, used to grind out *Annie Laurie* and *The Bonnie Banks o' Loch Lomond*." Careless hymn-singing and hymn-choosing offended Archie's sense of how much it mattered what people sang together, and he was extremely distressed by the random peppercasting of hymns which had no integrated part in the structure of a service.

137

Above all, the central risk of the institution, established and codified, was that it could forget that its meaning was love. Everything else to do with structure, liturgy, pastoral discipline was to be determined by that. Archie in fact reiterated on many occasions his moral conviction that a Puritan church was a thousand times preferable to a lax one, and that Pharisaism was a lesser sin than antinomianism; so he wanted no antithesis between law and love, seeing the former as a mode of structuring the latter. But he recognised that, on Scottish soil, religious anarchy was thin on the ground, and that legalism was much more likely to be the local problem. Contextually, he was

> "Speaking from within the Protestant tradition, and remembering the dangerous love of human beings, and especially of ecclesiastical human beings for clear-cut, authoritative rules and formulas out of which they may build static, defensive fortresses, colleges of inquisitors & dungeons for offenders: and within which they may settle down with dangerously clear consciences to the living death of legalism."

The actual lovelessness of church structures which were intended to manifest the brotherliness of the gospel wounded him deeply. He once confided to a ministers' group, meeting in Leighton House, Dunblane, a musing which was immensely self-disclosing:

> "I wonder if it's true that my generation of ministers never really knew the inner secret of fellowship *in the faith*; lived and moved tricked in disguises, alien to the rest of men and alien to ourselves; hidden behind the conventionalities of church life, hidden and starving.
>
> I've certainly come away from meetings of Presbytery feeling desperately lonely and starved. I've certainly come down from the pulpit feeling as though it had been a tomb, and I had not been dead in it, but had shouted for help without result. I wonder if, somehow or other, "fellowship" in the churches isn't sometimes the contiguity of marbles in a bag, touching minimally within a surrounding emptiness."

From a man who had served the church for over fifty years at the time, these were awful words. Perhaps Archie only risked such directness because he found it difficult, as he wrote to one old lady, "to thaw out my fellow-ministers." The disappointment is in one way a measure of how *uncynical* he was about the Presbyterian courts, for to *expect* Presbytery to be a nourishing and sustaining experience would be rare enough among ministers to be conspicuous. But then, Archie's earliest experience of the system had been in a Kelso manse, where his father would invite the whole Presbytery home after the meeting for tea and merry conversation.

What maintained Archie's faith in the church, not just as hope against the odds of sight, but as lived experience, was the undemonstrative quiet goodness of men and women he knew. He wrote, for instance, to Robert Begg, minister emeritus at Kippen, after his wife's funeral:

"This kind of tribute to a lovely quiet, serene, church-nurtured, church-centred life, outgoing in love and service, through shine and shade – this kind of tribute is the best kind of indication of what is best and deepest and loveliest and most lasting in the church's witness to God. No room for dejection so long as this thread of gold runs unbroken among all the less authentic strands."

It was not by quantitative measurement that Archie made the value judgment against all the weight of accusation which he knew the church deserved. He admitted with candour at a pre-Lund meeting that, "the wider you look in space and time, the more material you will find for your picture of a re-re-revolting institution." Yet the quality of some lives, even of some faces; of some parishes where the spirit of loving, prayerful service had got in through the pores as well as through the ears, these seemed to him such gold among the dross as to vindicate faith. The most significant fact was that the church had survived centuries of murky history, still able to inspire and invigorate such living, rare as it might be.

Archie' vision of the *reformanda* aspect of the church was more to do with the renewal of faith than with the altering of structures. He confessed to worry, in his typically unstrident and unbrutal way, that the energies of the church were going into relatively superficial questions of management, and that the Anderson Report and the Committee of Forty (successive Church of Scotland working parties in the seventies which spent many collective years on how the church could adapt to the needs of the late twentieth century) were dealing only with peripheral questions.

In this context, he had a running conversation with Norman Orr, a minister on both committees, who wanted to defend the concern with structures as a proper *faith* question, precisely to do with what incarnating the Gospel meant, particularly in urban contexts, where parishes were increasingly unnatural ways of defining community. At one point, in 1975, aware of Norman's personal concern as to the next stage of his own ministry after a robust University chaplaincy job, Archie wrote to him:

"Sometimes I have a kind of misty vision of a time for which men like you are being prepared, a very hard & sore time for the Church, which will call for insights and qualities of character not possessed by the ministers of my generation & only begun to be glimpsed by yours . . . .

At any rate, I feel in my bones & marrow that you & others like you will be much needed at some future date, however disappointing the situation may be just now in some of its aspects; and also, at any rate, that disappointment is often the school in which God trains men & women for some difficult task he has in store for them."

Above all, and more important even than the remarkable willingness to be open, uncensorious and hopeful in the face of an apparently declining institution, was the trust that the church's life was not to be justified by its works, but by the love and promise of God that it was the Bride of Christ. Deeper than all the criticism, that was the bulwark against despair. It was God's definition of the church, and not its self-understanding which identified it. And that definition loosened up the tense, potentially panicky introspection of ecclesiastical institutions. Archie's account of it unpacks the meaning of catholicity:

"This inclusive, comprehensive, unfastidious society which welcomes everybody on exactly the same terms, butcher, baker and candlestick-maker on the same terms as the learned scholar and the rich magnate and the cabinet minister. Note how wide is the conception I have uttered, I, a Presbyterian minister, include the candlestickmaker."

It was this potential for actualising catholicity, for manifesting the generosity of God which made Archie able to "bear all things" in relation to the churches' actual flaws and failures. And it was that which seemed him to make it vital that the internal divisions of Christendom should be visibly overcome, lest the inclusive love of God be misrepresented.

13   Towards symphony

"For we build citadels around our lives against each other, hoping thus
to find security, and fearing lest fellowship should rob us of our freedom.
So we blaspheme thee with our lives, even while we bless thee with our
lips, and run upon death, mistaking it for life and bliss."

Broadcast prayer

Archie's commitment to ecumenism was a direct implicate of what he
believed about the love and providence of God. It was, so to speak, the concrete
lateral extension in the life of the church of the inclusive, comprehensive,
unfastidious offer of salvation to all creation.

From the fifties onward, he was so identified with the controversial proposals
of the Bishops' Report that he admitted in the mid-seventies to being rather
sick, not of ecumenism, but of speaking about it; and of feeling like a scratchy
gramophone record worn by overplaying. He did, however, diligently accept
endless invitations to explain, defend and promulgate his vision of a united
church, since he felt that the "dogged processes of education" were the main
natural channel of progress. The supernatural channels were hidden in the
ripening time of God, and the mystery of prayer.

Archie was well aware of the risks of ecumenical self-righteousness, and
deplored it. In every context, he believed, to identify yourself with God against
your opponents was to prove your distance from him. It is therefore important
to assess how his wholehearted commitment to the Ecumenical Movement,
and his conviction that the Spirit of God was behind it, was compatible with
his sense of how tentative human truth-claims had to be. He was constantly
reiterating in sympathetic ecumenical circles the caveat:

"We who follow the ecumenical way must all the time be trenchantly
self critical, and give genuinely humble attention to the criticisms
directed at us, for the deadliest and subtlest enemy of every movement
is spiritual pride, especially the corporate kind."

The risk of detaching unity from renewal weighed heavily with him, and he
was scornful of the kind of "ecclesiological joinery" which would simply tack
together small pockets of cosy tribalism or of clerical self-exaltation. He was
open enough to hear the question of a friend who heard him express distress
about Lund: "Does it matter very much if conferences like Lund mark time?
Would you really expect much life to emerge by tying corpses together?" The

light by which ecumenical moves had to be judged was a "large enough ecumenical ideal, one to which the pursuit of Christian unity is integral, but which also all the time includes the missionary motives and the motive denoted by the words of *Life and Work, and connoting the claiming of the whole world for the empire of Christ.*"

That this should be also expressed in the structural life of the churches was not a timeless generalisation, but a vocation of the twentieth century Christian community. Archie was convinced that the Reformation had been necessary in its day, there being no other way, given papal reaction to internal Catholic reform movements, of witnessing to the freedom and truth of the Gospel. He saw in the growth of the denominations an instance of the way in which God would bring good out of evil:

> "God has over-ruled the sin which has entered into their divisions by granting to each of them in their separatedness special and unique gifts, e.g. grace and beauty in worship, fruitful emphasis on laity, devotion to preaching of the Word etc."

He was convinced that the practice of "unliturgical" and specific prayer was a valuable complement to the timelessness of set forms, and that the Presbyterian expression of the priesthood of all believers in the parity of ministers and elders in church courts was a valuable asset to the emerging church.

He even saw the immense competitive missionary outreach of the 19th century as a providential use of the church's divisions, making the initial urgency of evangelisation as thorough and wide-ranging as could be; and he was insistent that whatever shape the church of the future took, it should retain the splendid loyalties and achievements, virtues and values of separated branches of the church.

His basic stance, therefore, was not defensive and apologetic, a kind of Protestant grovelling for the sins of division. He was clear that there were elements of Romanism still unacceptable to Protestant conscience, and therefore on the agenda for any deep and serious conversation. But for deep and serious conversation, levels of trust had to be built up, requiring at least enough closeness to be within hailing distance, and at best, a sense that the conversation partner was a fellow-Christian with a different God-given perspective, from whom one had something to learn. It seemed to him that Vatican II had initiated a genuinely new phase of Roman Catholic/Protestant relations, and that the impetus of that should be sustained, not because it was easy or obvious, but because it was the next difficult rock overhang on the way up the uncharted hill of God.

What made him so confident that the Ecumenical Movement of the twentieth century was to be identified with the beckoning of God? In the first instance, it was the pressure of the younger churches, stated over and over again in the missionary conferences which followed the historic meeting in Edinburgh in 1910. The particular statement to this effect, from the Willingen Conference, quoted by the Church of Scotland's Inter-Church Relations committee, ran:

"Division in the Church distorts its witness, frustrates its mission, and contradicts its own nature. If the Church is to demonstrate the Gospel in its life as well as in its preaching, it must manifest to the world the power of God to break down all barriers and to establish the church's unity in Christ . . . .

We believe that unity of the churches is an essential condition of effective witness and advance. In the hands of the younger churches divided witness is a crippling handicap. We of the younger churches feel this very keenly. While unity may be desirable in the lands of the older churches, it is imperative in those of the younger churches."

This verdict seemed to Archie to be more worthy of attention than the various pleas of the old-established churches, if only because his gardening experience produced a suggestive analogy, that the vitality of a herbaceous clump is at its greatest round the edges: at the centre it is apt to be rootbound and desiccated.

The second reason for undoing the divisions of the past was that Britain itself, like the rest of Western Europe and the senior countries of the Commonwealth, was once again missionary territory. It seemed to Archie, sensitised by his experience of the *Religion and Life* weeks, and by twenty years of close encounter with the student world, that there really was a massive culture-gap between the axioms of the churches and the assumptions of the secular culture, a gap in doctrine and world-view, in ethics and in normative patterns for living. In trying to bridge that gap, it seemed to him, denominational differences were at least 95% irrelevant, a kind of specialised question in a Special Honours paper once all the general papers had been competently dealt with! To impose the divisions of the past, intelligible as they had been in the context, upon a sceptical world, struck him as a criminal irrelevance.

It was not that church unity was, in itself, a gospel, but it was, rather, a medicine to restore soundness and energy to the gospel-bearing churches, for he had no doubt that in the mid-twentieth century, "denominational Christianity was diseased Christianity." Much as he enjoyed some formulations of denominational pride – (one favourite was Dean Inge's, "the Church of England observeth a mean way between the meretricious gaudiness

143

of Rome and the squalid sluttery of conventicles") — he was clear that such confessional triumphalism was no longer tolerable. This judgment seemed to him to be confirmed by the *reductio ad absurdum* of the fission and splintering of the fabric of western Christendom as it was found above all in the U.S.A. He would quote, with slightly mischievous glee, from *The Yearbook of American Churches*, in which "the Church of the Universal Redemption" had twenty-nine members, and "the Church of Universal Emancipation gallantly reports as the firstfruits and earnest of Universal Emancipation a total of eighteen souls".

For a man who appreciated the loneliness of the prophet in the face of conventional religion, numbers, of course, proved nothing. But what seemed to him the give-away danger signal in such sectarian enclaves, and in the larger ghettoes of denominational pride was how happy they were with their isolation. In a paper on "Unity and Uniformity", given sometime after the Bishops' Report, Archie tries to articulate the difference between "desirable unity in essentials" and the kind of deadly uniformity that would cramp the variety and diversity of gifts and insights within a united church. He recognises the frequent plea that the church is all the better, and not any the worse for its different denominations, catering as they do for different types, styles, and manifestations of faith. This position is often combimned with the contention that *spiritual* unity is the real target, and may be combined with the continuation of the present denominations, more or less in their present form, though perhaps with some kind of federal relationship.

This seems to him, however, to be a weak position, even in relation to classical Reformation ecclesiology, far less to Pauline or early church understanding, where the commitment was still to identify theologically and pastorally the *one Church* (which is why such bitter disputes arose about inter-communion). It is not the church's business to be conformed to the sectarian groupings which are natural to human society in many spheres, but to challenge them. And if the challenge is merely verbal, not manifestly incarnated in the new creation of the church, it can be dismissed as a pious fiction. Besides, he suggests, is it not the case that the loudest cries against "monolithic uniformity" are raised by those who *want* a bogey-man to frighten people away from the costliness of working for unity? And may this not be a sort of unconscious hypocrisy, masking what is at bottom their own fear "lest the darling uniformities of their own denominational groups may have to be modified?"

What exactly were the modifications likely to be involved in the unity process was not clear to Archie, and indeed he thought they could not in principle be clear, since the situation was one in which the only thing to be said was *solvitur ambulando*. Ecumenical faith was not sight, as indeed no faith was sight, and the invitation to the denominations was not to sail for a visible harbour, but to be willing to slip their denominational moorings and set out towards open sea, committed to a common journey. He was clear that the sail would be no bland exchange of courteous pleasantries, and always reminded groups that "Everything the Christian knows about fellowship has been learned at the foot of a cross." But his experience of the actual costly ecumenical growth in understanding and trust through the British Council of Churches and the World Council of Churches had about it the taste of resurrection. It was in the context of speaking about the road to Christian unity that he most often invoked the image of an Arabic phrase sent him by a friend: *"February with wintry weather and cold sad blasts of wind, and the smell of summer in it."*

Certainly, as far as Scotland was concerned, he was clear that it was not July. When assessing what had gone on between 1952 and 1972, he came to the sad conclusion,

> "This failure, [of top-level negotiations between Presbyterians and Episcopalians and between Presbyterians and Congregationalists] must be interpreted to mean that Scotland has not been inspired by the vision of a Great Church which would incorporate the best features of the three historic traditions of church structure and government, and so has not given, or has not yet given, the lead in that great matter for which so many of us hoped.
>
> I am not forgetting, of course, that these top-level activities are still being pursued . . . . and pray that the "Multilateral Conversations" report will justify hope that a deadlock may be broken through.
>
> But, in default of that happening, I think I shall find myself forced to the conclusion that the admirable principle of Sabbatical rest should be applied to formal top-level negotiations."

This never meant, in Archie's mind, that belief in and prayer for a re-united Church of Scotland should be abandoned. (In fact in the fifties he had been involved with a couple of hundred other people on both sides of the border with another George MacLeod scheme called the *Panel of Advocates of the Church of Britain,* a venture presumably scuppered without trace by the sinking of the Bishops' Report. He thought that nothing less could body forth unmistakably, for all to see, that the Christian Fellowship was one in faith, hope and love.

What it did mean was that both the time-scale and the order of procedure might need to be revised. He thought it an error, though an error of commendable enthusiasm, that the Nottingham Conference of 1964 had pledged itself to aim for the inauguration of union by 1980. For there was no timetabling possible, he thought, for the slow processes needed to break through the amazing insulation of the denominations from one another, "shut up in our denominational enclaves." One could not put triggers to the ear of the Holy Spirit, far less the General Assembly!

"We must be both patient and impatient", he once said to a missionary conference, "the balance between the two being kept by sensitiveness to the leading of God's spirit. Still, I think you can reckon on the home-churches overdoing the patience bit, ... so you can be forgiven if you a little overweight the impatient end of the scale."

He was convinced that a central role in the process lay with the ecumenical theologians on Faith and Order issues, and regretted that the churches were inclined to dismiss them as peripheral to their own lives. In particular, he thought the central area to be explored was the connection between Christology (on which there was a large measure of agreement) and ecclesiology (on which there was not, especially as regards issues of ministry).

He was utopian neither about the coming church, nor about the apostolic one. Indeed he found it comforting that "for honest, sharp, prolonged ecclesiastical dispute there is apostolic precedent." But precisely that fired his commitment to work for reconciliation, for he saw in Acts 15 "not a hint that anyone proposed as a good way out of the difficulty the setting up of denominations, 'Orthodox Petrine and Jacobean' and 'United Pauline Gentilist'."

While the slow patient work of ecumenical theology was underway, the main progress, he came to think, would be not on the level of formal negotiating structures, but on a more domestic scale, at what has come to be called the grassroots level. He was comforted in his dismay about what looked like ecumenism in Scotland "grinding to an ignominious halt" by words of William James:

"I believe in the invisible molecular moral forces that work from individual to individual, stealing in through the crannies of the world like so many soft rootlets, or like the capillary oozing of water, and yet rending the hardest monuments of man's pride, if you give them time."

As signals of hope he cited the setting up of Scottish Churches' House, Dunblane; the Kirk Week experiences; the ecumenical experiment in Livingston New Town; and the existing co-operation in the sphere of Christian Aid. He was clear that England was further along this road of "grassroots ecumenism" than Scotland, mainly, in his judgment, because the latter had remained "largely immune to the beneficial virus" of the *Religion and Life* weeks. Even thirty years later, they seem to him to be a paradigm of the *right* kind of ecumenism; to have sprung out of concern for the setting right of the national life, not of church life; to have been focused on issues like home, education, commerce and industry, and not on what he called the "lice-hunting of ecclesiastical introspection." This did not mean that he wanted to polarise *Faith and Order* over against *Life and Work* to the detriment of the former. It was rather that he thought *Faith and Order* only got into gear and out of neutral under the pressure of questions which had to do with the life and death of the world.

He was well aware that ecumenical conversation might mask denominational empire-building intentions, and sensitive therefore to the need for almost ruthless self-scrutiny as to motive.

Long before the word was fashionable, he was insisting that the various conversations and negotiations must consist of genuine dialogue and not of a series of partisan monologues masquerading as dialogue.

"The Pharisee in the Temple prayed *with himself*, and thanked God that he was not as other men. There can be *Faith and Order* conferring of the same quality, the parties to it saying, "We are of Paul! We of Apollos! We of Cephas!" and some even having the assurance to say in an equally exclusive way, "And we of Christ!" No genuine listening for a voice from God through another's lips! No real, aching hunger for an advance in unity! Only a fixed determination to assert and defend a given point of view! How boring it can be! And how spiritually shaming when claim and counter-claim become edged with rancour and passion!"

In effect then, the pressure towards ecumenical risk seemed to Archie to be one with the pressure of the Sermon on the Mount which was so crucial to his entire ministry — a challenge to risk what, without God, was impossible — the genuine possibility of being more concerned about the planks in one's own eye than about the specks in one's neighbours, the actual realisation of love for the neighbour as potent and energetic.

He could, of course, also appreciate the day-to-day benefits which an integrated Church might bring; the end of wastefully overlapping effort; the pooling of scattered and straggling attempts to deal with problems which needed massively concentrated force; the orchestral elation of harmonies which had so far been practised only as the piccolo line or the trombone line in isolation. But the core of his commitment was not pragmatic but evangelical; a matter not of prudence, but of the deep repentance that was the only proper response to a God whose eye was sound and generous, and who promised that we should, in seeing him as he is, become like him. ·

14 Caesar, Christ and conscience

"Not yet has the church pioneered with any conspicious gallantry in the matter of peace. The image here is of a burglared house in which the householder comes downstairs, armed with a poker, and behind him comes his wife, exhorting him to trounce the malefactor, but not to get hurt any more in the process than he can help. The Church is the Bride of Christ, not the mistress of Caesar."

From a sermon, "What do ye more than others?" Armistice, 1935

Speaking in the thirties on "Ways of Peacemaking", Archie felt able to take it for granted that theology was supremely relevant to politics, and indeed, that any political schemes which did not take account of theology were like the sand-castles which children build on the shore. As with ecumenism, the central issue for him about political decision-making was whether or not faith meant trusting the power of God as actually effective, here and now, and not just in some transformed future, quite discontinuous with the realm of our moral effort. It seemed to him that not so to trust was a failure of Christian nerve, and even, particularly, of Protestant nerve. He was very sympathetic to a point made by Congar in *Divided Christendom*, which he quoted from time to time, that "Extreme Protestants do not believe in the real and actual gift of the Divine Life to human nature. They believe that this life is only promised, albeit truly promised, and it is regarded as purely eschatological."

If the church took seriously the claim that Jesus Christ is indeed God of God, the commands of the Sermon on the Mount could not be heard with a kind of distancing superior judgment that it would, of course, be naïve to take them as real marching orders. He deplored the position of Niebuhr in *Moral Man and Immoral Society*, where he suggests:

"Redemption is really deliverance from blindness to the inescapable tragedy of mortal existence, plus a hope beyond the grave [Congar's point!].Revelation thus involves no radical breach in the historical order regarded as the plane of moral effort, but only an illumination by which men are enabled to recognise sin as sin and to look for mercy at the last."

Archie's pacifism began (and very nearly ended) with the conviction that the revelation of God in Christ is a communication of power as well as an effusion of light; that the categories of social or political determinism are shattered by the irruption of Christ into our history, creating *from the point of entry onwards* a new order of existence which relativises the previous sanities of prudent common-sense. Unless one risked the new ethics of the Kingdom, it was mere pietism to affirm, for instance, the Chalcedonian definition of Christ's being. If one said on the one hand, "It's all very well for him, but not for us", that was *effectively* denying his real humanness. If, however, one said, "Well, first century enthusiasm in the light of mistaken expectations about the end of time" then one was *effectively* denying his identity as God.

In the same Armistice sermon from which the burglar-chasing image comes, Archie articulates this conviction about power and risk most directly, in the context of the responsibility of the Christian state (a category which in 1935 he could still use of Britain without irony or cynicism):

> "I believe that the teaching of Jesus does apply to state morality . . . .
> The world is resuming the old fatal way of competitive armament . . .
> because the so-called Christian states were too rich in prudence and fear,
> and too poor in penitence and faith. I believe that a new era will be
> ushered in, when, and only when, the Christian state ventures out upon
> the Christian thin ice . . . .
>
> Unilateral disarmament is not any kind of magic wand. Nevertheless,
> I do believe in unilateral disarmament in obedience to the word of Jesus
> and in the image of his death. Some day God will raise up a statesman
> . . . . I am nationalist enough to pray that that statesman will be a Briton
> and a Scot."

Archie was not persuaded by the kind of rationalisation which took the sting, so to speak, out of the commands of God. Both in personal and in corporate morality, he was clear that there was no guarantee that turning the other cheek would disarm the enemy. It might indeed goad him to further brutality. It was not the result, in that important but limited sense, which mattered. What counted was the fidelity. All the Biblical imagery, Abraham willing to sacrifice Isaac, Peter willing to step out upon the water, were to him prototypes of this kind of extravagant obedience, unsanctioned by any of the standard criteria of sane or responsible behaviour. The walking on the water story was a key one for Archie. At one point he suggested that if he were told he had the chance to preach only one sermon in his life, it would be on that story. But he did not blink the established factual and causal connections between events. As he said in another context, "There is a very sound traditional and prudential case for not trying to walk on water, and we had certainly better not try it — unless Christ commands it."

There is a remarkable parallelism between Archie's ecumenism and his pacifism. In both cases, one was dealing with commitment "against the odds"; with a renewal of reconciled co-existence on the horizontal level with one's fellows as testimony to the potent reconciliation wrought by God; and in both desperately aware of the need for self-scrutiny as to motive and intent. On one occasion, he reminded his fellow-pacifists:

"It is our plain duty to examine ourselves continually for the faults which are often laid against us — incompleteness in our understanding of the divine revelation, disproportion in our thinking, a militancy of attitude which consorts ill with our fundamental thesis, above all, spiritual pride, as though we were the people and wisdom would die with us."

Instead, as he believed, God would in the end sift wheat from chaff in all partial human apprehensions of the Divine truth.

This conviction that no-one sees it whole but God, rather than paralysing him, simply tempered his pacifism with the deepest courtesy and respect for those who had wrestled with the issue and come to the opposite conclusion. In the years before the Second World War, when he was a member of the Church of Scotland Peace Group, he found, as the thirties advanced, friends coming to the painful conclusion that there was no alternative to war, and he seems never to have harangued or scorned their personal decision. And his deep experience of simultaneous shared faith and divergent political readings of God's will in the Cloister Group confirmed his sense that, while he could take no other stance, he could not de-Christianise those who did. Not for him an orthopraxis which excommunicated others.

Even when speaking to boys of call-up age in the fifties, he was so far from pressurising them towards pacifism that he actually pointed out the reservations he had about his own advocacy of the position. These were

"i)   that being a minister in his sixties, he had never had to pay any considerable price of suffering for his pacifism;
ii)   that he had a profound respect for the "military virtues", comradeliness, loyalty, discipline, decisiveness etc.;
iii) that there were various forms of pacifism with which he had no sympathy, sentimental idealism, squeamishness erected into sanctity, prudential pacifism, the kind of passive resistance which is still an act of coercive intent, and the militant pacifism whose spirit is still aggressive."

What he specified as the only kind of pacifism he was advocating was "theological or Christian pacifism", which was a commitment to take the way of the Cross in relation to whatever assailant. This meant recognising the "haunting tune of action" with which Jesus "set to deeds" the way of God's opposition to evil. That way, he recognised, was quite horrifying to the instincts of the natural man, repugnant even to his moral sense of justice. But to believe in God's forgiveness, to receive it, was precisely to accept the overthrow of "normal" morality; for God maintained unswerving goodwill towards every assailant, and refused to retaliate. Even for God, the cost of this was the apparent "satanic checkmate" of the cross. For us, fragile in mortality, it meant holding the like goodwill and the like refusal "livingly together to the utmost human limit — which is death — in the faith that death is not a limit for God, but can be transfigured by Him into resurrection."

What Archie consistently called "ethics" was in some ways so antithetical to ethical commonsense that his entitlement to use the word might be disputed. Most moral philosophers who take seriously any view of there being an objective right and wrong simultaneously credit man with some native facility for recognising or intuiting good and bad, normally called conscience. Archie himself appealed to that occasionally *en passant*, using phrases like "any decent man" or "anyone capable of moral reflection." Pacifism did not belong here for him. It was in one sense a heroic stance, entirely inspired and enabled by the impact of standing at the foot of the cross, where all heroism and all ignominy were put in perspective. At the same time, Archie thought that such an attitude was widely recognised and even steadily practised by many people on the domestic scale, for instance, by parents who, "by a blend of limitless patience and steadfast beneficence" would "gradually convince the small egotist of the stupidity of egotism, and nurture good social character."

What the church and the Christian state needed to do was to make and incarnate the imaginative and moral leap which widened this stance across boundaries of family, creed and nation. The conviction that such a widening was not demanded by the Gospel, or that it was not possible for "fallen" human beings, revealed, as he tartly remarked of Mr Niebuhr, "A level of wisdom to which the New Testament hardly attained." Ecumenism was the process of breaking the boundaries in the realm of church denominations. Pacifism was the process of breaking it in the political world. This seems to have been what he meant by saying, as he was wont to, that pacifism was, at bottom, taking forgiveness seriously.

Just as denominational pride was the taproot of resistance to ecumenical brotherhood, so nationalism was the taproot of resistance to strenuous peacemaking. From the twenties onward, Archie became increasingly doubtful whether the sovereign nation state was the best model of political organisation. Between the wars, he was a serious champion of the League of Nations, even on one or two occasions recommending support for it from the pulpit in Galston or Gilmorehill as the most cogent practical contribution to peace.

His own trust in the machinery of nation-states was severely dinted by his sense of Allied default on disarmament policy between the wars. On one occasion he came back from a summer visit to Austria in 1931, and spoke of "having to stand silent and shamed in the presence of a young Austrian teacher" who had made it clear to him the German-speaking people had begun to despair of good faith among the Versailles signatories.

While believing that each man must wrestle in the privacy of his soul with God on the question of bearing arms, he had no illusions about the status of national propaganda which exalted the nation-state's survival to an absolute value. That was idolatry. And, characteristically, he concerned himself with the idolatry of his own political regime rather than with that of anyone else. He took seriously the mote and beam parable.

Even here, he could he funny. On one occasion, having mapped out the various ways in which, formally, the *"Render unto Caesar"* verse could be taken, [Were all things God's, and some also Caesar's? Were some things God's and other things Caesar's? Were all things Caesar's and only some God's?] he admitted to liking the rendering of the text which ran, "Give unto Caesar the things that are God's". He enjoyed too telling the story of a corporal in the Black Watch who was told to get a hut ready for a religious service. When the padre went to inspect it, he found behind the rostrum a scroll bearing the motto, "Scotland for ever!" He told the corporal to change it into something religious, and when he went back, found the scroll carrying the motto, "Scotland for ever and ever, Amen."

It was, however, for the purveying of jingoist triumphalism, and even more for the religious sanctification of it, that Archie reserved his most crackling anger, not only because it let the preciousness of life be cheapened, but because it cheapened it for a phoney ideal. And when the church allowed itself to be "pulled out of the gravitational field of the Word" by such propaganda, it had, he thought, fallen into the constant danger that besets a state church, of becoming subservient rather than prophetic in relation to the nation's life.

It was for him not just diplomacy, but an act of intended reconciliation that when he preached at Armistice services, he would not dwell on anything which further polarised antagonisms about the pacifist issue, and he was sincere and steadfast in that.

"I hold that on Remembrance Sunday no word ought to be spoken which cannot fairly be expected to command the assent of, at any rate the great bulk of Christians, whether they are still believers in "the just war", or untroubled militarists or pacifists of one brand or another — prudential, political, theological, what not."

He did, however, admit to friends that he found Armistice Day services quite stressful on the human level, since he was aware of so much in the atmosphere, and sometimes in the personnel, which was straining against his vision of the occasion. It was not that he wanted a company of committed pacifists; his

Cloister Group experience had been a convincing demonstration of the possibility of deeply shared faith across the pacifist/non-pacifist frontier. But he could not move easily among the military establishment, as he sometimes had to, for instance, in the course of his Moderatorial year of office, and he was appalled by the church, when it failed to point out the distance between the ways of even a just war, and the way of Jesus. He was clear that love could, and indeed on occasions must, involve severity and even anger. But war's impersonal organised killing, its reduction of the enemy to thinghood, taking the sting out of his death or wounding, that seemed to him to be an unacceptable kind of lie. One might feel forced to wage war, but even in that forcing, one should recognise the situation as one incompatible with the life of the Kingdom of God, one which, by its very nature, "belongs to the Kingdom of Satan."

More specifically, he felt strongly that modern warfare was quite a different phenomenon from the old picture of brave soldiers fighting to keep their wives and children safe. And he would brook no softening of language to describe, for instance, Britain's policy of saturation bombing in the Second World War.

> "It is splendidly courageous for a bomber's crew to fly hundreds of miles across defended enemy territory, and a wonderful feat of technology and airmanship when its load of bombs is dropped accurately on an open city, but by no possible stretch of courteous language can it be called a "chivalrous" or "gentlemanly" operation. To kill women and babies by the thousand is simply barbaric and beastly."

Or again,

> "It has always been an anomaly that to knife a man in a back alley because he has done you wrong is morally monstrous, but to bayonet a man in a battle is not just pardonable but morally magnificent. Patriotism has always obscured this anomaly beneath national flags: and orthodoxy muffled it in its eloquent doctrine of the 'just war'."

The scale and cost of armaments, and that in a world stalked by famine and disease for so many, combined with the destructive power of the atomic bomb, seemed to him to turn the war scenario into something so grotesque that its claim to virtue or valour could no longer gain credibility with any sane person. "And yet, the official churches have gone on piously protesting their horror of war and ritually blessing the banners and the bombs."

Archie was inclined to read the menace of the nuclear threat in a darkly provident way, albeit rather tentatively. He was unambivalently convinced that, humanly speaking, the arms/finance complex was insanity, "rationalised devilry". Theologically speaking, he wondered:

> "Can we say that, in the providential rule of almighty God, mankind has been allowed to run this madness, this badness to the extreme where it exposes itself as madness and badness?"

In his last years, he seems to have found the prophecies of Jeremiah more and more articulating his own feelings about the present state of western political and military policy. A few months before his death, in the course of an interview with Ian MacKenzie, he was asked what he thought of the possibility that God would let the earth be annihilated. "That's the question," he said, "whether God has, in the incarnation so insinuated himself into the very fabric of the cosmos as to make it indestructible." "Yes", said Ian, and "what's your answer?" and Archie replied, "I swither, I swither." The swithering, it should be noted, was neither about the providence of God, nor about the reality of incarnation, but about whether the virtual destruction of this earth might be compatible with both, an instance on the major scale of the kind of educative punishment which the Old Testament prophets so regularly identified in their national disasters.

The acceleration of the nuclear race in the twentieth century seemed perhaps to be a sign that God's patience was snapping, and that we might have to go through hells of self-inflicted global suffering to be persuaded of the folly of our headstrong stupidities. This possibility, of either environmental or military global destruction, was, of course, something he hoped we would avert, by the repentance of the nations, but it is clear that he contemplated it; and that even the contemplation of it failed to dissuade him of the ultimate providential love of God.

This steadiness of faith was possible because the mortality of the world and of us in it, was one of the facts which he believed faith must not blink, and which any truthful nurture and politics must enable us to face. While deploring the sentiments of pining 19th century hymns like "Earth is a desert drear", he deplored as much the secular sentimentality of living as if death did not exist, and existing, did not threaten the meaningfulness of all our culture. While acknowledging the morbidity of the typical Victorian nursery sampler, the fragility of this beautiful, wonderful earth was for him a datum that no account of reality could fudge.

It was, in the last resort, because the braggadocio of chauvinism was so untruthful about our common vulnerability that Archie so hated it. And the collusion between church and state in this area was, to him, the most sinister betrayal of the gospel. He reserved some of the most scathing lines from his many occasional poems for this *mesalliance*.

"The fighting man must be a fighter,
Wearing a helmet, not a mitre.
He needn't rack his brains; his bishop
A glittering shoal of proof will fish up
That the English patriot's selfless cause
Has always mirrored God's own laws.

Is Jesus worship all baloney,
The Church a hive of sanctimony?
And Bible texts that preach of love
And gentleness a holy nonsense,
A velvet camouflage above
Sir Winston's gospel, Lyndon Johnson's,
Stalin's and Heath's and Tricky Dick's,
The gospel of the nation-state,
The call to make it rich and great
By dint of power politics,
By rocket-rattling, furtive spying,
And arts of diplomatic lying?

Let Heath conduct the Christmas carols
Of village children: let Sir Alec,
Addressing the United Nations
Drip Honey from his bland orations
And wear the self-same dove-grey tunic
He wore above his shirt in Munich,
So long as fools with wits aberrant
Don't wreck our nuclear deterrent.

Lets tell the G.I. in Vietnam
Our version of an ancient psalm.
"God is our refuge and our stay,
And though we make of earth a hell,
He loves the stars and stipes too well
To castigate the U.S.A." "

Those who knew Archie in the thirties and forties, either in Glasgow
University or in Iona were certainly under the impression that he was a Labour
voter, and certainly some of his remarks about the maldistribution of wealth
have a socialist ring. However, Mrs Armstrong, his housekeeper in Doune at
the time of his death, testifies to many amiable political arguments with him
(she was a Scottish Nationalist, and he used to compare her to the spiky

ornamental thistles in the garden) and is sure that, latterly at least he voted Liberal. Apart from one public utterance in the '30s to the effect that the rise of the Labour Party was the most significant event in Britain's secular history over the last fifty years, he does not seem to have made much public comment on party politics, and little private comment, even among friends, which would allow him to be confidently pigeon-holed in these terms. His family's political ethos seems to have been Liberal. His mother wrote him an amusing letter during the war from Troon about how Madge and Minnie had scolded her for accepting a proferred lift to the polling station from the Conservative candidate's agent, who had not withdrawn his offer of it when she told him directly that she was not going to vote that way. The girls were afraid that the sight of her in the Conservative car might lend weight to that campaign!

Whatever his voting record, Archie was certainly convinced that the democratic freedoms of the Christian as citizen should be exercised as fully as possible, and commented disapprovingly on the gravestone of an American which bore the supposedly triumphant epitaph,

"Here lies the body of a Christian man.
He never cast his vote."

At the same time, he was sure that it was not through politics that the Kingdom of God would be brought in, but only through the unconditioned freedom of God. The political ethics of the Kingdom were, in the eyes of secular prudence, impractical and subversive, intemperate and incautious, since turning the other cheek must seem to commonsense a recipe for disaster; but the Sermon on the Mount demanded no less, and if the church were to fulfil its mission as the icebreaker of God, it could not, in good faith, take itself out, so to speak, by helicopter. Rather it had to bear its strange message of the unlimited love of God, by being, among the horizontal structures of the world, an earthed microcosm of that love.

15   Life in a straight line

"If I may use the metaphor in this place, biographies are the horse's mouth, whereas the volumes of systematic theology are the racing calendar."

New College Union Presidential Address

If Archie was listening to his own funeral and memorial service orations, he must doubtless have done the celestial equivalent to tut-tutting, and called for a little more of the "Scotch causticity" recommended by Sir Walter Scott. The tribute paid by Stuart McWilliam in Kilmadock parish church, where Archie had faithfully and unobtrusively worshipped for more than two decades; and those by Lesslie Newbigin and Oliver Tomkins in St Giles a month later, were full of the sense that words could not do justice to the man, "a prince among men", as Lesslie Newbigin put it.

Stewart McWilliam said, towards the end of his address, that he had never known anyone loved by so many different kinds of people. Archie's capacity to inspire that sort of response across the whole spectrum of social, political and theological positions signalled the fruitfulness of what he sometimes called "the ministry of friendship". From landed gentry to miners' wives, from Iona Community radicals to the headmasters of select private schools, from "conservative evangelicals" to sophisticated liberal theologians, people felt at home with him, even though they might never have felt at home with one another.

Archie himself, in the course of his Biblical Studies lectures on Ezekiel, made a significant aside to contention that Ezekiel, "for all his reforming zeal, like most priests, was a conservative." He said to the class:

"The more I see of human nature, the less I am disposed to limit its possibilities and forcibly to thrust individuals into psychological pigeon-holes and categories held to be mutually exclusive. After all, there are such phenomena as very great men, and the greater a man is, the more complex he often is, exhibiting in his own person a union, or it may be a struggle, between qualities more usually exhibited separately in different personalities."

It was certainly the judgment of Norman Porteous, a former principal of New College, with decades of Scottish experience behind him, that Archie was possibly, of all that slaughtered generation to which he belonged, the outstanding man. His versatility enabled him to move through the diverse pioneering jobs he did as if each was in turn made for him, though he was often forging them almost *ex nihilo*. And there are clear indications that he could have done many more things with equal competence. Lord Reith, for instance, disclosed over a lunch-table that he had very nearly appointed him as head of Religious Broadcasting in the twenties. And in almost every new career decision he made, he was actually excluding at least one or two others which would have been quite plausible and even attractive to him. Yet Archie carried his own complexities of decision-making so light that they were almost invisible, and the question of what in him was struggled for is hard to answer, since he was rarely self-revealing, at least in the sense of making comment on his own character.

He was clear, indeed, that the privacy of the soul/self was one pole of any mature life, needing development, nourishment and judgment just as much as its social and gregarious pole. He made recurrent comment about the importance of the wilderness in any properly balanced spiritual growth, and noticed how often prison or exile had been part of the maturing of the genuinely great. On the retreats which he frequently led he often advocated, and therefore probably practised, a minimum of an hour a day in silent communion with God.

In dealing with others in the process of wrestling with faith and disbelief, he had immense patience, tact and delicacy. Quite often, he had to handle the kind of inner panic of people who wished they could believe, but couldn't, and his gardener's sense of time stood him in good stead here, resisting any forcing, and demanding nothing except the integrity of the searching. This must have been one of his gifts even as a very young man, for even when he was a student, and teaching at St. Mary's in Melrose, he was trusted as spiritual confidant by one, Kate Wilson, the headmistress of the twin Abbey School for girls, who was full of scruples about her own incapacity to believe and her entitlement to give religious instruction to her pupils. She was at the time twice Archie's age.

In his Galston days, too, he had said candidly to his congregation:

"I do not want any young men or women to sign in advance of experience the complex statement of Christian belief which has been formulated in creeds and theologies. I trust indeed that they will be led to understand these in due time."

Throughout his chaplaincy days too, he was always encouraging people not to fudge their intellect, and not to chafe because they did not see, so long as they were looking straight; and it is clear, from the number of retreats he was asked to take, that many people found themselves immensely deepened by his gifts in this area. It is perhaps a fair judgment that it was in this context, even more than in preaching or academic teaching, that his particular fusion of abilities could best express itself. He would warn people against a false sense of sanctimonious silence, and give them permission to blow their noses in the normal manner, and with the normal loudness; and then, with remarkable acumen, move into the designated field of discourse and draw people into a process of reflection which commanded intellectual, moral and spiritual attentiveness without straining, and at the same time allowed them the enjoyment of wit and anecdote precisely apt for the occasion. There was a complete absence of sepulchral piety, and yet a deep sense of reverence in handling high things.

One of the hardest things to understand, from outside, is how Archie managed to live as happily as he did with a Calvinist anthropology, while being so open to the liberalism of someone like Charles Raven, whose very name, as Archie once said, guaranteed the package it was attached to. His sense of the gravity and pervasiveness of sin was a constant check on any facile optimism, and while he designated as "benign" the Calvinism of his United Free Church upbringing, it led him to judge himself and the mass of mankind in fairly negative terms, at least when the question was theoretical. "There is something detestable about human nature". "In the light of Christ, I am a morally deformed and disreputable creature." Although such statements are always put in the context of even deeper affirmations of God's redeeming and renewing potency, they manifest what the congress of Orthodox theologians in Moscow, 1953 called "*la psychologie pessimiste*" of Protestantism. What is remarkable is that Archie's handling of his own existence, while clearly disciplined and self-scrutinising, gave to those he met, the feel of a man who was at home in himself; and his encounter with others was so consistently full of interested delight as to produce a sense of wellbeing and worth in those he dealt with. That such deep geniality should be able to co-exist with such self-renouncing beliefs needs much pondering.

Another area where Archie seems to have contained within himself positions which seem, *Archie remoto*, very nearly contradictory, is that of nature, and in the Pauline sense "flesh". It was one of his central and guiding convictions, forged back in his late schooldays, that if faith was to be worth pursuing, it must have room for everything good under the sun. Sometimes he spoke in terms which were almost pantheist, ("All nature reveals God"), and he could celebrate, in his eighties, "our glorious young Scottish soccer players", as he had, in his twenties, been bowled over by the Dresden art gallery head of a Christ who rejoiced to be flesh. He was constantly delighted by physical landscape, and reminded people that a glimpse of something beautiful in the natural world might, like a good joke, be one of God's angels, even before a text of Scripture.

At the same time, he seems to have felt more distaste for the "sins of the flesh" than for any other, even if his official theological diagnosis was that pride was the taproot of all other sin. Emotionally, however, pride was more congenial to him, being so to speak, a vice aspiring to more than it was entitled to, a kind of Promethean striving. On the other hand, sins like drunkeness or promiscuity seemed to him simply squalid and unmanly, a failure to grasp the proper hierarchy of the self, in which reason mastered and judged passion. This Platonism took many forms. It was his recurrent *en passant* swipe at paganism, that it generated and approved "the crudeness, the materialism, the lasciviousness above which mere nature-worshippers find it so difficult to rise". Speaking to the World Association for Christian Broadcasting in 1966, he characterises the Gentile context of the Bible as

> "a sun-loving conscienceless exuberance of living never far from ugly sensualities, and often sliding into them."

And in his 1971 Lent broadcasts, he contrasts the austerity of the Sermon on the Mount with its pagan counterparts, where

> "the unbridled sensuality of the pagan world had led to a situation where sex had sprawled over into everything else: the very stars and flowers were scrawled over with erotic legends, like the scribblings with which prurient boys find satisfaction in defacing the walls of public buildings."

Though normally he insisted, in the light of the Resurrection, that the trans-figured life of the Kingdom must include and not exclude the transfiguring of body, he could speak, in the context of an intercessory prayer, of the communion of saints, "with whom the souls of the faithful, after they are delivered from the burden of the flesh, are in joy and felicity." The indulgent carnality of post-war Cologne sickened him almost more than the horrors of the war, and he could find nothing commendable in giving the body its head, whether in relation to food or drink or sexual appetite (though he found something a little opaque in the logic of Paul, whose Christian permissiveness about food did not extend to a like liberty about sex). At the same time, he welcomed the new candour, if not the new permissiveness of the late twentieth century, finding it much healthier than the furtive atmosphere of Victorian England. And he did believe that "there is ecstasy of the body and ecstasy of the mind, but there is nothing to compare with the simultaneous ecstasy of body and mind."

On the whole, however, his moral weight fell on the side of strict and ethical and rational control, which probably explains why he found Pharisaism a less awful threat to the church than antinomianism. The only significant chink in his theoretical ethical severity seems to have been Beethoven, for whose music he was willing to make all allowances. He found Beethoven's eccentric social boorishness unjudgeable, as if it fell outside the realm of ethics altogether, and was merely an epiphenomenon of genius. Normally, however, laxity distressed him in any sphere. He was, as he grew older, sometimes horrified by what seemed to him the slipshodness of much contemporary preaching, and by the same phenomenon in general dilettante reading. Something in him demanded, aesthetically as well as morally, hard discipline, since anything wrought with less was likely to be swept away on tides of populist appeal to the fast result, the cheap solution. One of his central words of rebuke was "shoddy". Another was "mushy". "He has a mushy mind" was almost his most damning comment.

He schooled himself severely, and judged himself, as he thought proper, more stringently than anyone else. At times, his self-appraisals seem so at odds with the man perceived by others, that it is hard quite to credit them as accurate self perceptions. He apologises, for instance, that his sermons are less systematic and scholarly than those of his father and his great-uncle, whereas to most hearers, Archie's liveliness of image combined with clarity of thought must have been an immense aid to theological digestive processes, and the sequences of sermons he gave at Galston and Gilmorehill are in fact unusually un-text-hopping, even if they fall short of his original plan for a forty-year sequence. He felt that during his moderatorial year so much had been left undone, whereas most observers were amazed by the verve and energy which this seventy-three year old brought to every journey and every meeting from one end of the country to another.

He felt that his own besetting sin was vanity, and said as much both to Harry Galloway and to his friend Hugh, who admitted that he occasionally felt that Archie was intellectually arrogant, but thought that in most cases he had every right to be! It may have been sensitivity to that tendency which made him so severe on anyone who tried to mask their own defects, like the writer who sent an uncomplimentary letter back to his publisher with the words, "I return your letter, for I should not like my biographers to find it in my files of correspondence."

George Stewart gently chid him for a kind of self-pity which was potentially destructive, but on the whole thought he was *too* moral, and suggested to him that the Gospel allowed a glory of absolution which his religion did not yet allow.

The relationship between ethics and Gospel was always one of Archie's preoccupations, and it was fitting that the Gospel reading at his memorial service should be John 14, with its direct linking of the two, "If you love me, you will keep my commandments." He was himself convinced of the priority of God's unearned and forgiving love, but placed the absolute character of moral demand as yet a further token of his generous trust in us, to which the only decent response could be penitent and grateful obedience.

His vision of the good life was not, however, one of constant unremitting struggle with a worse self, but of a growth in what would be called, in traditional language, sanctification: that is, of goodness becoming fluent. In almost the same breath as his critique of Gentile sensuality, he could empathise with the Gentile critique of Judaism, with their distaste for

> "the bleak disturbing figure of the Jew who seemed to exhale winter round about him. The Jew with his inexorable law and his haunted conscience: the awkward and angular Jew with his tiresome scruples and eternal moral fussiness: the detestably exclusive and infuriatingly superior Jew."

The people he most loved and admired were not spikily and scrupulously good, but graceful. He recognised this quality in others, pre-eminently in George Stewart, and in Graham of Kalimpong, and called it, most often "charm". For him that was no superficial attribute, but the attractiveness and allure of enfibred goodness, rooted by much practice in the soul, and becoming second nature. He often used it as a synonym for "grace" in Biblical contexts.

Archie's own "charm" was abundantly manifest, whether in genial welcome to his house, or in his rich gift for anecdote which often bit and healed at the same time. He loved the crazinesses of the human race, and collected jokes and stories which made the point, sometimes in surrealist modes. He liked, for instance, the story of the man who came home with his pay packet, took out the money and handed the empty pay packet to his wife. Asked by a friend why he didn't just throw it on the fire, he replied, "It's the principle of the thing." Or the joke about the psychiatrist who was met emerging from his house looking immensely under stress, and asked by his colleague if he was all right. "No", he replied, "I need to see a psychiatrist." "But you *are* a psychiatrist" protested the other. "I know, but I charge too much."

In church circles too, he relished the idiosyncratic. So, for example, he marvelled at the unverifiable claim of Newton Flew, an ecumenical ally of the war years, to the effect that, by some incontrovertible calculus, 78% of the world's theologians shared a common faith. His Biblical Studies classes were regaled as they worked on the book of Acts with an account of how Principal Alexander White had preached on the story of Eutychus, his entire sermon consisting of three sentences:

> "What are we to make of this incident by way of edification? The lesson seems to me very clear: it is that even an apostle may preach far too long. And as example is more important than precept, I shall not say one word more except Amen."

As a paradigm of ineptly targetted utterance, he loved the glorious ineptitude of V.H. Stantol, as he blithely began a sermon to the college servants of Trinity College, Cambridge, opening with the words,

> "The ontological argument for the existence of the deity has of late years, I grant you, mainly owing to the onslaught of a destructive and largely Teutonic criticism, been relegated to a subordinate place in the armoury of the Christian apologetic."

Archie himself loved the sonorities of words, and had a marvellous ear for the cadences of strong prose. His vocabulary was richly Latinate, enough to send hearers scuttling for the dictionary to find the meaning of such polysyllables as *apolaustic* or *dyspnoea*. He hated Americanisms like *timewise*, and once, in his British Council of Churches days, ended a letter to an exiled correspondent in the States with the words, "I see you have adopted the American spelling of *honour*. *Facilis descensus Averno*." It saddened him that words became debased, that "nice", for instance, should have become such a minimal compliment as to be almost an insult. Though he thought there was some risk of free prayer becoming a distraction, if the hearers listened to the prayer instead of praying through it, his own public prayers had a sharpness and toughness in which every word counted. For instance,

> "By love of ease, by fear of pain and disrepute, by skilled blindness to the claim of our neighbour, by langour in service and prudence in sacrifice, we have made the Cross of Christ of no effect."

Or, at the opening of Leighton House in Dunblane,

> "And grant that to all who look upon this figured cross, it may be a perpetual teaching and incentive, a rebuke to sloth and selfishness, an inspiration of love and self-forgetting, a promise of life beyond death in the image of the death and resurrection of the Lord."

Partly because his own sense of language was so deft and secure, he found immense pleasure in malapropisms; cherishing especially his old Aunt Jane's injunction to look up a scriptural verse in the *Concrudence*; and the comment of a Swedish divine after a Faith and Order conference, that the whole thing had *wonderfully* manifested *complete unanimosity*. He delighted in the misdeeds of his unbaptised typewriter, which produced, as the final heading of a talk on temperance, the words clearly visible to the Chairman as "One Last Pint". Or, for a school prizegiving, "Sindays" for "Sundays". This must have been a genetically inherited pleasure, for the only time he remembered seeing his father laugh in the pulpit was when he found that his newly-acquired typing machine had produced the title "David and the Shortbread" for "David and the Shewbread".

He was also a skilfully wicked punster, saying for instance of the more extreme ascetic neglect of the body, "We fail to see the connection between the sublime and the pediculous;" or, of decent reticence about the inmost being of God, "You can't unscrew the inscrutable."

One could happily produce an anthology of his invariably trenchant epigrams: "Miracle is the lawful offspring of religion, and not a bastard begotten upon credulity." "God is running a universe and not a Jobiverse." "Priggishness is simply the puppyhood of Pharisaism." He was both collector and composer of limericks, finding the latter pursuit a way of filling in sleepless nights if he had been awakened by May, or was lying awake in case she needed him. The results would be chortlingly shared with friends:

> "I simply detest the euphonium
> It wounds me to hear the thing blownium.
>> In frankness dear sir,
>> I greatly prefer
> An instrument sweeter of tonium."

Or,

> "A young Trappist monk in Algeria
> Of silence grew wearier and wearier
>> Till at length with a shout
>> From his cell he burst out
> And murdered the Father Superior."

Both as preacher and speaker his command of vivid, arresting prose was evident, though more muted in preaching, where he wanted his hearers not to be struck by the language, but to find it a vehicle transparent of truth. In particular, he loved to begin talks with a coruscating sentence which at once disarmed his hearers and could not but engage them mentally and expectantly. Examples of this are legion, but one or two suffice to give the flavour:

> "What I have to offer to the group this evening amounts, alas, to little more than a plateful of lukewarm tapioca pudding — an agglutinous agglomeration of half-baked suggestions rather than any very carefully shaped and articulated theme."
>> (on The Old Testament and Nihilism)

Or,

164

"It is an impossible assignment to reduce this sturdy, rowling, sometimes wild and dangerously-burned ecclesiastical bullock to a forty-minutes cube of historical oxo."

(on The History of the Scottish Church)

Or, addressing the Educational Institute of Scotland on Education and the Home,

"Few men would be better disqualified than I for standing before you this afternoon. I have no children of my own. Any pedagogical relation I have dates back to half a century ago. And there is no television set in my home."

All linguistic playfulness delighted him, and he had a delicate touch, knowing by a kind of interior sonar the right balance between teasing, flattery, real intellectual challenge and coat-trailing. The flattery was venial and superficial, like his habit of attributing "Reverend" to people who were merely "Mister", during his Moderatorial visit to Nigeria, on the grounds which he blithely disclosed to Bob MacDonald as "harmless, while giving a certain glow of satisfaction to those who know".

He could be caustic, and appreciated the sardonic, but his gift was rarely to target the barbs directly at those he was addressing, so that if the cap fitted, people might recognise rebuke, but without the sting of personal recrimination. So, for instance, he would raise the question of whether the ministry had lost its collective Christian nerve, by quoting a remark of Louis XIV on a sermon, that it was "a remarkable utterance for learning and comprehensiveness. There is no subject under heaven or earth which it did not touch, if only it had mentioned the Christian religion." Or he could say to an elders' conference,

"I find it safe to distrust people who speak as though they were a lump wiser than the Apostle Paul, and perhaps just a modest wee bit ahead of the old-fashioned programmes laid down by Jesus' word and example."

When dealing with particular people, by contrast, Archie seems to have had, and possibly to have cultivated, the gift of noticing the best in them. In a narrow fundamentalist he would see, above everything, his zealous love of God. Of an ex-moderatorial colleague who had repeatedly opposed the Church of Scotland's ecumenical outreaches, he could write to a friend with whom he had no need to disguise his feelings, "I think he is deepening." When Einstein was given an honorary degree by Glasgow University, what struck Archie most was the unself-conscious and childlike gaze he had, that of a man used to "looking out of his own eyes" (though in this case he also confessed to an impulse to cut his hair from behind!).

He seems not to have spoken much about his feelings at marrying too late to have children, and close friends say that it was one of the areas where his acceptance of providential wisdom was quietly integrated into his sense of his own life and its possibilities. If anything, the role he most naturally adopted several times in his life was that of father to adult son, a relationship which meant an immense amount to him with, for instance, the diverse personalities of Lesslie Newbigin, and of two sons of neighbours, Ronnie Buchanan in Bank Street, a kicker over of traces, and Douglas Burnet in Doune. There are several tributes by parsonical fathers, the most famous being Raven, whose own children showed anti-clerical, and even anti-religious tendencies, that Archie impressed them as no other professional minister did. In similar vein, Mrs Lois MacKinnon, a daughter of the manse in the thirties, recalls how natural it seemed to them to call Archie by his Christian name while they wouldn't have dreamed of doing it with any other member of the Church of Scotland Peace Group, not even with significantly younger ones.

He enjoyed dealing with children, and could enter their world of seeing and feeling with an engaging and unpatronising directness. Apparently, he never took those he was baptising into his own arms, for fear of dropping them, but preferred to baptise them in their parent's arms. Watching small children gave him many images of faith. He noted the little boy who was learning to dive at the Arlington Baths Clubs at Glasgow where he swam nearly every day, and recognised what trust it took for the child to accept his father's instructions to let his feet be the last part of him to enter the pool. He registered the trustful confidence of the three-year old son of an old college friend, who, on one occasion when his father had locked the study door so that he and Archie could enjoy uninterrupted conversation, melted their resistance to disturbance by saying with quiet emphasis, "But Daddy, this is *me*." And he was delighted by the filial pride of another neighbour's child, whose father was five foot four in his stocking soles, and who met Archie on the pavement, looked appraisingly up and down his six-foot-two length, and announced matter-of-factly, "My daddy's taller than you." Above all, he prized the *Emperor's New Clothes* role of children, and used many times in sermons an anecdote told him by George Cockin, sometime Bishop of Bristol. Archie would retell it with immense gusto:

"In the corner of a railway carriage, there sat, under the curling brim of the latest thing in bowler hats, an exquisite young man, a tailor's dream of a young man, − suit cut to perfection, umbrella rolled to an unbelievable slimness, one manicured hand resting elegantly on the handle of the umbrella while the other toyed daintily with a virgin pair of doeskin gloves. From diagonally opposite, a small girl gazed unflinchingly, and then asked in a piercing voice, "Mummy, what is that funny man for?"

It was the harvesting of such little moments, the attentiveness to all that went on around him that made Archie so lively an illustrator of the interconnectedness between faith and life. He saw things and people with a fresh, unjaded and undoctrinaire eye, and was immensely alarmed when a bout of anaemia in his old age left him temporarily listless, and in a state of *accidie*.

Though he did not do much autobiographical reminiscence with his wide range of friends and visitors, it is clear from the overview which his papers give that a few incidents in Archie's own past were immensely important to him, and became, over the years, points of reference for his own sense of himself. Some have already been mentioned: his childhood discovery of the hidden moon; his school friend finding Christianity a pallid evasion of full-blooded life; his Galston co-op manager; the communion service at Tambaram. There were many others, accumulating over the years a kind of patina of significance.

One was being in Germany in his student days when a small earthquake took place, not a full-blown earthquake, but a little tremor, enough to make the pictures jump sharply off the walls as if saluting, and then jump back again. No damage was done, but the episode became for Archie a symbol of the precariousness of things if God suspended his normal sustaining of them, and it was the shock of earthquake which seemed to him the most compelling image for the loss of faith. Another was a visit to a small Northumberland church, where he was impressed by the naturalness of a picture of grazing sheep on one of the stained-glass windows. All of a sudden, one of the sheep raised its head, and he realised that only a trick of the light had made him think it was a picture, and that he had, all the time been seeing a three-dimensional world. This was his vignette of the opposite phenomenon, the realisation of God, or of the potency of Scripture, taking one by surprise as belonging to a dimension of reality not previously appreciated, but compellingly coming alive. Yet another was a gardening competition which had been arranged among a few keen gardening friends in Galston, with the proviso that on a certain July day they would inspect one another's gardens for the excellence of the displays. A cold, wet spring and early summer had ensured that everything was badly behind, but as they approached one garden, their eyes were met by a riot of colour. It took closer scrutiny to ascertain that the glorious display was produced by the owner having tied on to every plant as a joke, heads of multi-coloured paper. The phoney garden was a recurrent image of surface spirituality, unwarranted by the shallow condition of soil quality and care.

Time fascinated him. He would often reflect to those impatient of progress in mission that it was 2.2 million years ago that the light of the Andromeda nebula had left its source; or that it would take, according to the calculations of "an ingenious and presumably leisured scholar", two hundred and seventeen billion years to exhaust the permutations of the first ten moves in a game of chess, even if every man, woman and child on earth played steadily at a rate of one set per minute. Against this, the fact that it was less than a million days since the death of Christ seemed to him to put impatience in the right perspective. This macrocosmic perception had its microcosmic correlate in the fact that within mere decades, the few grains of Maquis wheat planted in Canada in the 1920s were producing enough grain to feed a nation and to export; or in the proliferation of Shirley poppies from a handful of seeds.

Such calculations, which would daunt many with a sense of the insignificance of human life, against the cosmic timescales and mindless prodigality of nature, in fact only reinforced Archie's sense of the patient providence of God, who need not hurry, and certainly need not be stampeded into producing fast and flashy results. yet it did not cut the nerve of his conviction that mission was, from the human point of view, the imperative priority of the church. This was less because he feared for the souls of the unsaved (*that*, he was clear, was God's business, which he would do well and lovingly; Universalism, however struck Archie as an illicitly speculative position beyond what the church could legitimately preach) than because he was sure that the whole earth was made for the worship of God who had, in the Incarnation, insinuated himself into the very fibre of the world's life.

To appraise such a life would be impertinence. What is clear is that scores and hundreds of people found in him a quality of humanness rare in their diverse experience, even the memory of which, at a distance sometimes of fifty years, could generate animation and delight in the faces of those who knew him. One feels that if the Church of Scotland went in for canonisation, he would be, by popular acclaim, a prime candidate.

Given the impact he made on so many circles of church and national life, it is amazing that his name occurs so little in the documentation of the century's ecclesiastical history, and that, even in most accounts of ecumenical developments in the thirties and forties, he is often mentioned, if at all, merely in a fleeting, one or two line reference. Adrian Hastings, for instance, in his vast documentation of English Christianity, even if he is scrupulously not straying north of the border, might have been expected to include Archie's name in the context of the British Council of Churches, or of the wartime witness of the churches in the European peacemaking context. That it does not appear in the index, when so many like Paton or Temple acknowledged his indispensable service to the ecumenical cause, suggests a remarkable level of limelight-avoidance, a genuinely self-effacing and unself-seeking commitment which allowed him, for all his physical, intellectual and moral "bigness" to remain publicly unobtrusive.

The Church of Scotland is still thick with people, most of them over forty now, and many over seventy, who cherish memories or encounters with the man, even if it was only one occasion, a sermon or a retreat or a conference. But the almost universal reaction of the under-forties to whom I said I was writing about Archie Craig was "Who?". The fragmentation of the church into polarised and mutually suspicious wings of liberal and conservative, each with their exclusive theological heroes; the failure to find imaginative ways of engaging the secular world; the widespread mediocrity of religious cultural life; the failure to explore lively forms of alternative ministry; the dragging slowness of ecumenical advance; the theological pauperisation of the laity; the shrill insistence on *entitlement* to be listened to; the predictability of moral statement, and the poverty of neighbourliness; all these insert into the mind the niggling question of whether in fact the church can·cope with his quality of searching and strenuous and uncomplacent faith, except as a proudly exhibited museum specimen.

Archie, however, would not have crumpled into despair. He would have wagged his head, and clasped his hands and nodded his understanding of one's dismay, and then said, "But you know, there are remarkable things happening, really remarkable things." And he would have produced some small encounter he had had, or a conversation, or the news of eastern Europe, and would remind one of the molecular forces of growth in apparently barren February soil.

What those who share none of his sense of a God at work would make of such a response, and indeed of such a life, is hard to guess. Would they marvel that such a palpable quality of realism and truthfulness could coexist with a belief system which strikes them as so discredited and bankrupt? Would they be tempted to put it all down to the indoctrinatory power of a benignly Calvinist upbringing on the thought and emotional structures of a happy manse boyhood? Would they see in it the corruption of a fine intelligence, the seduction of a humane conscience into moral codes less flexible than they could have been; the infinitesimal evasion of the hardest critical historical questions; an understatement of the role of sexuality in human life and well-being; the projection of an almost Stoic self-discipline onto the cosmos; the blinkering of the eyes by too much Christian company?

Or would they be tempted by such a life into entertaining the possibility of God more seriously? Would they recognise the intimacy of the connections between dogma and generosity, between the capacity for laughter and the sense of cosmic atonement, between the deep interest in whatever "other" crossed his path and his vision of a world transfigured into its proper beauty?

To recreate the integrity of the man by words is not possible. But if, as he believed, the communion of saints interpenetrates the life of the world, not just by the sinews of memory, but in initiating presence, he may be sharing the chortling anticipation of God that we will yet know one another even as we are known. And he will be at home in that knowing.

Appendix 1 Acknowledgements

Rev. Bobby and Jennifer Anderson
Mrs Jane Anglin
Mrs H. Armstrong
Rev. William G. Baker
Very Rev. Robin Barbour
Rev. Robert W.A. Begg
Rev. Louden Blair
Alan Booth
Ms Chris Brown
Rev. Graeme Brown
Dr and Mrs and Douglas Burnet
Professor David Cairns
Mrs Ethel Cairns
Rev. Bill Christman
Captain J.B. Coutts
Mrs Edith F. Currie
Mrs Catherine Davidson
Canon F.W. Dillistone
Col. and Mrs F.A. Fargus
Rev. Ron Ferguson
Rev. Margaret Forrester
Mr A. Forrester-Pato
Eric Fenn
Jean Fraser
Rev. Donald Geddes
Rev. Professor Alan Galloway
Mr Craig Galloway
Mr Ritchie Gardiner
Rev. David Gourlay
Rev. Nelson Gray
Bishop Alastair Haggart
Mr Donald Hamilton
Rev. Fergus Harris
Mr Gordon Hector
Sir James Howie
Dr Eleanor Jackson
Mr Alistair Johnston
Very Rev. Bill Johnstone
Mr R.D. Kernohan
Mr A.B. Kerr

Dr and Mrs Fred Levison
Dr R. Stewart Louden
Rev. David Lyon
Mr Ian McColl
Rev. Bob Macdonald
Rev. Donald McFarlane
Rev. Johnson Mackay
Mrs Molly MacKichan
Rev. Steven Mackie
Prof. Donald MacKinnon
Mrs Lois MacKinnon
Mr Colin P. Maclean
Miss Jenny Maclellan
Dr Fraser McLuskey
Mr MacMurtrie
Rev. Stuart McWilliam
Miss Anne Malvenan
John Marsh
Mrs Sarah Baird Moffat
Bishop Lesslie Newbigin
Rev. Norman Orr
Professor Norman Porteous
Miss Purves
Bishop Pat Rodger
Miss Mabel Small
Mrs Helen Smith
Bishop Oliver Tomkins
Mr Derek Walton
Mrs Alison Weir
Rev. Andrew Wylie

Edinburgh University Archives
Glasgow University Archives
Kelso High School Log
New College Library
Ministry of Defence
National Library of Scotland
Selkirk Archives Library
Selly Oak Library, Birmingham
Trinity College Library

Appendix 2   Bibliography

1   Published work of Archie Craig.

A Christ-like church? Church of Scotland Forward Movement Congress
Booklet, no 4 Edinburgh, 1931
Christian Faith and Practice. Course for Bible Classes. With O.B.
Milligan and D.M. Baillie. Edinburgh, 1934
University Sermons. James Clarke & Co. 1938
Christian Witness in the Post-War World. Editor and introduction.
S.C.M. Press, 1946
A Scottish Reflection on Lund. The Ecumenical Review, vol.V, no.2,
pp.117-122. 1953
God comes four times. Radio Advent talks. Publ. S.C.M. Press, 1954
Preaching in a Scientific Age. The Warrack Lectures for 1953.
S.C.M. Press 1954
The Lost Treasure of Christian Unity. Introductory speech to the Inter-
Church Relations Report. St. Andrews Press, 1957
The Church in the World. Moderator's closing address to the General
Assembly. Edinburgh, 1962
Jesus. Four Lenten Talks. B.B.C. 1968
Foreword to *A System of Christian Doctrine* by David S. Cairns.
St. Andrews Press, 1979

2   Other books providing useful background, or illustrating particular
interests and concerns of Archie Craig at each stage of his career.

George M. Reith *Reminiscences of the U.F. Church General Assembly,
1900-1929.* Moray Press, 1933.
T.R. Glover *The Jesus of History.* S.C.M. 1917
George S. Stewart *The Lower Levels of Prayer. Addresses and other
Records.* Tambaram Madras Series, vol.VII. Oxford University Press,
1939
Eric Fenn *Learning Wisdom.* S.C.M. Press 1939
W. Temple (ed) *Is Christ Divided?* Penguin Books, 1943
Ernest A. Payne *Thirty Years of the British Council of Churches.*
BCC, 1972
R.P.C. Hanson *The Summons to Unity.* Edinburgh House Press, 1954
Mabel Small *Growing Together: the Ecumenical Movement in Scotland,
1924-64.* Scottish Churches Council, 1969

Dr Eleanor Jackson *Red Tape and the Gospel*. Phlogiston Publishing, 1980

The Anglican-Presbyterian Conversations. St. Andrews Press, 1966

Ian Henderson *Power without Glory*, 1967

Adrian Hastings *A History of English Christianity, 1920-1985*. Collins, 1986

David S. Cairns *A System of Christian Doctrine*. St. Andrews Press, 1979

Index

Alexander, Douglas 73
Alexy, Patriarch 89
Armstrong, Mrs H. 166 ff., 155
Azikwe, Mrs 102

Bach, J.S. 8
Baillie, D.M. 28, 53, 90
Baillie, John 28, 48, 90, 129
Baird, Mistress 38
Barbour, R. 74
Barclay, W. 77
Bartlett, P. 64
Barth, Karl 48, 122, 129, 131
Bea, Cardinal 104
Beethoven, 8, 161
Begg, Robert 139
Bell, Esther G. 11 ff.
Bell, George 63 ff.
Birmingham, Bishop of 129
Bliss, K. xii, 66, 69
Bowman, A.A. 46, 48, 53, 119, 122
Brander, Rev. 19, 23
Buchanan, R. 166
Bultmann, R. 124
Burlingham, R.E. 65 ff.
Burnet, D. 112, 118, 166
Burnet, T. 102, 109, 116 ff.

Cairns, David S. 48, 67, 129
Cairns, David 4, 14, 107, 108, 113, 125
Calvin, J. 94, 105, 120, 133
Cameron, Lawrence 31
Campbell, A., 108
Campbell, John 111
Carlyle, Thomas 33
Carter, H. 63
Casals, P. 111

Christman, B. 108 ff.
Churchill, W. 155
Cockin, G. 166
Congar, Y. 148
Congreve, Fr. 55
Coutts, Dr. John (Jack) 51 ff.
Coutts, Capt. Ben 52
Craig, Alice 19 ff., 23
    Alick (father) 2 ff.,
        13 ff., 18 ff., 21,
        22 ff., 24 ff.,
        32, 110, 161, 164
    Alick (nephew) 52
    Bessie 2 ff., 13
    Bob 72
    Forrest 19 ff., 21, 23, 25
    George 2
    Hetty 3
    John 19, 21, 22, 25,
        44, 114
    Madge 3 ff., 19 ff.,
        22 ff., 24 ff., 31, 45,
        53, 67, 156
    Margaret (nee Forrest)
        2 ff., 19, 21, 22 ff.,
        24 ff., 29, 31, 40 ff.,
        45, 110, 111, 156
    Minnie 19, 25, 45, 53,
        67, 156
    Stuart 10, 114
    Willie 3, 15, 21
Crick, Dr. 127
Crumpler, Dorothy 65
Currie, Mrs. 23

Davidson, N. 82, 84
Dawson, Mr. 118
Dinwiddie, M. 83

Dixon, McN. 122
Donn, T.M. 93
Dougall, Miss 122
Drummond, Mr. 37
Dryburgh, George 97 ff.
Dunn, John Petrie 28
Dulles, John Foster 63

Einstein, J. 165
Elmslie, W. 55, 67

Falconer, Ronnie 24, 83
Fargus, Shiona 117 ff.
Farmer, H.H. 46, 48, 129
Fergusson, Sir B. 79
Fisher, Geoffrey 66, 68, 92, 93
Flew, Newton 162
Fordyce, James Christian 43, 115
Forrester, Isobel 82
Forrester-Paton, A. 61
Fox, H.W. 55, 66, 67
France, Anatole 136
Fraser, Donald 43
Fraser, Jean 68, 81

Galloway, Harry 33 ff., 40, 47, 161
        Sammy 36
        Craig 34
Gardiner, Ritchie 12
Glover, T.R. 15
Gourlay, David 77, 109, 113
Graham, James 53, 162
Gray, Nelson 73, 88, 118
Gray, John R. 103
Grieve, George 66
Grou, Pere 55
Grunewald, 119

Haggart, A.I.M. 86
Hamilton, John 12
Hastings, A. 168
Heath, E. 155

Henderson, Ian 92, 124
Herklots, H. 67, 68
Hetherington, H. 48, 53,
        74, ff., 95, 100
Hildebrandt, F. 64
Hinsley, Cardinal 59
Hodgson, Leonard 64, 67
Hodgson, Ralph 130
Hogg, Mr 39
Home, Sir A. 155
Howie, Sir James 80
Hume, Theodore 66
Hunter, Leslie 69

Inge, Dean 143
Iredale, Eleanora 61, 69

Jackson, Eleanor 60, 63
James, William 146
Jenkins, David xii
Jerusalem, Patriarch of 105
Johnson, Lyndon 155

Keats, 9
Kemp, John 6, 10
Kemp-Smith, N. 10, 29, 44
Kennedy, H.A.A. 15, 20, 32
King, Dr Alex 104
Knox, John 94

Laidlaw, John 18, 23 ff., 117
Laidlaw, Leslie 81
Laidlaw, May (later Craig)
        18, 23 ff., 80 ff., 88, 100,
        105, 108–118, 164
Lamont, D. 48, 74
Leiper, H. 66
Louden, Dr S. 104
Louis XIV, 165
Luther, 94
Lyon, D. 117
Lyon, Lord 101

MacAlister, Principal 44
McColl, Ian 92
McDiarmid, Hugh 92
Macdonald, Bob 102, 165
MacDonald, Ramsay 22
MacGregor, Garth 51
MacGregor, W.M. 43
MacKenzie I. 154
Mackie, Robert 46, 82, 115
MacKinnon, Mrs. L. 166
Mackintosh, H.R. 15, 34
Maclay, Lord 45, 53
Maclean A.J. 104
Maclean, Colin 24
Maclean, Norman 72
Maclellan, J. 39 ff.
MacLeod, George 45 ff., 51, 72 ff.,
    133, 145
MacMurtrie, Mr. 111
McWilliam, S. 101, 157

Main, Archibald 43 ff., 46
Maitland, J. 84
Maltby, Russell 46, 86, 137
Manson, W. 90
Martin, Alexander 15, 28
Martin, Hugh 82
Maud, John 70
Micklem, Nathaniel 66
Miller, Harry 29 ff., 43, 55
Moberley, Walter 70
Moffatt, J. 80
Morley, J. 108
Muir, E. 130

Newbigin, Lesslie ix, 47, 52, 61, 81,
    111, 157, 166
Niebuhr, Reinhold 63, 131, 148, 151
Nixon, R. 155

Oldham, J. 4, 16 ff., 56, 60 ff., 65,
    67, 69, 70, 82, 123

Oman, J. 48, 129
Orr, Norman 139
Otto, R. 119

Parry, Kenneth 67
Paterson, W.P. 16
Paton, W. 60 ff., 64 ff., 68,
    70, 167
Patrick, D. 66
Peake, A.S. 77
Pitt-Watson, I. 92, 95, 98
Pope John XXIII, 102 ff., 109
Porteous, Professor N. 30, 40,
    48, 157
Pringle-Pattison, Seth, 10 ff.

Quarnier, W. 129

Rainy, Principal 61
Raven, Charles 46, 48 ff., 64 ff.,
    88, 129, 159, 166
Reeves, Marjorie 70
Reith, George 39
Reith, Lord 158

Sackville-West, V. 111
Sanderson of Oundle, 79
Say, David 67
Sayers, Dorothy 130
Schlapp, Otto 12
Scott, Sir W. 116, 157
Shelley, 131
Sheppard, Dick 51
Shillinglaw, A. 95
Slack, Kenneth 84
Small, Mabel 65, 67, 82 ff.
Smith, G.A. 78
Smith, J.W.D. 74, 126
Smith, Mrs 30
Smith, R. Gregor 88, 96, 124
Somerville, S. 102
Soper, Donald 88
Spellman, Cardinal 104

Stalin, 155
Stantol, V.H. 163
Stevenson, R.L. 130
Stewart, George S. 32, 37, 40 ff., 48,
    51, 55, 122 ff., 129, 133, 161 ff.
Studdert-Kennedy, G. 36, 130
Swift, Dean 114
Symons, W.G. 70

Taylor, Denis 81
Temple, William 39, 56, 63 ff., 68,
    70, 130, 167
Tensing, 133
Thomson, M. 116
Tindal, W. 74, 97
Tolstoy, L. 130
Tomkins, O. 66, 157
Torrance, T. 120
Trevelyan, J. 70
Trevor-Roper, H. 137
Tribe, Reginald 67

Unwin, E.C. 55

Van Dusen, Pitney 63, 115
Vidler, Alec 51
Visser 't Hooft, W.A. 62
Von Hugel, F. 48 ff.

Walker, Hugh 10, 13 ff., 17 ff., 21,
    74, 81, 115, 161
Wardle, 78
Welch, A. 15
White, Alexander 162
Whitehorn, Roy 93
Wilde, Oscar 136
Willebrands, Cardinal 104
Wilson, Kate 158
Wordsworth, 130
Wright, Dick 13, 15, 17, 24
Wright, Kenyon 117

Zvi, B. 105